Jesus the Pharisee

Contents

Preface

The present book takes up themes which I have adumbrated in previous works and gives them more detail and substance. I have used a style which, I hope, makes the book, in large part, accessible to the ordinary reader; but I have also added much new material that should be of interest to professional scholars. One section, the Appendix, being largely based on an academic article ('The Washing of Cups', *Journal for the Study of the New Testament* 14.3, 1982), is suitable mainly for professional readers, but I hope that non-professionals will be able to derive some interest from it.

That Jesus was a Pharisee will seem a startling thesis to many, but I hope that it will seem less outrageous to the reader as he or she continues to read the book. The derogatory image of the Pharisees, which has been implanted in the Western mind by certain passages in the Gospels (though modern scholarship has rendered these more and more doubtful) is countered by a different picture given by other New Testament passages that, unfortunately, have had much less impact. Also, the monolithic image given of the Pharisees in the derogatory passages takes no account of the variegated nature of the movement as evidenced in the available extra-Testamental literature. To correct the prevailing image of the Pharisees is an urgent matter, in view of the part this image has played in the demonization of the Jews, resulting finally in the horrors of the Holocaust.

In quoting from the Hebrew Bible and the New Testament, I have used a somewhat complex policy. I have often preferred the old AV version to the modern NEB. This is for two reasons: AV often gives a more literal translation than NEB in its concern for modern idiom; and also I have been reluctant to abandon AV in passages with a familiar ring for readers of English literature. On the other hand, sometimes NEB is preferable as incorporating the results of modern scholarship, and for this reason too I have sometimes used the translation offered by the Jesus Seminar volume *The Five Gospels.* Occasionally, I have been dissatisfied with all the available translations and have offered my own.

I have found a congenial background to the writing of this book in the Centre for Jewish Studies at the University of Leeds, and wish to thank its director Dr Eva Frojmovic and its constant supporter and participant Professor Griselda Pollock for their help and encouragement. I wish to thank also my friends in the Leo Baeck College, London, who supported me for the many years of my sojourn there. In the development of my views on the New Testament I have often had to face opposition, but have had a sympathetic hearing from scholars whose views I value very much, particularly Professor E. P. Sanders and Professor Graham Stanton. In writing the present book, I have built on the life-work of Paul Winter, whose book *On the Trial of Jesus* (1961) set me on my path, and who stated unequivocally (p. 133), 'In historical fact, Jesus was a Pharisee.' He also wrote, 'If the evangelists portray Jesus as being in violent opposition to the Pharisees, they depict a state of affairs which had come about several decades after the crucifixion' (p. 134).

My chief thanks, however, as always, must go to my dear wife Cynthia, who has selflessly devoted herself to furthering my work and has helped me in innumerable ways, from the handling of the (to me) recalcitrant computer, to the provision of sage advice and criticism on my writing at every stage.

Abbreviations

Arak.	*Arakhin*
AV	Authorized (King James) Version
Avod. Zar.	*Avodah Zarah*
B. Bat.	*Bava Batra*
B. Metzi'a	*Bava Metzi'a*
b.	Babylonian Talmud
Bek.	*Bekorot*
Ber.	*Berakhot*
Ecc. Rab.	*Ecclesiates Rabbah*
Gen. Rab.	*Genesis Rabbah*
Git.	*Gittin*
Hag.	*Hagigah*
Hor.	*Horayot*
Hul.	*Hullin*
Kel.	*Kelim*
Kidd.	*Kiddushin*
Lev. Rab.	*Leviticus Rabbah*
m.	Mishnah
Mak.	*Makkot*
Miqv.	*Miqva'ot*
NEB	New English Bible
Neg.	*Nega'im*
Nid.	*Niddah*
Pesah.	*Pesahim*
Pesiq. Rab.	*Pesiqta Rabbati*
Qoh. Rab.	*Qohelet Rabbah*
Ros. Hash.	*Rosh Ha-Shanah*

RV	Revised Version
Sanh.	*Sanhedrin*
Shabb.	*Shabbat*
t.	Tosefta
Ta'an.	*Ta'anit*
Tem.	*Temurah*
Ter.	*Terumot*
Toh.	*Tohoroth*
y.	Palestinian (Jerusalem) Talmud
Yevam.	*Yevamot*

Who Were the Pharisees?
The Incident of Gamaliel

Who were the Pharisees? This might seem an easy question to answer. According to Josephus, the New Testament and the rabbinic writings, the Pharisees were the dominant religious grouping of the first century CE, at the time when the Jerusalem Temple was still standing. In the Gospels, the Pharisees are treated from a hostile standpoint, but their dominance and authority among the majority of the Jewish people is not questioned. It is the New Testament that says that 'the Pharisees sit in Moses' seat' (Matt. 23.2, AV). According to Josephus, the Pharisees had the allegiance of the people, who followed their religious rulings and regarded them with the highest reverence. According to the rabbinic writings, the Pharisees were the movement from which the rabbinic movement itself derived; the leading Pharisee teachers, Hillel and Shammai, are called 'the fathers of the world', by which, no doubt, the rabbinic world is meant, (since the rabbis certainly did not intend to raise the authority of Hillel and Shammai above that of canonical figures such as Moses, the Prophets and Ezra).

In recent years, however, this picture has changed in the eyes of many scholars. Especially under the influence of Jacob Neusner,[1] the Pharisees have dwindled into a small sect, comprising only one of the many 'Judaisms' of the first century. The rabbinic claim to continuity with the Pharisees has become suspect; instead the theory has gained ground that this claim was an unhistorical attempt by the rabbis to acquire traditional authority for their own assertion of dominance and for their own enactments. It has been stressed that the rabbinic writings are late; the earliest of them, the

Mishnah, was composed at about 200 CE. Various doubts have been
thrown on the accounts found in Josephus and the New Testament,
each being alleged to have motivations for exaggerating the influence of the Pharisees.

Moreover, doubt has been cast on the assumption that Pharisees
and 'scribes' in the New Testament are to be regarded as alternative
and equivalent terms. Sometimes Jesus is questioned or attacked by
Pharisees, sometimes by scribes and sometimes by 'scribes and
Pharisees'. Who, then, were the scribes? Perhaps, it has been
argued, they were a separate group altogether from the Pharisees.
Even more puzzling, then, is the expression that sometimes occurs
(for example, Mark 2.16, my translation) 'the scribes of the
Pharisees'. Perhaps this means that other groups, the Sadducees for
example, also had scribes.

The view upheld here is that the scribes and the Pharisees mentioned in the New Testament are members of the same movement.
They are mentioned together so frequently that the authors of the
Gospels must have thought of them as very closely identified.
Sometimes a story told in one Gospel about Pharisees becomes
a story about scribes in another. The evidence of the rabbinic writings is important here. They sometimes use the word 'scribes' as
equivalent to 'rabbis', as in the expression 'the words of the scribes'
(*divrei soferim*) when it is desired to distinguish rabbinic from
Toranic ordinances.

Compelling also is the evidence of the New Testament, Josephus
and the rabbinic writings that the Pharisees/scribes were the
dominant religious party in Jesus' day, and that there was strong
continuity between them and the rabbinic movement. If they were
not prominent and authoritative in their day, it is hard to see why
the rabbis should think it worthwhile to manufacture a continuity
with them. Moreover, the argument (particularly put forward by
Jacob Neusner) that Pharisee/Sadducee controversies mentioned
in the Mishnah are second-century rabbinic concoctions has been
much weakened by the publication of the MMT document of the
Dead Sea Scrolls (see Chapter 11, note 1 on p. 210), which shows
that these same controversies were actively pursued in the first
century.

The gap in time between the Mishnah and the first century is to some extent an illusion. The Mishnah was indeed written down as late as 200 CE, but it is not a composition of that date, but a compilation of materials many of which clearly existed in an earlier period. There is even evidence that the Mishnah itself is only the latest of a series of compilations, constructed on a similar plan, the earliest of which dates to about 100 CE. One rabbinic work, *Megillat Ta'anit*, actually dates, by common scholarly consent, from the first century itself. Moreover, the Targumim (translations of the Hebrew Bible into Aramaic), though edited in the second century, were partly composed in the first century, and contain some interesting pre-Tannaitic halakhic interpretations that escaped the process of revision, throwing light on the continuous process of development of halakhah from the first to the second century. Many of the rabbinic leaders mentioned and quoted in the Mishnah were born and spent their youth in the first century. This applies not just to Hillel and Shammai and their immediate followers, whose activity was entirely in the first century, but even to prominent figures whose main work was in the second century, such as Joshua ben Hanania and Rabbi Eliezer (see p. 116). So the gap is by no means as enormous as it is often represented to be.

The testimony of Josephus that the Pharisees were revered by the vast majority of the people seems plain enough, yet some modern scholars have felt impelled to suspect Josephus' motives in saying this. Neusner's theory was that Josephus shows a change of attitude from his earlier work, which was much less favourable to the Pharisees, and this change had a political motivation: the rabbis of Josephus' later days were consolidating the authority granted to them by the Romans by claiming continuity with the Pharisees, and Josephus decided to bolster this claim by propaganda aggrandizing the status of the Pharisees. This speculation has been abandoned by one of Neusner's closest disciples, Anthony Saldarini,[2] who has pointed out that every stage of the reasoning exhibits flaws: Josephus did not change his attitude to the Pharisees in his later work, his alleged political association with the rabbis of his day has no historical basis, and the alleged alignment of the rabbis with Roman power had not yet taken place in Josephus' lifetime.

We may thus attach great importance and credence to Josephus'
statement about the Pharisees, especially as it is the testimony of
someone who, on the whole, had a negative attitude towards them:

> they are able greatly to persuade the body of the people, and
> whatever they [the people] do about divine worship, prayers and
> sacrifices, they perform them according to their [the Pharisees']
> direction; insomuch that the cities give great attestations to them
> on account of their entire virtuous conduct, both in the actions of
> their lives, and in their discourses too.

Further, Josephus says about the Sadducees: 'They are able to do
almost nothing of themselves; for when they become magistrates,
unwillingly and by force sometimes they addict themselves to the
notions of the Pharisees, because the multitude would not otherwise
bear them' (*Antiquities* 18.3–4).

Josephus is here asserting that the Pharisees' influence extended
to the rites of the Temple (since he stresses that the sacrifices were
offered in accordance with Pharisee principles). Yet Saldarini dismisses as unhistorical the very same statement when made in the
rabbinic literature. He also dismisses rabbinic claims that the
Pharisees created the liturgy – yet Josephus makes the same assertion.[3] Saldarini, while combating the theory of Josephus' propaganda aims in relation to the Pharisees, fails to follow through this
insight when he disregards the consonance between Josephus and
the rabbinic writings. In particular, he rejects or at least doubts the
rabbinic claim that the Sadducees in practice bowed to Pharisee
rulings because of the pressure of popular opinion, though Josephus
makes a point of this. In general, Saldarini adopts a sceptical
approach towards rabbinic assertions about the Pharisees, but fails
to appreciate the significance of the agreement of rabbinic statements with those of Josephus, whom he admits to have been free of
rabbinic influence. The rabbinic agreement with Josephus casts an
entirely new light on the question of rabbinic historical links with
the Pharisee movement; instead of interpreting the rabbinic statements as mythical, we must acknowledge that the rabbinic literature
shows accurate knowledge of the religious situation of the first
century and must be taken seriously.

Saldarini, while freeing himself in some respects from the scenario of Neusner, still cannot accept the well-attested fact that the Pharisees were not just one sect among many, but represented the views of the vast majority of the Jewish people. Yet Saldarini at least accepts that the Pharisees did not regard themselves as a sect like the Dead Sea Scrolls sect, cutting themselves off from the people as a whole, but on the contrary made every effort to mix with the people and appeal to them by what Josephus calls their 'discourses' (a term which, as we shall see, pp. 92–99, links the Pharisees to Jesus and his parables and sermons). One of the sayings attributed to Hillel, the greatest Pharisee leader, is, 'Do not separate from the community' (how this saying can be reconciled with a commonly-alleged meaning of the word 'Pharisee' is discussed below, pp. 78–81).

Josephus is also at pains to stress the Pharisees' high reputation for 'entire virtuous conduct' among the people (here Josephus' change of vocabulary from 'people' to 'cities' cannot be given the sociological significance which some scholars have seen). This description is very much at odds with the diatribes against the Pharisees in the New Testament as oppressors and hypocrites who were actually hated by the people. Yet the odd fact is that certain passages in the New Testament itself contradict this hostile picture. Prominent among these dissident passages is the account given in Acts 5 of the role of Gamaliel in saving Peter and his associates from the condemnation desired by the High Priest, who is described as a Sadducee. Here is the description of Gamaliel given in this passage: 'a member of the Council rose to his feet, a Pharisee called Gamaliel, a teacher of the law held in high regard by all the people' (Acts 5.34, NEB). Then follows Gamaliel's speech, in which he pleads for mercy for Peter and his associates, 'For if this idea of theirs or its execution is of human origin, it will collapse; but if it is from God, you will never be able to put them down, and you risk finding yourselves at war with God' (Acts 5.38–9, NEB).

The full significance of this passage is obscured by the fact that Gamaliel is described as merely 'a member of the Council' and as 'a Pharisee'. It is not revealed by the author of Acts (probably Luke) that Gamaliel was not just an individual Pharisee, but the leader of the whole Pharisee movement. We learn this information from the rabbinic literature, in which Gamaliel figures prominently, and there is no reason to doubt this evidence. As the leader of the Pharisees, Gamaliel naturally carried all the other Pharisee members of the Council (or Sanhedrin) with him when the matter came to a vote, and Peter was duly rescued from death. Yet the impression left by the text is that Gamaliel was a lone individual who by some miraculous means persuaded the other Pharisees to acquit Peter, which otherwise they would not have been inclined to do. This is certainly the interpretation that was accepted by Christian exegetes, who even invented a legend that Gamaliel was a secret convert to Christianity. He is located together with other individual Pharisees, such as Nicodemus (John 3.1) and probably Joseph of Arimathaea ('a secret disciple for fear of the Jews'; John 19.38, NEB) who felt sympathy for Jesus despite the general Pharisee hostility to him.

Yet the author of Acts must have known that Gamaliel was not just an ordinary Pharisee but the leader and chief representative of the Pharisees, the immediate successor of the great Hillel, and he must have realized that many of the readers of Acts would also know this. It is therefore a problem that this episode was included even though it throws the greatest doubt on the whole Gospel picture of Pharisee hostility to Jesus and his movement. Peter was brought before the Sanhedrin at the instigation of the High Priest on a charge of spreading the message of Jesus. If Jesus had indeed been the person depicted in the Gospels as a blasphemer and Sabbath-breaker who so aroused the hatred and anger of the Pharisees that they constantly sought his death, why did the leader of the Pharisees defend Jesus' chief disciple and even state that Peter's advocacy might be 'from God'?

Modern scholars (while rejecting traditional Christian explications) have generally underrated the significance of this problematic passage, and tried in various ways to explain it away (or perhaps they have understood its significance only too well). The historicity of the episode has been doubted, especially on the ground that Gamaliel, in his speech, mentions Theudas as a figure similar to Jesus, though we know from Josephus that Theudas belonged to a later date. This is hardly a reason to doubt the historicity of the reported stance of Gamaliel, since Luke may very well have got a detail wrong in his attempt to reconstruct Gamaliel's words, while correctly reporting Gamaliel's overall attitude; but in any case, the problem remains, 'Why did the author of Acts go out of his way to attribute support for Peter to a prominent Pharisee, and indeed credit the Council representatives of the Pharisee movement as a whole with the rescue of Jesus' chief disciple?' The problem is not so acute in the later rescue of Paul from the High Priest by the Council Pharisees (though this episode, too, is instructive in showing the gap between the Pharisees and the High Priest, a gap much obscured in the Gospels), since here Paul misleadingly identified himself as a Pharisee, not as a Christian; but here in Acts 5 there can be no doubt that the account represents the Pharisees as siding with someone who declared himself unequivocally a follower of Jesus.

A recent explanation is that of Saldarini. His view is that the author of Acts includes a number of remarks favourable to the Pharisees because one of his aims is to assert continuity between the early Christian Church and Judaism. The Gamaliel episode is thus understandable in the context of this aim. Here Saldarini is following the line taken by Jack T. Sanders,[4] whose more detailed formulation will be considered below.

It can be seen at once, however, that when we compare the other 'favourable' remarks with the Gamaliel episode, we see a world of difference. They all concern the tendency of individual Pharisees to join the Jesus movement, or to show sympathy for it as individuals. None of them suggests a tolerance of the Jesus movement as a whole by the Pharisee movement as a whole. On the contrary, Acts strongly reinforces the picture of the Gospels of the Pharisees as implacable enemies of the Jesus movement. Moreover, one particular aspect of Acts drives home an anti-Pharisee message: the story of the persecution by Saul (later Paul) of the Jerusalem Church. This is imputed to Saul's Pharisaic zeal. It is true that this intolerance conflicts puzzlingly with the attitude of Saul's alleged teacher, Gamaliel. But this only reinforces the uniqueness of the Gamaliel episode. That the author of Acts records both Saul's intolerance and

Gamaliel's tolerance is one of the most remarkable puzzles of New Testament studies.

The only feeble attempt in Acts to minimize this revealing incident was to suppress the actual position of Gamaliel among the Pharisees as their leader and chief representative. The survival of this incident in the narrative goes far beyond Saldarini's concept of a desire, on Luke's part, to present a picture of 'continuity' between the Jerusalem Church and Judaism; the incident portrays instead an actual solidarity.[5] Gamaliel is asserting his approval of the Jesus movement as showing no trace of heresy, and therefore as sharing the main tenets of the Pharisaic movement itself. He compares it with other movements which attempted a messianic coup without promulgating any doctrines that conflicted with Pharisee ideas. These messianic movements actually arose out of Pharisaism. In the case of Judas of Galilee, whom Gamaliel mentions, the testimony of Josephus is that the movement of Zealots which he founded 'agree in all other things with the Pharisaic notions; but they have an inviolable attachment to liberty' (*Antiquities* 18.23). The only difference between such messianic movements and the Pharisees as a whole was that most Pharisees adopted a cautious 'wait-and-see' attitude towards messianic claims and preferred (like Gamaliel himself) to await the outcome, while contemplating the daring aims of the messianic movements (arising from their 'inviolable attachment to liberty') with sympathy and hope.

Gamaliel's defence of Peter is very far-reaching in its implications. It means that Peter was not advocating Jesus as a divine Messiah, but merely as a human messiah whose aim was to liberate the Jews from the Roman yoke. Otherwise, Gamaliel would certainly not have supported Peter and the Jesus movement. The attitude of Jesus' disciples is actually portrayed by Luke/Acts itself, when it represents Jesus' immediate followers as saying, 'We had been hoping that he would be the man to liberate Israel' (Luke 24.21, NEB), and even requesting the resurrected Jesus if he would now 'restore the kingdom' (Acts 1.6, AV). Jesus' movement was patriotic and insurrectionist; it aimed at liberation from the Roman occupation. It had no notion of elevating Jesus to divine status. It also had no aim of abolishing the Jewish religion; the Jerusalem

Church shows no sign of doing this, but is portrayed in Acts as very observant of the Jewish laws. As E. P. Sanders pointed out, 'If Jesus taught that the Torah was at an end, his disciples show no sign of having learnt this from him.'[6] Sanders concluded that Jesus did not actually teach the supersession of the Torah. The book of Acts portrays Peter as a very observant Jew, who had never tasted any food forbidden by Jewish law. Of course, one of the main themes of Acts is the gradual education of Peter into an anti-Torah attitude; but this implies that he did not learn this from Jesus himself. The adherence of Peter and the other disciples to Judaism is explained in the Gospels by the concept of the 'stupidity of the disciples', who never understood what Jesus was really teaching. But this concept is very questionable, and is best explained as an *ex post facto* attempt by the later Pauline Church to reconcile the Torah-observance of the Jerusalem Church with the alleged anti-Torah teaching of Jesus. The point that is relevant to the present discussion, however, is that if Peter and his associates were preaching the supersession of the Torah, they would never have attracted the support of Gamaliel.

Another implication of the Gamaliel incident is that the trial and condemnation of Jesus himself never happened. This conclusion has been reached by many scholars for other reasons, chiefly the inherent contradictions of the accounts given in the Synoptic Gospels, and the lack of knowledge they show of the procedure of the Sanhedrin. Also, a very weighty consideration is that the Fourth Gospel does not mention any Sanhedrin trial of Jesus at all, but instead describes an interrogation of Jesus carried out by Annas, the father-in-law of Caiaphas, the High Priest, and by Caiaphas himself, without any judicial procedure (John 18). Here the Fourth Gospel, though in many respects the least historically reliable of the four Gospels (being replete with Christology of a late character) shows that it has access to sources other than those used by the Synoptic Gospels of which it is independent; another important example of this is the Fourth Gospel's omission of all reference to the institution of the Eucharist in its account of the Last Supper.

While fully aware of the unhistoricity of the trial described in the Synoptic Gospels, scholars have not appreciated the importance, in this connection, of the Gamaliel incident in Acts 5. If Peter,

Jesus' chief disciple, was defended by the leader of the Pharisees, Gamaliel, at a meeting of the Sanhedrin on a charge of being a follower of Jesus, where were the Pharisees, and particularly Gamaliel, at the trial of Jesus himself? If Gamaliel saw no harm in the Jesus movement, how could he have seen any harm in the founder of the movement, Jesus? If such a trial had taken place, would he not have given the same reasons for acquitting Jesus, and declared that his messianic claim should be judged by its results and that it might turn out to be 'from God' and that its opponents might, in the event, be shown to be 'enemies of God'? Note that Gamaliel appears, in the trial of Peter, to be completely unaware of any charge of blasphemy against Jesus, that is, that he had claimed divine status. Does not this show that no such charge was ever made against Jesus? This is further proof that the earliest followers of Jesus (known as Nazarenes and later as Ebionites) did not regard Jesus as a divine personage, but as a claimant to the title of 'Messiah', which in Jewish parlance of the time carried no connotation of deity, but meant merely 'King of the Jews'; its literal meaning being 'the anointed one', since every Davidic king was anointed with a special mixture of oils at his coronation ceremony, so that every Davidic king (even those who 'did evil in the sight of the Lord') had the title of 'Messiah' (this did not apply to non-Davidic kings, such as the Hasmoneans, who were not called 'Messiah').

The only way, then, that Jesus could have been condemned at a Sanhedrin trial is if there were no Pharisees present at it, and especially if Gamaliel was not present at it. Yet Gamaliel was definitely the leader of the Pharisees at the time of Jesus' trial, which took place only a short time before Peter's trial. But can we conceive a meeting of the Sanhedrin without the presence of Pharisees, who (as the trials of both Peter and Paul show) actually constituted the majority of the members of the Council? This would be like a meeting of the British House of Commons in which some important decision was passed without the presence of the majority party. Such a meeting could hardly be regarded as a valid parliamentary session, and a report that such a meeting occurred would simply not be believed.

It is actually a remarkable fact that the Pharisees make hardly any appearance in the Gospel accounts of the trial of Jesus. The Gospel of Luke omits all mention of them, and the other Gospels make only obscure hints at their presence. This is very surprising in view of the prominence given earlier to accounts of conflict between the Pharisees and Jesus. If the Pharisees had indeed sought Jesus' death on many occasions because of his Sabbath-healing, why did they not seize the opportunity to come forward at his trial with this very accusation, which the Gospels assert so strongly to be a capital charge in Pharisee law? In the event, the Gospel accounts of Jesus' trial do not even mention this allegedly serious charge as a reason for condemning Jesus. So the absence of the Pharisees is one more piece of evidence that the alleged conflicts between the Pharisees and Jesus on the question of Sabbath-healing also never took place; a conclusion that is confirmed by the copious evidence from rabbinic sources that the Pharisees did not forbid Sabbath-healing but actually encouraged it, using arguments identical with those attributed to Jesus in the Gospels (for example, Jesus' dictum 'The Sabbath was made for man, not man for the Sabbath' is found in the Talmud precisely in a context of justifying Sabbath-healing, see p. 124).

Thus the implications of the Gamaliel incident are indeed multiple and far-reaching. This incident alone, if taken seriously, is sufficient to invalidate the majority of the Gospel story: the alleged conflict between Jesus and the chief Jewish religious authorities, that is, the Pharisees, the alleged trial of Jesus as a blasphemer, the concept of Jesus' mission as a divine visitant intent on suffering crucifixion in order to bring salvation, and the alleged responsibility of the Jews, rather than the Romans, as the betrayers and killers of Jesus, a charge that gave rise to the demonization of the Jews. We must look further, however, at the attempts that have been made to minimize the importance of the Gamaliel incident; attempts that arise in some cases, it may be plausibly supposed, from awareness (conscious or unconscious) of its destructive implications for the whole Christian anti-Jewish and pro-Roman myth.

On the whole, the chief strategy has been simply to ignore the incident altogether. W. G. Kümmel's celebrated *Introduction to the New Testament*[7] contains no discussion of the Gamaliel incident, and does not even include the name of Gamaliel in the index. It is hard to believe that this acute scholar saw no special difficulties in the incident worthy of discussion. The same author's *The New Testament: The History of the Investigation of Its Problems*[8] shows the same total lack of interest in this subject. Even the comprehensive *Dictionary of Biblical Interpretation* edited by R. L. Coggins and J. L. Houlden[9] contains no article about Gamaliel, no mention of him in the index, and no mention of him even in the article about the Pharisees.

Consultation of some school textbooks shows a preference for the view that Gamaliel was simply showing a practical, commonsense approach in advocating a 'wait-and-see' policy towards the early Christians. No appreciation is shown for the difficulty that Peter was preaching a doctrine that (according to the previous narrative) had been recently condemned as so blasphemous and destructive of Judaism that its originator had been hounded to death. It is as if Pope Innocent III in the twelfth century were to advocate a 'wait-and-see' policy towards the Albigensians instead of launching a crusade against them as dangerous heretics. The very fact that Gamaliel advocated a 'wait-and-see' policy shows that he saw nothing heretical or blasphemous in Peter's preaching, but only an announcement of historical or eschatological developments that might or might not occur and in any case could occasion only hope (or disappointment), not condemnation.

The only extended discussion of the topic that I have been able to find is that of Jack T. Sanders, in his valuable book *The Jews in Luke-Acts*.[10] It cannot be said, however, that even Sanders appreciates fully the problematic nature of the Gamaliel incident and its implications.

Sanders is struck by the number of instances in Luke/Acts where the Pharisees are treated in a friendly manner. On the other hand, he acknowledges that Luke/Acts also contains some very unfriendly episodes concerning Pharisees, including even some conflict stories between Jesus and the Pharisees not contained in the other Gospels, the attitude of which is much more uniformly anti-Pharisee. Sanders sees here a problem that requires resolution: why this mixture of friendliness and unfriendliness towards the Pharisees in Luke/Acts? His solution (rather like that of Saldarini discussed earlier, though Saldarini is more concerned with the question of continuity) lies in Luke's attitude to the Jewish Christians. Luke is aware that the Jewish Christians who comprised Jesus' earliest followers and who constituted the Jerusalem Church had an attitude towards religious practice and belief that was indistinguishable from that of the Pharisees. Luke's friendly allusions to Pharisees, then, are all gestures towards rapprochement with the Jewish Christians, and do not preclude a most unfriendly attitude towards the Pharisees themselves as persecutors of Jesus and Christianity.

This explanation can hardly be regarded as satisfactory, especially in relation to the Gamaliel incident, which Sanders treats as just one more instance of pro-Pharisee sentiment in Luke/Acts, not different in kind from the other most striking instance, the warning (recorded by no other Gospel) given by the Pharisees to Jesus that saved his life from Herod Antipas (Luke 13.31). The latter incident is certainly striking; yet it does not involve the entire Pharisee movement and can be read as a friendly act performed by a group of uncharacteristic Pharisees, or (as Sanders would prefer to say) Pharisees having much in common with the Jerusalem Church rather than with the Pharisee movement as a whole. Some Christian commentators, beginning with Loisy, even read the incident as a trap set by the Pharisees, but there is no ground for such an interpretation, which clearly arises from reluctance to see any good in any Pharisees in view of the dastardly behaviour attributed to them in the rest of the narrative. What distinguishes the Gamaliel incident is its representative character. Sanders' explanation of the friendly Pharisees elsewhere in Luke/Acts (existing alongside a plentiful supply of unfriendly Pharisees) as symbolic representatives of the Jerusalem Church has merit; but this does not begin to explain the Gamaliel incident.

My own view is that Luke simply overreached himself. He did, as Sanders explained, want to present a composite picture of good Pharisees/bad Pharisees. The good Pharisees were those who were sympathetic to the Jesus movement, and even comprised a large proportion of the Jerusalem Church, thus providing the continuity that Luke primarily sought. The bad Pharisees were those who were

totally opposed to Jesus and his followers. To portray his good
Pharisees, Luke used sources which the other Gospel-writers suppressed, and these sources provided some of the most authentic
materials to be found in the Gospels, on the principle of *tendenz*
criticism (see Chapter 12, p. 157, for fuller explanation of this term)
that what goes against the *tendenz* is liable to be trustworthy. Luke
went some way towards giving the game away when he included the
incident of Pharisees saving Jesus' life: this incident is at the very
least surprising in view of the general Gospel picture of the
Pharisees as hostile to Jesus. But Luke, going beyond his intentions,
gave the game away entirely when he included, from his authentic
sources, the Gamaliel incident, which threw brilliant light on the
true, historical relationship between the Pharisees and Jesus. Here
Luke relied on the obfuscation by which he portrayed Gamaliel as
just one Pharisee among many, and therefore as just another
Nicodemus ; he did not fear a reaction inappropriate to his purpose
because he was writing for Gentile readers to whom the name
Gamaliel meant nothing. He did not know that a voluminous Jewish
literature would later arise embodying traditions in which this same
Gamaliel featured as one of the fathers of rabbinic Judaism and as
the leader of the whole Pharisee movement. Luke's incautious use
of his sources (in contrast with the policy of suppression of the other
Gospel-writers) resulted in the preservation of precious documentary evidence of the history of the early Church and its relationship to Pharisaic Judaism.

The Jerusalem Church:
Peter, Paul and James

As we have seen, the explanation given by Jack T. Sanders of the pro-Pharisee references in both Luke and Acts is that the author, Luke, while strongly opposed to the Pharisee movement (as he shows in his anti-Pharisee references) wished to placate the large body of Pharisees who had attached themselves to the Jerusalem Church, either by actually joining it as members, or as acting sympathetically towards it.

We must now consider further the significance of the prominence of Pharisaism in the early Church, and what this tells us about Jesus himself.

The evidence of Acts is that the early Church regarded itself as a branch of Judaism, not as a new religion. Its members were fully observant Jews, who practised all the laws of the Torah, including circumcision, the dietary laws, the observance of the festivals and fasts of the liturgical year. Moreover, they showed great respect for the rites of the Temple and frequently attended it (Acts 2.46), in order to offer sacrifices, taking care to attain a state of ritual purity by the prescribed washings before entering the Temple grounds. In fact, their observance of Temple rites went far beyond that of other observant Jews, even Pharisees. We know this not only from the text of Acts, but also from Church traditions, which attributed special assiduity to James, Jesus' brother, the leader of the early Church, in Temple-attendance (Hegesippus, quoted by Eusebius, *Ecclesiastical History*, 2.23). Some scholars, finding this evidence disturbing, have attempted to throw doubt on the plain statements of Acts to this effect. This is a striking example of a phenomenon fairly common in modern New Testament scholarship: pious scepticism. Where acceptance of a text runs counter to fixed Christian beliefs, Christian scholars are very willing to be thoroughgoing sceptics and to deny the historical truth of the text in question. Sometimes the only scholars who are willing to believe the evidence of the New Testament are non-Christians; a strange reversal of the situation in previous generations.

An important corollary of this devotion to the Temple is that the leaders of the early Church did not regard themselves as priests. A mark of the foundation of a new religion is the creation of sacraments, administered by a newly-formed priesthood. It was when Christianity instituted the sacrament of the Eucharist and founded a priesthood with the function of administering this sacrament, that it truly became a separate religion from Judaism. In the early Church, this had not yet happened. The evidence of Acts is that the Jerusalem Church knew nothing of the Eucharist rite. This evidence is supplemented by that of the *Didache* (a large part of which is an early document of the Jerusalem Church), which describes a rite of wine and bread (in that non-eucharistic order) without any mention of these as the blood and body of Christ; the rite described is thus simply the Jewish Qiddush, which precedes the Sabbath or Festival meal. The earliest description of the Eucharist rite is that of Paul in 1 Cor. 11.23–30, and his words are best interpreted as signifying that he received instructions about this sacrament not from the tradition of the Jerusalem Church, but by a direct communication from the heavenly Jesus in a vision describing the institution of the Eucharist by Jesus at the Last Supper.[1] Paul's vision was then incorporated, in various inconsistent ways, by the writers of the Synoptic Gospels into their accounts of the Last Supper; though the lengthiest Gospel account of the Last Supper, that of John, omits all mention of the Eucharist.

The most obvious conclusion from the above is that the Eucharist was not instituted by Jesus in historical fact. Therefore, Jesus was not the founder of Christianity as a separate religion from Judaism. For Jesus, the sacraments of the Jewish Temple, administered by the Aaronite priesthood, were still valid, and no new sacrament had supplanted either the Temple or the priesthood. (He told the leper whom he had cured to perform the appropriate sacrifice in the Temple, Matt. 8.4; even when attempting to reform the Temple by overturning the tables of the money-changers, he did so on the ground that they were profaning the house of God – this shows reverence for the Temple, not the irreverence which some have seen in the incident.)

The creator of the Eucharist was not Jesus but Paul, who based it on his vision in which the heavenly Jesus instructed him in the matter. As the founding prophet of a new religion, Paul regarded himself as far superior in authority to the leaders of the Jerusalem Church, who had been in contact with the earthly Jesus, but unlike Paul did not receive constant instructions from the heavenly Jesus. Paul makes this position clear in his letters, but the book of Acts, anxious to preserve continuity between the Pauline Church and the Jerusalem Church, lowers the status of Paul to equality with the Apostles, and portrays the Apostles, especially Peter, as slowly overcoming their lack of understanding of Jesus' intentions and progressing to a Pauline position.

A key passage in the alleged education of Peter towards a Pauline position is the episode of Peter's dream in Acts 10. Peter has a dream or vision in which he sees

> creatures of every kind, whatever walks or crawls or flies. Then there was a voice which said to him, 'Up, Peter, kill and eat.' But Peter said, 'No, Lord, no: I have never eaten anything profane or unclean.' The voice came again a second time: 'It is not for you to call profane what God counts clean.' (Acts 10.12–15, NEB)

The moral of this story is not that the dietary laws are to be abolished, for it is carefully explained that the 'profane' animals are a metaphor for Gentiles, who are to be admitted without distinction into the Christian movement. What is interesting, rather, is what is taken for granted; that Peter is a totally observant Jew, whose association with Jesus has never led him to relax in any way his observance of the laws of clean and unclean animals. If Jesus declared the abolition of the Torah, why is Peter so unaware of this? Or (if the story is regarded as unhistorical) why does the author of

Acts take it for granted that Peter, at this point, was untouched by any notion of the obsolescence of the laws? Even though the author of Acts wishes to describe a gradual change in Peter's attitude, he does not venture to suggest that any such change was brought about by Peter's association with Jesus, which left him, on the contrary, a fully-observant Jew.

But did not Jesus explicitly abolish the Jewish dietary laws? When he came into conflict with the Pharisees in the matter of hand-washing before meals (Matt. 15; Mark 7), he said that defilement comes from what goes out of the mouth, not from what comes into it; and the author of Mark's Gospel adds: 'Thus he declared all foods clean' (Mark 7.19). (This translation of the some-what enigmatic Greek clause *katharizon panta ta bromata* is found in RV and NEB and other translations, and is based on Church tradition). These words do not appear in the parallel passage of Matthew; and most scholars regard it as a late explanatory addition to Mark's Gospel. But the NEB translation of the clause is probably wrong; the Jesus Seminar suggest instead the translation, 'This is how everything we eat is purified,' which simply continues the previous theme of physical purgation, and comprises Jesus' own summary of his previous words. If this translation is correct, the clause may not, after all, be a late explanatory editorial addition. This text, then, cannot be cited as proof that Jesus abrogated the Jewish dietary laws. This could be suspected, in any case, from its lack of contextual relevance, since the passage is concerned with hand-washing before eating food, not with the content of the meal. The interpretation given to the clause later testifies only to the eagerness of members of the Pauline Church to attribute their own rejection of Torah laws to Jesus. The incident of Peter's dream shows that Jesus gave no such instructions to his disciples, who continued to observe the dietary laws so meticulously that Peter, even in a dream, was horrified at the idea that he was being told to flout them.

But surely there is a well-known incident in the Gospels that runs contrary to the thesis that Jesus did not found the Church and had no intention to abandon Judaism, its sacraments or its priesthood? The whole institution of the Christian priesthood, and especially the Papacy, bases its credentials on the incident (Matt. 16.15–19) in which Jesus singled out Peter as the Rock on which he founded his Church. Peter was not an Aaronite priest, and his appointment as the Rock involved the abolition of the previous priesthood, the hereditary successors of Aaron, the brother of Moses. True, this incident does not mention the Eucharist as the sacrament taking the place of the sacraments administered by the Aaronites, but it does, surely, announce the advent of a new priesthood, no longer hereditary, but based on the Apostolic Succession.

Some scholars have argued that this incident is spurious, inserted to bolster the claims of the Church of Rome as legitimate successors of the first Pope, St Peter. I do not take this line, however, but on the contrary, regard this incident as one of the most authentic and historically-based passages in the New Testament. A reason for this confidence in the authenticity of the passage is its possession of a thoroughly Jewish tenor. It contains several expressions that are plain 'semitisms' (that is, expressions that embody idioms characteristic of Hebrew or Aramaic, and not of Greek); hence it is most unlikely that this passage was concocted by some non-Jewish interpolator.

Nevertheless, the passage, properly understood, does not portray Jesus founding the Christian Church, or appointing Peter as its first Pope.

The word *ecclesia*, usually translated as 'church', occurs only once more in the New Testament, when it has the meaning 'community'. Of course, in later post-New Testament times the word came to have the specialized meaning of 'Church', that is, the Christian organization. But Jesus had no such meaning in mind, and when he told Peter that he was the Rock on which he would build his *ecclesia*, he meant only his community in general, which was not necessarily a new religious community, since Judaism contained many communities which did not sever their connections with Judaism in general. Thus in reading the passage as a validation of the Papacy, later commentators were importing a meaning of *ecclesia* that did not exist in Jesus' time.

But what kind of community did Jesus have in mind? And why did he use the expression 'Rock'? This is evidently an expression of leadership, but what analogies can we find to it in Jewish culture and tradition?

Even more pressing and puzzling is a question that makes the whole passage problematic in the extreme. If Jesus was here appointing Peter, in a dramatic way, as leader of his 'community', why is it that the leadership of the early Church passed not to Peter but to James, the brother of Jesus? The answer to this question will throw light on the whole early Church and its relationship to Jesus. It will also throw light on Jesus' own aims, and his attitude to Judaism.

Let us have before us the whole passage (found only in Matthew), in which Peter is appointed as the 'Rock':

> 'And you,' he asked, 'who do you say I am?' Simon Peter answered: 'You are the Messiah, the son of the living God.' Then Jesus said: 'Simon, son of Jonah, you are favoured indeed! You did not learn that from mortal man; it was revealed to you by my heavenly Father. And I say this to you, You are Peter, the Rock; and on this rock I will build my church, and the powers of death shall never conquer it. I will give you the keys of the kingdom of Heaven; what you forbid on earth shall be forbidden in heaven, and what you allow on earth shall be allowed in heaven.' (Matt. 16.15–19, NEB)

It is instructive to compare this passage with a passage in the Hebrew Bible, where the prophet Isaiah predicts to Shebna that a man called Eliakim will soon be appointed in his place as King Hezekiah's chief minister:

> And it shall come to pass in that day, that I will call my servant Eliakim the son of Hilkiah; and I will clothe him with thy robe, and strengthen him with thy girdle, and I will commit the government into his hand; and he shall be a father to the inhabitants of Jerusalem, and to the house of Judah. And the key of the house of David will I lay upon his shoulder; so he shall open, and none shall shut, and he shall shut, and none shall open. And I will fasten him as a nail in a sure place. (Isa. 22.20–23, AV)

This passage shows some remarkable similarities to the Gospel account of the appointment of Peter.[2] Instead of being a Rock, Eliakim is fastened 'as a nail in a sure place'; but the connotation of utter stability is the same. Instead of being given 'the keys of the kingdom of Heaven', Eliakim is given 'the key of the house of David'. This last instance is more similar than it may appear; 'the kingdom of Heaven' is actually equivalent to the 'house of David'. Jesus is here using the expression he always uses when referring to the liberated Israel which he hopes to bring about: the Land of Israel, instead of being under the rule of Rome, will be under the rule (kingdom or kingship) of God. So Jesus is appointing Peter to a position of leadership in a country whose monarch will be another David; Jesus himself, the rightful heir to the throne of his ancestor David. This explains why Jesus' successor at the head of the Jerusalem Church was not Peter, but James. For a king is naturally succeeded not by by his Prime Minister, but by his nearest relative, even though the Prime Minister may continue to serve under the new monarch. This explains also why the successors of James in the leadership of the Jerusalem Church were also close relatives of Jesus. The Jesus movement was not a new religion, but a monarchical movement aiming to restore the ancient Jewish monarchy. The founder of Christianity as a religion separate from Judaism was not Jesus but Paul.

Very striking is the similarity between the charges given to Eliakim and Peter. On the one hand, Peter is told, 'what you forbid on earth will be forbidden in heaven, and what you allow on earth will be allowed in heaven'; and on the other hand, Eliakim is told 'he shall open and none shall shut, and he shall shut and none shall open'. What the Greek of Matthew means literally, is 'what you bind on earth shall be bound in heaven, and you loose on earth shall be loosed in heaven'. To 'bind' is a typical rabbinical expression for 'forbid', and to 'loose' is a typical expression for to 'permit'. This is one of the striking semitisms in the passage (clearer in the AV than in the modern NEB version quoted above – the NEB, striving for modern colloquial English often suppresses authentic Hebrew idioms and their valuable associations).

What does Jesus mean when he tells Peter that what he binds

(forbids) on earth will be bound in heaven, and that he looses (permits) on earth will be loosed in heaven? The term 'heaven' here is not just a synonym for 'God' (as in the expression used earlier 'kingdom of Heaven', a common rabbinic expression *malkhut shamayim*). This time it means the abode of God, the meaning which comes most naturally to Christian readers (who misunderstood Peter's possession of the 'keys of the kingdom of Heaven' as meaning that he was destined to become a guardian angel standing at the portals of heaven, deciding whom to admit and whom to reject). But how can Jesus give Peter the power to make decisions that even God has to accept? Does this exalt Peter to a supernatural role with ascendancy even over God?

Again we can understand this matter with the aid of the rabbinic literature. A rabbinic passage that throws much light on Jesus' charge to Peter concerns the famous Rabbi Joshua ben Hananiah, who disagreed, on one occasion, with the decision of the court of Gamaliel II about the date they had assigned for the Day of Atonement that year (this was in a period when there was no fixed calendar, and the beginnings of months were decided by observation of the moon):

Rabban Gamaliel sent him [Rabbi Joshua], saying, 'I charge thee that thou come to me with thy staff and thy money on the Day of Atonement as it falls according thy reckoning.' R. Akiba went to R. Joshua and found him sore perplexed. He said to him, 'I can teach you from Scripture that whatsoever Rabban Gamaliel has done is done right, for it is written, "These are the set feasts of the Lord, even holy convocations, which ye shall proclaim" (Lev. 23.4). Whether in their proper season or not in their proper season, I know no other set feasts save these.' Rabbi Joshua then went to Rabbi Dosa ben Harkinas [who had previously disagreed with Rabban Gamaliel's decision] and said to him, 'If we come to inquire into the lawfulness of the decisions of the court of Rabban Gamaliel, we shall need to inquire into the decisions of every court that has arisen since the days of Moses until now . . .' He took his staff and his money in his hand and went to Jabneh to Rabban Gamaliel on the day which fell upon his reckoning on the

Day of Atonement. Rabban Gamaliel stood up and kissed him on the head and said to him, 'Come in peace, my master and my disciple! – "my master" in wisdom and "my disciple" in that thou hast accepted my words.' (*m. Ros. Hash.* 2.9, Danby's translation)

Here we see the concept that God accepts the decisions of the rabbinical court, whether they are objectively right or wrong. This corresponds to Jesus' declaration to Peter, 'What you forbid on earth shall be forbidden in heaven, and what you allow on earth shall be allowed in heaven.' Jesus did not mean here to give Peter a right of individual decision, but to appoint him to a position as Head of the Court, like Rabban Gamaliel, whose decisions were arrived at by majority vote. The principle of majority decision, so vital to modern democracy, is also regarded as vital in rabbinic decision-making, and is enforced in the Talmud in various stories such as the above. The most startling of these stories is that of the attempted revolt of Rabbi Eliezer (*b. B. Metzi'a* 59b) who, seeking to overturn a majority decision that went against him, actually called to God to come to his support. A voice from heaven then came and said, 'Rabbi Eliezer is right', upon which, on the initiative of Rabbi Joshua (the same rabbi who figures above as the opponent of Rabban Gamaliel), the voice from heaven was ruled out of order! The principle of majority rule was instituted by God himself, who could therefore not infringe it without logical contradiction. The sequel to this amazing story (which was condemned as imbecilic by Christian disputants in a medieval Jewish–Christian disputation) was that God laughed, and said, 'My children have defeated me.' God, according to the story, was actually pleased that the human court had asserted its rights against Him (for further discussion of this story, see p. 58).

Thus the decisions of a human court were regarded as human and fallible, yet in an important sense also as God-given, since the right to make decisions by majority vote was instituted by God. Being fallible, such decisions could be reversed, if necessary, by some succeeding court, but meanwhile they had the force of law, even for those who had voted against them. This is the subtle, rabbinic version of the rule of law, which in the later Christian Church took the crude form of a doctrine of infallibility of the Church (which however did not become a dogma until the twentieth century, before which time a doctrine rather similar to the rabbinic one held sway).

Thus we may conclude that Jesus' words to Peter comprise an appointment to a post similar to that of Rabban Gamaliel II (grandson of the Gamaliel mentioned in Acts 5), that is, Head of the Assembly in which law-making took place. For Rabban Gamaliel too presided over a court whose decisions were accepted by God: what they bound on earth was bound in heaven, and what they loosed on earth was loosed in heaven. When Rabban Gamaliel's court decided on a certain date for the Day of Atonement, God marked up that date on his calendar in heaven, even if, objectively, it was the wrong date.

Thus the appointment of Peter by Jesus displays not only a striking linguistic feature that marks it as authentic (the use of 'bound' and 'loosed' in the sense of 'forbidden' and 'allowed', Hebrew *'asur* and *patur*), but also a theoretical feature (the conception that God has undertaken to abide by decisions of the human Assembly of Sages) that marks the incident as authentically rabbinic (or more exactly at this period, Pharisaic). Among Jewish religious trends, only the rabbinic movement, and before them the Pharisees, had this daring conception of the God-given authority of human fallible decision-making. The Dead Sea Scrolls sect, for example, had no such conception, as is shown by the style of their writings, which unlike the rabbinic Mishnah and Talmud contain no atmosphere of equal discussion and vote-taking, but rather consist of apodictic utterances intended to be regarded as unchallengeable and canonical.

The medieval Christian condemnation of the story about Rabbi Eliezer requires some comment. The story seemed to confirm the Christian charge that the Rabbis had arrogated to themselves the right to override Scripture. Here was a story that even portrayed the Rabbis as overriding God himself. This was sheer blasphemy, and confirmation of the New Testament account in which Jesus accused the Pharisees, 'Why do ye also transgress the commandment of God by your tradition?' (Matt. 15.3, AV). Yet the New Testament also seems to concede that the Pharisees had a certain humility in their claims, for it asserts that Jesus taught with a kind of authority beyond what the people were accustomed to: 'For he taught them as one having authority, and not as the scribes' (Matt. 7.29, AV). There is a contradiction here: the scribes or Pharisees had the confidence to override Scripture, yet they taught without claiming authority. This paradox actually reflects a reality. The rabbinic movement claimed the right to make laws, or to hand down as traditions the laws made by their predecessors, some of which certainly seemed to go against the plain sense of Scripture: for example, they taught that the precept, 'an eye for an eye' was not to be taken literally, but referred to monetary compensation for injuries inflicted. Yet at the same time, their law-making was always at a human level, arrived at by discussion and persuasion, and if agreement proved impossible, by majority voting. This was not a process of 'authority', yet it showed a confidence that their unauthoritative mode of procedure had God's approval. This paradox was, however, too subtle to be appreciated by their opponents, who simply saw the Pharisees as setting up their own authority against that of God. Their chief opponents in this regard were the Sadducees, who criticized the Pharisees for following traditions and instituting laws that were not contained explicitly in Scripture.

But Jesus was certainly no Sadducee, and his apparent adoption of a Sadducee antagonism to the 'traditions' of the scribes is no doubt a later addition to the text. It was these very traditions that humanized the literal meaning of the scriptural text, reducing its punishments, improving the condition of women and instituting reforms of all kinds, as Josephus makes plain, when he contrasts the leniency of the Pharisees with the harshness of the literal-minded Sadducees (*Antiquities* 13.10.294). The medieval Christian critique does little justice to the humanity and sophisticated concept of scriptural interpretation shown in the Talmudic stories.

3

Jesus and Hand-Washing

In the previous chapter we confronted the question of whether Jesus set himself against Pharisaic interpretations of the biblical text. I adopted the perhaps unexpected line that if Jesus had done so, he would have been taking a reactionary line similar to that of the Sadducees. For the interpretations of the Pharisees were in the direction of reform and humanization of the sometimes harsh commandments of the written text.

But surely, it will be objected, this was not always the case. The general impression we gain from the New Testament is that the decrees and interpretations of the Pharisees were in fact burdensome and enslaving. For example, a well-known text (in a heavily anti-Pharisee chapter) shows Jesus saying about the Pharisees: 'For they bind heavy burdens and grievous to be borne, and lay them on men's shoulders; but they themselves will not move them with one of their fingers' (Matt. 23.4, AV). Here the Pharisaic regulations are seen as a mass of unnecessary restrictions which oppress the people and divert their attention from vital considerations of morality and spirituality. Another familiar text from the same chapter is: 'Woe unto you, scribes and Pharisees, hypocrites! for you pay tithe of anise and mint and cummin, and have omitted the weightier matters of the law, judgment, mercy and faith; these ought you to have done, and not to leave the other undone' (Matt. 23.23, AV; see Luke 11.42) (this latter text, however, finally comes round to accepting the minutiae of Pharisaic law as necessary, but complains that the perspective and emphasis is wrong; this charge is somewhat different and will require further discussion; actually even the first Matthew text takes the same viewpoint by preceding the verse quoted above with the injunction: 'All therefore whatsoever they bid you observe, that observe and do').

As a test case, let us go back to the incident discussed in Chapter 2 where Jesus rejects the Pharisaic regulation about hand-washing before meals. On the face of it, this incident is a criticism of the Pharisees for making an unnecessary fuss about hand-washing before meals. This is criticized, it appears, as an over-materialistic approach, since it depends on the idea that people can be polluted by failure to observe purity laws, whereas, Jesus urges, only bad thoughts really cause pollution. Impurity cannot be absorbed through the mouth, but only created by the mouth itself when it expresses malicious thoughts.

This interpretation, however, cannot be correct, because it would convict Jesus of total misunderstanding of the Jewish purity laws. The apex of misunderstanding is when Luke represents the Pharisees as practising total immersion of the body before meals (Luke 11.38). He uses the Greek word *ebaptisthe*, which can only refer to total immersion, whereas the other Gospel accounts refer explicitly to the washing of hands – the English translations cover up Luke's howler by simply translating his word as 'washing' instead of 'immersion'.

To practise total immersion before meals would certainly be an exaggerated expression of concern for purity. Perhaps Luke was not really so ignorant as to think that this was Pharisee practice, but was rather afraid that his readers would regard the washing of hands before meals as mere civilized behaviour, rather than as obsessional self-purification, so he changed the story accordingly, from hand-washing to immersion. After all, the washing of hands before eating has always been a practice of civilized communities whether ancient or modern. It is surprising that commentators have invariably omitted to mention this point, but have taken it for granted that Jesus was perfectly justified in criticizing a practice of elementary good manners.

But, it will be objected immediately, Jesus was not criticizing hand-washing as a practice of etiquette and hygiene, but as a practice of ritual purity. Ritual purity was not a matter of washing away dirt, but of washing away imaginary impurities arising from sources (listed in Leviticus) which were regarded as polluting, even though, from a physical point of view, the person might be shining brightly with cleanliness. Indeed, on the contrary, a person might be physically dirty, yet ritually clean (for example, if he had immersed himself for ritual purity purposes in a muddy pool). Physical cleanliness and ritual purity are two different things; and it was the concept of ritual purity that Jesus was criticizing, not that of physical cleanliness.

But was he? In my opinion, a close reading of the passages in the Gospels shows that Jesus cannot have been criticizing the ritual washing of hands, but was indeed criticizing the sanitary or hygienic washing of hands. My reasons are these:

1. In Jesus' time there was no Pharisee law requiring the washing of hands for ritual purity purposes, except for priests (who had previously immersed) about to eat the holy priestly food (*terumah*). The only kind of ritual purity washing practised by ordinary people was immersion of the whole body, since this is the only kind actually mentioned in Scripture, and this was never practised as a preliminary to eating a meal. The ritual purity washing of hands for ordinary people was first introduced over thirty years after Jesus' death. It is practised by ordinary Jews today (before a meal containing bread) as a token practice 'in remembrance of Temple times', not as an actual purifying rite (since it is quite insufficient to remove ritual impurities affecting the whole body). Jesus was not a priest, nor were his disciples, so there would not be any criticism from the Pharisees about his or their omission to wash their hands ritually.

2. Quite apart from the ritual washing of hands, all Jews, as a civilized community, practised the sanitary or hygienic washing of hands before eating. This practice is well attested in the literature, as having been practised long before the ritual practice of hand-washing was instituted in about 66 CE. It is a great mistake to think that the only form of purity known to the Jews was ritual purity. Sanitary washing was strongly advocated because it was regarded as a duty, even a religious duty, to safeguard the health of the body by washing away from the hands any sub-

stances that might prove toxic to the body if introduced. In fact, hand-washing, of a hygienic nature, was practised even during the course of meals; compare the modern practice of using finger-bowls, when moving from one course to another.

3. It is this internal toxicity that Jesus was concerned about in his words about hand-washing, or rather, which he wished to discount as an unnecessary and materialistic worry. In his opinion, concern for health showed lack of faith in God, who had arranged the human body in such a way that it eliminated naturally any toxic substances.

4. Ritual impurity was never regarded as affecting the interior of the body, but only its surface.[1] Jesus' remarks about the interior of the body are thus totally irrelevant to the topic of ritual impurity, though they are very relevant to the topic of sanitary impurity, which may indeed cause danger to health by affecting the interior of the body.

It may be as well at this point to have Jesus' remarks before us, in order to reinforce my point that Jesus was objecting not to ritual purity practices, but to hygienic purity practices:

> Do you not see that nothing that goes from outside into a man can defile him, because it does not enter into his heart but into his stomach, and so passes out into the drain (this is how everything we eat is purified)? (Mark 7.19, Jesus Seminar translation)

What Jesus is saying here quite plainly is, 'Don't worry about being poisoned by anything you eat, because God has arranged the human body in such a way that harmful substances are evacuated and thus rendered harmless.'

Only a determination to read Jesus' remarks as a comment on ritual purity has prevented people from understanding these plain words.[2] Also, the words have been hard to accept in their plain meaning because they seem rather foolish. Surely Jesus cannot have been advocating total indifference to the harm that can be caused by unhygienic eating?

I am not arguing that Jesus was quite as foolish as this. He must

have been aware that it was inadvisable to eat food that was known
to be poisonous, and he did not think that the process of normal
evacuation could deal with really noxious substances. But he did
think that it was going too far to assume that hands in their normal
condition could cause harm to the body that had to be nullified by
a routine practice of washing. And in this, he was following the
opinion of a highly respected section of the Pharisee movement,
the Chasidim, who rejected the majority Pharisee regulations on
hygienic matters as showing lack of faith in the protective power of
God.

It is known that the Chasidim refused to accept the hygienic
regulations instituted by the Pharisee majority. For example, it was
a Pharisee regulation (recorded *m. Ter.* 8.4 and *y. Ter.* 23a) that
liquids left uncovered at night should be thrown away, because of
the danger that a snake may have sipped the liquid and left some of
its venom. This was not a ritual purity regulation, but entirely
hygienic; the Pharisees did not think that anyone would become
ritually impure by drinking such liquids, but they did fear that the
result might be bodily harm through the imbibing of snake-venom,
and they regarded it as part of their duty, as guides of the people,
to institute health measures of this kind, just like local health
authorities in modern communities. The Chasidim, on the other
hand, because of their reliance on the protection of God, preferred
to ignore these health regulations. One story told about a prominent
Chasid, Hanina ben Dosa, was that he was actually bitten by a
scorpion, but it was the scorpion that died, not the Chasid (in an
English parallel story, 'the dog it was that died'). Here the Chasidim
went even further than Jesus, because they thought that God would
protect even from actual poison, not merely from ordinary physical
impurity. Even the Chasidim, however, did not think that such
extraordinary divine protection was available for every Chasid, but
only for outstanding saints such as Hanina.

In general, there was a difference of opinion on hygienic matters
between the general run of Pharisees and that section of them
known as Chasidim. It was a common-sense Pharisee principle that
'one should not rely on a miracle' (*b. Pesah.* 64b, *b. Ta'an.* 20b), but
the Pharisees did not condemn the Chasidim, who ignored this

principle (to some extent), but rather admired them as unusual individuals, who, because of their saintliness, could afford to omit the precautions necessary for ordinary people. It is a great mistake to think (as some scholars have argued) that there was an irreconcilable rift between the Pharisees and the Chasidim. On the contrary, the rabbinic literature contains many admiring stories about the spiritual feats of the Chasidim, whom they regarded as part of their movement, and on whom they called in times of crisis, especially when a prolonged drought called for prayers for rain or when prayers were required for someone suffering from a dangerous illness. But it is characteristic of the Pharisees that they never regarded saintliness as the norm. They regarded their own task as ministering to ordinary people, from whom virtuoso spiritual performances should not be demanded, and the hygienic regulations formed part of this concern.

Thus it is possible that a disagreement arose between the Pharisees and Jesus on the question of hygienic hand-washing; but such a disagreement would not be of a serious nature, but part of a general difference in approach by which the Chasidim sought to attain a standard of saintly behaviour which the mainstream Pharisees thought inappropriate for ordinary people and therefore refused to include in their code of rules.

In many of his sayings (for example, 'take no thought for the morrow'), Jesus appears as typical of the Chasidim, but this by no means takes him out of the Pharisee movement, which contained a wide range of religious types. Geza Vermes, in his well-known book, *Jesus the Jew*,[3] identified Jesus as a member of the Chasidic movement, similar to Hanina ben Dosa. But he made the mistake of thereby taking Jesus out of Pharisaism. The many admiring stories about the Chasidim in Pharisee literature were discounted by Vermes as disguising the irreconcilable conflict that actually existed between the Pharisees and the Chasidim. The admiration expressed in these stories was interpreted as interpolations; the later rabbis wished to take advantage of the high reputation of the Chasidim by pretending that they too were Pharisees, and therefore they 'rabbinized' these figures and played down the tension and conflict that historically existed between them and the Pharisees. This approach had the the advantage, too, of explaining why the Gospels are so anti-Pharisee, and portray Jesus as in serious conflict with the Pharisees. Taking their cue from Vermes, a whole school of New Testament scholars have taken up the notion of 'rabbinization', and have sought to recover the Chasidim as highly idiosyncratic individuals who had little or nothing in common with the Pharisee movement, despite later attempts to 'rabbinize' them. Thus John Dominic Crossan has produced a picture of Jesus that is very similar to Vermes' Jesus, except that he is no longer 'Jesus the Jew', but a Hellenistic wandering Cynic, indifferent to societal priorities – with the difference that while Vermes' Jesus was indifferent to politics, Crossan's Jesus has a generalized unconventionality that makes him oppose all authority-figures, political or non-political, and not only the Pharisees.[4]

The rabbinic stories about the Chasidim do not disguise that tension did exist between the main body of the Pharisees and the Chasidim. But this tension was on minor matters, such as the maintenance of hygienic regulations, as described above. In essentials, the Chasidim were at one with the non-charismatic Pharisees, with whom they were on terms of friendship. The view that the tension was very serious has no firm foundation in the data; such arguments could be used to show that an eccentric saint, such as Francis of Assisi, was not a Catholic (he, in fact, was at times in tension with the Pope, who nevertheless greatly admired him). For example, the tension that did exist between the normative Pharisees and the Chasidim is shown by the existence of a term 'foolish Chasid' (*chasid shoteh*), sometimes found in the literature.

An example given of a such a foolish saint is that of one who forbears to come to the rescue of a naked drowning woman; his reluctance to overcome his prudish horror of nakedness leads to the possible death of a fellow human being. This example is very enlightening about the whole relationship between the normative Pharisees and the Chasidim, and about the general attitude of the Pharisee movement in general. The Pharisees admired high moral standards, but envisaged the possibility that standards could become so strained and unrealistic that ordinary common-or-garden morality could be endangered. The duty to save the life of a person, whether male or female, in danger of drowning is part of ordinary, elementary ethics, incumbent on anyone whether a Chasid or not. To by-pass this duty in the interests of a lofty sense of sexual morality has no moral merit at all. The 'foolish saint' thus turns out to be lower in the moral scale than the ordinary unpretentious individual who dives in to the rescue without giving a thought to sexual proprieties. Yet note that this judgement does not dismiss the notion of sainthood as such. The very fact that there is such a thing as a 'foolish saint' confirms that there is such a thing as true sainthood, which is unattainable by the majority, but which has not severed its links with common humanity and everyday reality.

A serious mistake of Vermes was to confuse hygienic precautions with ritual purity laws. This made him think that because the Chasidim opposed sanitary precautions, they were also opposed to the ritual purity laws. In fact, the opposite was the case: the Chasidim were more meticulous in observance of ritual purity laws than the general run of Pharisees. This was because the ritual purity laws were regarded as having spiritual, rather than physical, relevance. They were laws which brought man and God together; their chief application was to prepare human beings to enter the Temple of God in Jerusalem, but they also were essential for those wishing to enter the Temple on High through mystical experience. We do not know how far the Chasidim were connected with techniques of mystical experience, as found in non-Judaic religions (for example, special techniques of posture and breathing), but such practices appear likely in view of their specialized practice of prayer. We are told, for example, that when Hanina ben Dosa prayed for the life of the son of his friend Yohanan ben Zakkai, he adopted a posture (sitting down with his head bowed between his knees) that is well-known from meditative practice in religions (such as Hinduism) in which mystical practice is central. Later medieval Jewish mysticism knew of such techniques for inducing special raptness, but our knowledge of the techniques of their Talmudic precursors is very sparse, probably because the rabbinic writings, including the Talmuds, regarded mysticism as peripheral to the true business of Judaism, and therefore purposely repressed any extended discussion of such matters.

Yet the question arises, 'Even if Jesus can be accommodated within the ranks of the Pharisees as a member of the Chasidic movement, does he not come under the definition, outlined above, of a "foolish Chasid"?' Even a 'foolish Chasid' was regarded as a member of the Pharisee movement, though one who misunderstood an important Pharisee principle; yet if Jesus had the reputation among the Pharisee majority of being a 'foolish Chasid', this would certainly have lowered his status considerably and perhaps have led to some sharp exchanges which might have formed the basis of the exaggerated conflict-scenes which we find in the Gospels.

Jesus' repudiation of Pharisee hygienic regulations (as described above) would not have led to his being stigmatized as a 'foolish Chasid', a term reserved for a tiny minority of Chasidim whose practices led to serious infringements of Torah law. After all, the example given of a 'foolish Chasid' (one who failed to come to the rescue of a naked drowning woman) was not a case of the flouting of rabbinic regulations, but of neglecting a major Torah principle 'Thou shalt not stand against the blood of thy neighbour', that is, the duty of rescue from immediately threatening death. The regulations ignored by the Chasidim were mere precautions, and the Chasidim were never given the appellation 'foolish Chasidim' on this issue, especially as the rabbis did believe that such precautions could be safely ignored by people of saintly stature, whose special religious status would protect them. The disagreement was simply on the ground that the example of the Chasidim might bring danger to people of lesser stature, who might overestimate their own immunity.

The statements attributed to Jesus which put him in the category of the Chasidim (though not in that of the 'foolish Chasid') are those expressive of pacifism and quietism and also those expressive of indifference to worldly concerns. They may be listed as follows, together with their parallels or near-parallels in the Talmudic records regarding the Chasidim:

Resist not evil (Matt. 5.39, AV)
[Say not thou, I will recompense evil (Prov. 20.22, AV)]

'Whosoever shall smite thee on thy right cheek, turn to him the other also' (Matt. 5.39, AV).
[Rabbinic: 'To those who curse me may my soul be dumb' *b. Ber.* 17a]

'Take therefore no thought for the morrow' (Matt. 6.34, AV).
[Rabbi Eliezer the Great said: 'He who has bread in his basket, and says, "What shall I eat tomorrow?" belongs to those who are small in faith' *b. Sotah* 48b]

Here it should be noted that the rabbinic parallels are not exact, because they are put forward as counsels of perfection, not as universal principles applicable to all human beings. Moreover, the rabbinic parallels are put forward as guides to the practice of the speaker himself, as declarations of abnegation of the speaker's own rights, not as the denial or abolition of the rights of others. Thus Jesus is represented as saying that if someone takes away your coat, you should give him your cloak too (Matt. 5.40). This is an admirable precept for the individual saint, who hopes to shame a bully into discovering his own conscience, but if elevated to a general principle of morality, it would abolish all the moral effort that goes into the protection of the weak against the strong. Surely it is an important point of morality to stand up steadfastly for the rights of others. The story is told of Spinoza that, after the death of his parents, his sisters tried to deny him all his rights of inheritance (on the grounds of his heretical views). Spinoza fought this attempt in court, and won his case; but to show that his resistance was actuated by principle, not greed, he immediately handed over the sum assigned to him by the court to his sisters. This was an act inspired by the Jewish sense of sainthood, rather than the Christian understanding of the words of Jesus: a true Christian, following Jesus as generally understood, would not have fought the court case at all, but would have handed over the whole inheritance to the sisters without a fight. The principle for which Spinoza was fighting was one of wide application; that legal heirs should not be deprived of their inheritances. He wished to establish this principle, not for his own sake, as he was indifferent to money considerations, but for the sake of legal heirs everywhere, whom he would have betrayed if he had merely succumbed to the bullying of his sisters.

But have the words of Jesus been correctly understood – or was his attitude actually closer to that of Spinoza? Jesus is reported to have said, 'Resist not evil.' This saying is actually a part-quotation from the Hebrew Bible, but there is a very significant difference. The Hebrew Bible (Proverbs) says, 'Recompense not evil.' This means 'Do not retaliate against an evil act done to you by doing an evil act in return.' It does not mean, 'Do nothing at all in return.' In the form attributed to Jesus, 'Resist not evil,' the saying is a very dubious expression of would-be saintliness. If practised against Hitler, this precept would have led to the subjugation of the whole world to Nazism. As it happens, Gandhi, the apostle of non-violence did advocate a policy of appeasement towards Hitler. But not many people nowadays would believe that such a policy would have induced a change of heart in Hitler. A policy that succeeded in British India (where massacre was at first tried as a deterrent and then abandoned as impossibly contrary to the British ethos) would not have succeeded against a remorseless psychopath, at the head of a whole nation imbued with his spirit of fanaticism. 'Resist not evil' is a discredited moral precept, the formula of appeasement, and the abandonment of the world to the rule of bullies and psychopaths. Trollope has one of his characters say, 'If someone takes my hat I do not believe in handing him my coat too; the next thing is, he will be taking my trousers.' This is an interesting expression in fiction of Christian hesitancy about Jesus' precept: the character concerned is portrayed as lacking in spirituality, yet Trollope, as a practical man of the world (though a convinced Christian) cannot help sympathizing with him in this matter. Christian ambivalence, as a matter of historical record, about Jesus' alleged quietism will be discussed shortly.

But did Jesus actually say, 'Resist not evil'? I think it probable that (as so often) he was simply quoting Scripture, and what he actually said was, 'Recompense not evil.' But it is not impossible that he actually said, 'Resist not evil,' but like other Pharisee Chasidim, he was pronouncing a counsel of perfection intended only for the few, not a general principle of morality for the guidance of ordinary people. On the contrary, he would be in favour of resisting evil when it was directed against other people: otherwise, he would be washing his hands of the obligation to come to the rescue of a neighbour threatened by violence or oppression ('Thou shalt not stand against the blood of thy neighbour', Lev. 19.16, AV). Not to retaliate when one is oneself attacked is saintly, according to the Chasidic code. But not to intervene to protect the life of one's fellow-man is mere cowardice and selfishness. According to a rabbinic law of great antiquity, there was a right of 'citizen's arrest', which came into play when one saw a person fleeing from a 'pursuer' (*rodef*) intent on murder. It was a positive duty to come to the rescue, at the risk of one's own life, and also at the risk of depriving the pursuer of his life, if no other method of rescue was possible (here there was a strong requirement for detailed subsequent enquiry to ensure that no undue violence was used, but only enough for the purpose of rescue). But on Jesus' advice, as usually understood, the would-be rescuer should stand aside and watch the murder being committed without interference. There is thus a great need to interpret Jesus' more extreme sayings in the light of the Pharisaic Chasidism of his day.

Similarly, Jesus' sayings about taking no thought for the morrow should be interpreted in the light of Chasidism. The rabbinic writings make clear that for most people, taking thought for the morrow is not only permitted but highly desirable. There are some rare souls who can throw themselves on the mercy of God for their sustenance, and devote their lives to meditation. But there is great danger here not only of encouraging ordinary people to allow themselves and their families to slip into penury or starvation, but also of encouraging charlatans to sponge on their hard-working neighbours on the pretence of living saintly lives far above the need for self-provision. There is a rabbinic saying that is at the opposite pole to Jesus', 'Take no thought for the morrow', and yet, ultimately, is not at variance with it. The rabbinic saying is: 'It is better to skin animals in the street for a living than to say to one's neighbours, "I am a great man; come and feed me"' (*b. B. Bat.* 110a). In some societies, holy mendicancy is encouraged (Hindu fakirs, Franciscan friars), but in Pharisaic Judaism, while support of beggars is regarded as a great duty, the beggars themselves are never sanctified; indeed, it is regarded as more meritorious to provide the beggar with a means of livelihood by giving him work to do. Taking no thought for the morrow is indeed advocated in several sayings, but no one is encouraged to take no thought for today. The rabbinic approach is well illustrated in one passage of the New Testament, Jesus' thoroughly Jewish prayer 'the Lord's Prayer', which contains the words: 'Give us this day our daily bread.' This confines one's worry to one day, but to gain sustenance for that one day, one is expected to work.

It is thus not a mistake to regard Jesus as taking a view that excludes him from the constant worry about the future that is the lot of the ordinary man; but this does not take Jesus out of the Pharisee movement, but rather identifies him with one section of it, namely the Chasidim, who elected to live a life that even they did not advocate as a general policy. At the same time, it is important to take into account another consideration: that Jesus regarded himself as living in the Last Days, when taking thought for the morrow was contraindicated simply because there was not going to be any morrow, at least in the sense of a normal tomorrow. At any moment, a new (but not supernatural) world would burst out into being, and all counsels of prudence would prove beside the point. This is where Jesus' adherence to the principles of Chasidism ties in with his conviction of the imminence of a messianic period. In fact, it is probable that this conviction of the imminence of the 'kingdom of Heaven' played a part in the lives of all those who lived the Chasidic life. This is where what appears to be an apolitical view (indifference to the calculations that form the substance of politics) joins hands with a strongly political view (the expectation of the overthrow of the Roman Empire and the advent of a new system of world governance, 'the kingdom of Heaven').

This is why certain people who might seem very otherworldly in their way of life (for example John the Baptist, the wandering desert-dweller and preacher of repentance) were seen by the authorities as a political threat (it is clear from Josephus, *Antiquities* 18.5.118, that John the Baptist met his death for political reasons, not for the *grand guignol* reasons given in the New Testament). In

Judaism, a renunciation of ordinary politics might go along with a revolutionary brand of politics that would alarm all persons in political authority, especially the Romans and their henchmen the High Priest and his entourage. When, as in Jesus' case, the conviction of the imminence of the 'kingdom of Heaven' went along with a conviction that he, Jesus, was himself the promised Messiah who would usher in God's Kingdom and act in the role of earthly king of Israel, a collision-course with the powers-that-be became inevitable (though this self-identification as the messianic king came somewhat late in the course of Jesus' career, at the time of the Salutation of Peter).

The above characterization of Jesus as a Pharisee, but an unusual one in that he belonged to a minority group of Pharisees known as Chasidim and also because he had active messianic hopes in which he himself played a central role, is at odds (though not entirely) with a view of Jesus that has gained popularity in recent years (though there are already signs that its popularity is waning). I am referring to the view of John Dominic Crossan and his adherents, who see Jesus as a kind of Diogenes figure – a wandering hippy or self-elected outcast, who despised all norms and authorities, and saw himself in the role of a peasant philosopher similar to the Greek Cynics. It is necessary to examine this view of Jesus, which would cut Jesus off from Pharisaism altogether, though it does take account of certain authentic features presented in the Gospels, that is, those features that identify him as a Chasid.

4

The Leper and the Tax-Collector

A good test-case for the Crossan theory is the incident of the healing of the leper by Jesus. The incident is reported in Matthew as
follows:

> And behold, there came a leper and worshipped him, saying,
> Lord if thou wilt, thou canst make me clean. And Jesus put forth
> his hand, and touched him, saying, I will; be thou clean. And
> immediately his leprosy was cleansed.
>
> And Jesus saith unto him: See thou tell no man; but go thy way,
> and show thyself to the priest and offer the gift that Moses com-
> manded, for a testimony unto them. (Matt. 8.2–4, AV; parallels in
> Mark 1.40–44; Luke 5.12–14)

At first sight, this passage is a great blow to Crossan's general
picture of Jesus as an anti-Establishment figure implacably opposed
to the ceremonial rites and sacrifices of the Temple. After curing the
leper, Jesus reminds him that a cured leper is enjoined by the Law
of Moses to undergo a purification procedure which includes a
sacrifice in the Temple (Lev. 4.3–10). This seems to show that Jesus
had respect for the Temple and its sacrifices, and had no wish to
abolish it or them.

Crossan, however, avoids this conclusion by putting a special
emphasis on the word 'clean'.[1] Jesus says to the leper, not 'Be thou
cured', but 'Be thou clean'. It is then said, not 'his leprosy was
cured', but 'his leprosy was cleansed'. This shows, according to
Crossan, that Jesus was claiming to be able to carry out purifications
and thereby abolishing the prerogative of the Temple. The whole
incident, therefore, instead of being an endorsement of the Temple,
becomes an attack on it.

In that case, why did Jesus, having 'cleansed' the leper insist that he should undergo the purification ceremony in the Temple?

Crossan explains this primarily as a later addition to the story, which in its earliest form told only of a cure or cleansing and did not contain anything about the Temple. Crossan also lays stress on the detail that, in Mark's account of the incident, Jesus actually touches the leper, thus flouting the laws of impurity. Here Crossan falls victim to the error (now exposed as such by various authors) that it was regarded as a sin to incur ritual impurity: in fact, in all rabbinic treatment of the subject, ritual impurity is regarded as simply an inevitable accident of life, which requires correction by immersion if the person concerned wishes to enter the Temple (the only kind of ritual impurity that is regarded as sinful is corpse-impurity if wilfully incurred by a priest, and even here exceptions were made for emergencies). Thus by touching the leper, Jesus was not in any way flouting rabbinic regulations: on the contrary, if such contact was necessary for the completion of his cure, this would be praised as a holy act, since curing the sick is in all rabbinic thought a meritorious deed. There was no more meritorious act than burying the dead, yet all involved in this became ritually impure: which shows clearly that to regard the process of becoming ritually impure as sinful is mere confusion.

The Temple authorities never claimed to be able to perform cures of leprosy or any other disease. They dealt only with lepers who had already been cured, and their purification rites were enjoined by Leviticus as transition rites conveying thankfulness for the cure and preparation for resumption of ordinary life. Thus it was perfectly logical for Jesus, after curing the leper, to enjoin him to go to the Temple to become 'cleansed'. If the man said to the priests, 'I have been cured of leprosy by Jesus,' the reaction of the priests (if they knew of his previous condition) would be to consider the possibility that Jesus was the promised healing Messiah. This may explain why Jesus was so insistent upon the leper's going to the Temple, rather than leaving this to the piety of the man himself.

It seems that Crossan is reading far too much into Jesus' use of the expression 'Be thou clean'. The expression 'clean' was probably used popularly as a synonym for 'cured', especially in the case of a leper, whose illness conferred uncleanness, and whose cure would lead inevitably (after the prescribed procedures) to ritual cleanness. It seems that Crossan here is clutching at straws, to rescue a passage that in its main outlines affirms Jesus' loyalty to Mosaic Law and to the Temple.

No doubt, if this incident appeared only in the Gospel of Matthew, it would be cited as an example of Matthew's alleged special concern to judaize Jesus (by depicting him as showing reverence to the laws of Moses). But the incident (including Jesus' injunction to undergo the Temple cleansing) appears in all three Synoptic Gospels, and is thus one of the best-attested incidents in Jesus' career, since it would have been easy for Mark and Luke to recount the healing episode while omitting the Temple-injunction and the reference to Moses. All three Synoptic Gospels attest to Jesus' loyal adherence to the Law of Moses, and to the rites of the Temple.[2]

Indeed, as Mark tells the story, the words 'for a testimony unto them' take on a significance which is the direct opposite of what Crossan wants them to mean (that is, to show them that Jesus has taken over the cleansing function previously performed by the Temple rites). For Mark juxtaposes these words to the injunction 'say nothing to any man' (Mark 1.44, AV). Thus Jesus particularly wanted the priests to be aware of his healing (not his cleansing) power, so that he could enlist them in advance on his side in his coming messianic campaign. Healing was one of the activities predicted by the Hebrew prophets for the Messiah. While Jesus, at this point, did not want to make public pronouncement of his messianic claim, he wanted to bring it to the attention of the priests who would be particularly useful allies to him when he finally appeared in public as 'son of David' and messianic king. While the Sadducee High Priest and his entourage could be expected to oppose this claim, as they opposed all messianic claimants (who threatened their position as hangers-on of the Roman Occupation), the rank and file of the priests were Pharisees (as Josephus and the rabbinic writings attest) and looked forward eagerly to the day when Roman rule would end, and an independent Jewish state would arise under the revived Mosaic constitution. Jesus is here appealing explicitly to the rank-and-file priests, not to the quislings surrounding the High Priest.

The fact that the whole incident of the cured leper is lacking in the Gospel of John is proof of its authenticity rather than the opposite, for it runs counter to John's whole picture of Jesus as a divine figure who owned no allegiance to Moses and had no hesitation in overruling him. John had every motive for suppressing a story that shows just the opposite – that Jesus revered the Law of Moses and adjured his cured patient to follow it, and to provide evidence to the priests both of his messianic power of healing and of his adherence to the priestly code.

Crossan's interpretation of the leper incident is part of a campaign by the Crossan group to dissociate Jesus altogether from the Jewish laws relating to ritual purity. Indeed, Marcus Borg, a disciple of Crossan, sees Jesus as engaged in a major way in countering and nullifying the ritual purity laws, which Borg sees as fundamental to Jewish religious society and as especially stressed by the Pharisees. This is an approach that misunderstands Jewish ritual purity law as similar to ritual purity law in Hindu society and in tribal societies, demarcating society into superior and inferior groups and reducing the lower groups to outcast status. Borg, in fact, thinks that he is adopting a comparative anthropological approach to the study of the Jewish ritual purity laws, and thus portraying Jesus as champion of the outcasts in Jewish society.

We may now consider another key incident that concerns (or is alleged to concern) the topic of ritual purity. Among the alleged outcasts of Jewish society whom Jesus is thought to have befriended in direct contravention of accepted mores were the tax-collectors. The Gospels say that Jesus was criticized by the Pharisees and others for associating with tax-collectors and sinners and in particular for sharing meals with them. Commentators have often said that this criticism arose from considerations of ritual purity, which was especially important in the sharing of meals. This explanation arises from a misunderstanding of the place of ritual purity in Judaism. It also involves importing ritual purity considerations into texts which do not mention them (not once in the New Testament is it said that tax-collectors were ritually unclean). The topic of

Jesus' alleged flouting of ritual purity rules has already been raised in an earlier chapter in connection with the washing of hands, and the same topic has been imported, in a very unconvincing way, into the incident of the leper. The topic of the alleged impurity of tax-collectors, however, will enable us to examine the whole issue in a broader way, and to show how profoundly the ritual purity code in Judaism has been misunderstood in much of the scholarly literature on the subject. Many misunderstandings have arisen from misreadings of passages in the rabbinic literature.

A prominent example of misunderstanding of this kind is the interpretation often given of a passage in the Mishnah:

> If taxgatherers entered a house all that is within it becomes unclean. Even if a gentile was with them, they may be believed if they say 'We did not enter', but (if a gentile was with them) they may not be believed if they say, 'We entered but we touched nothing.' If thieves entered a house only that part is unclean that was trodden by the feet of the thieves. (*m. Toh.* 7.6)

This has been interpreted to mean that tax-collectors suffered from an extraordinary degree of ritual impurity, since they affected everything in the house with impurity merely by entering it. That this cannot be the meaning of the passage is indicated by another Mishnah passage:

> If tax collectors entered a house (so too if thieves restored stolen vessels) they may be deemed trustworthy if they say, 'We have not touched.' (*m. Hag.* 3.6)

The meaning of these two passages is as follows. If Jewish tax-collectors entered a house, all within it becomes unclean, whereas thieves do not render all the contents of the house unclean. This is not because tax-collectors are uniquely unclean, but because tax-collectors are assumed to touch everything in the house (in order to assess the value of its contents), while thieves touch only items they are interested in stealing. On the other hand, if the tax-collector returns and declares to the house owner that he did not touch anything (that is, he entered but only looked at the objects he was assessing), he is believed, since as a Jew he is assumed to have some regard for truth and fellowship, especially as he has taken the trouble to return to explain matters. But if the tax-collector was accompanied by a Gentile supervisor at the time of his first entry, even if he later returns and declares that he did not touch anything he is not believed, since it is assumed that his fear of his supervisor (who would have regarded mere looking as negligent) would have been stronger than his regard for his fellow-Jew. His present declaration, therefore, is regarded as motivated only by a desire for self-exculpation and ingratiation, and is not believed. A thief, on the other hand, who returns what he stole and declares that he did not touch anything else, is believed without qualification. Only the items which he is returning to the owner of the house are reckoned to be unclean since he manifestly touched them. He has demonstrated his trustworthiness by his repentance, and did not have any special reason to touch other items in the house (here this Mishnah simply repeats the ruling of the Mishnah previously quoted).

A number of conclusions follow from the above explanation of the two Mishnah passages. First, the idea that the mere entry of the tax-collector into a house caused all within it to become unclean may be dismissed. Uncleanness can be transferred by the tax-collector to an object only by his touching it: if he entered the house but did not touch anything, everything remains clean. The only question mooted is whether he can be believed when he says he did not touch anything.

In the ritual purity system of Judaism, there are only three instances of an impurity-source causing all contents of an enclosed space to become unclean even without physical contact with actual objects. Two are biblical – the corpse in the tent (Num. 19.14–16), and the dead 'creeping thing' that falls into the space of an earthenware vessel (Lev. 11.33), and the other probably rabbinic: the 'leper' who enters a 'habitation' (*m. Neg.* 13.7). Apart from these, impurity is imparted only by contact or pressure or (in the case of corpse-impurity) by 'overshadowing' (that is, presence directly above or below the source of impurity). Thus for a tax-collector to cause impurity to the contents of a house merely by entering it would be contrary to all principles of the system, whether biblical or rabbinic.

Next, it is also contrary to all such principles for a person to be unclean simply because of his profession or status in society. A tax-collector is not automatically unclean just because he is a tax-collector. Tax-collectors were in general regarded as 'sinners', because they extorted excessive sums on behalf of the Roman occupying authority, often using methods of torture; their procedure is described fully by Philo (*On Special Laws*, IV). But sinners were not made unclean by their sin. The remedy for sin was repentance and not purification. The sources of impurity are clearly stated in Leviticus (corpse, leprosy, menstruation, gonorrhoea, etc.) and they are the same for every member of Jewish society from the High Priest down to the humblest labourer. If a tax-collector wishes to be ritually clean (having contracted one of the above kinds of impurity), he can undergo the prescribed purification and become cleansed of his impurity, whatever it may be, just like anyone else. He remains a sinner, but is now a sinner in a state of ritual purity.

It is the perennial question, 'Why was Jesus crucified?' that motivates the misrepresentations of the Jewish laws of ritual purity. It has always been tempting to scholars to give the answer: 'He was crucified because he flouted the ritual purity laws.' In recent years, this line (deriving from nineteenth-century scholars Emil Schürer and Ferdinand Weber, and reinforced more recently by Joachim Jeremias and the Jewish scholar Jacob Neusner) has received an impetus from anthropological studies, which have shown various primitive societies (in addition to the more familiar and more sophisticated society of Hinduism) as dominated by concern for ritual purity. One anthropologist, however, Mary Douglas, has resisted this trend, by pointing out that the Jewish ritual purity laws, as found in Leviticus and the rabbinic writings, show a fundamental difference from the purity-dominated societies which she studied in Africa: the Jewish laws never use purity to demarcate societal divisions: 'They maintain absolutely no social demarcation . . . no one is excluded from the benefits of purification.'[3]

The only feature that remotely supports the idea of purity as a form of demarcation is the fact that the priests had to pay more attention to purity than non-priests. This was because the priests, in the course of their duties, had to enter the Temple far more often than non-priests, and also because priests ate the holy food or *terumah*, for which ritual purity was required. (Most of the priests were poor, and this food, an agricultural tax, constituted their main source of livelihood.) Moreover, priests were forbidden, unlike other Jews, to incur corpse-impurity (except for a close relative) so avoidance of, or purification from impurity loomed more prominently in their lives. On the other hand, this did not make the priests into an isolated class, since any impurity incurred from contact with ordinary Jews could easily be purified away, and therefore there was no need to practise sedulous avoidance of ordinary folk, who were habitually in a state of impurity except at festival-times (when they visited the Temple). In practice, the main difference was that the priests visited the ritual-purity pool more frequently. Ordinary non-priestly Jews were not forbidden to incur corpse-impurity or any other form of impurity; this fact alone refutes the mass of so-called scholarly material that takes for granted that impurity was regarded as sinful and conferred a stigma.

Ignoring the warning of Mary Douglas, some scholars, notably Marcus Borg, have jumped to the conclusion that first-century Jewish purity laws did demarcate divisions in Jewish society, putting certain classes beyond the pale. On this view, it was because Jesus sought to break down these purity-derived divisions that he fell foul of the Jewish authorities and thus met his death. The misunderstanding of the law as it affected tax-collectors, analysed above, is just one of the many misunderstandings which have distorted the rabbinic evidence to produce a fantasy of a society wracked by purity-based divisions.

Marcus Borg has sought to confirm the picture of the isolation of whole classes of society by quoting certain rabbinic passages which show disapproval of certain trades or professions. For example, the following seven trades are described as 'despised', and their practitioners as 'outcasts', though Borg does at least make the proviso that 'the status of "sinner" or "outcast" was not inherited, and thus did not have the rigidity found in some caste systems':[4] 'Gamblers with dice, usurers, organisers of games of chance, dealers in produce of the sabbatical year, shepherds, tax-collectors and revenue farmers' (*b. Sanh.* 25b). These people, however, did not form any 'identifiable social group', as Borg suggests, they were individuals whose activities disqualified them from performing certain functions. The first four categories are people excluded from being witnesses or judges (*m. Sanh.* 3:3), because they were regarded as having withdrawn from the 'settlement of the world' (that is, the duty of contributing to the building of a just society). Nothing is said about such people being outcasts or being affected by ritual impurity. Shepherds, on the other hand, were regarded as robbers, since they allowed their animals to graze on crops. Again, no ritual impurity was involved. This denigration of shepherds was strictly confined to social conditions of the time, when bitter conflict existed between farmers and shepherds. If a blanket condemnation of shepherds were intended, this would have had to include the Patriarchs and Moses.

Tax-collectors and revenue-farmers were also regarded as robbers, because they collected more than was due, using violence. Again, no ritual impurity was involved.

Borg[5] quotes *m. Toh.* 7.6, with the usual misunderstanding that tax-collectors were unusually defiling. This error is discussed above.

Borg also quotes a passage citing members of trades suspected of immorality: workers in the transport trades, herdsmen, shopkeepers, physicians, butchers, goldsmiths, flaxcombers, handmill cleaners, peddlers, weavers, barbers, launderers, bloodletters, bath attendants, and tanners.[6] In context, Borg appears to be saying that all these categories were relegated to a state of ritual impurity.

The passage quoted is a comment on the unsatisfactoriness of all methods of making a living, compared with the blessedness of freedom from toil and contemplation of the Torah: this is an exaggerated expression of idealism comparable with Jesus' protest against making a living when he said, 'Consider the lilies of the field, how they grow; they toil not, neither do they spin' (Matt. 6.28, AV). If someone were to conclude from this that Jesus regarded all toilers and spinners as sinners, he would be making the same error as Borg and Jeremias in relation to this passage in the Mishnah. Other passages in the rabbinic writings could be quoted to prove the exact opposite: that self-absolution from toil is sinful, and that all trades and professions, however loathsome, are preferable to idleness or dependence on others (see p. 37).

In any case, the passage quoted is a pericope of aggadic material appended to the end of a tractate and certainly not intended to have any serious halakhic application.[7] It consists of aphorisms uttered by some rather eccentric and extra-normative rabbis. To take only one example, the condemnation of physicians is contradicted by the whole noble Jewish tradition of medicine; some of the greatest Jewish religious figures, including Maimonides and Nachmanides, were physicians. The citation of this passage is a prime instance of taking material out of context to prove a large social thesis. To take the eccentric aphorism of the otherwise unknown Abba Guria, for example, as proof of a social reality, that is, the alleged ostracism and deprivation of rights of whole classes of essential and respected professionals, tradesmen and artisans, is an example of flawed method.

Borg has some special remarks on tax-collectors. He says that they were unusually defiling and incapable of repentance, but the chief objection to them was their association with Gentiles. Here too he says that Gentiles were defiling, but also mentions that quisling behaviour was involved; this last point is the only valid one. He does not mention the violent gangster methods associated with tax-farming, as described by Philo.

It is true that by a rabbinic decree of about 66 CE, a degree of ritual impurity was assigned to Gentiles, previously regarded as free of ritual impurity, a condition that, by the Torah, applied to Jews only.[8] But this did not mean that those who associated with Gentiles for their livelihood were excluded from the usual means of purification, which they were at liberty to use whenever purity was required (usually at festival times when the Temple was frequented). So this consideration (of unusually frequent association with Gentiles) does nor make tax-collectors incorrigibly unclean.

As for Borg's remark that tax-collectors were regarded as incapable of repentance, the text which he quotes (*b. Bek.* 94b) actually means the opposite of what Borg thinks. It means that robbers, including tax-collectors, can and do repent, and the rabbis (under the persuasion of Rabbi Judah the Prince) made it specially easy for

them to repent by advising their victims to adopt the selfless policy
of voluntarily refusing attempted restitution – otherwise other
robbers might be deterred from repenting. Other passages (see particularly *t. B. Metzi'a* 18.26) say that it is difficult for tax-collectors
to repent because it is so difficult for them to make restitution to
their victims.[9] They should therefore seek to restore the wrongly-
acquired money by contributing to public works, such as the water-
system – in this way some of the benefit would be bound to reach
their victims. Note that Jewish conceptions of repentance regard
restitution as an essential element: mere emotional remorse is not
enough, if one's victims have not been recompensed for the losses
they have suffered. On the other hand, it was regarded as a praise-
worthy act for the victim to waive the recompense when offered (see
above).

The New Testament story of Zacchaeus, the repentant tax-
collector (Luke 19), is much illuminated by reference to the rabbinic treatment of the subject. Objections were made to Jesus' being
a guest of Zacchaeus, 'a sinner'. But the answer to this came when
Zacchaeus made public repentance; this would put an end to the
objections from the Pharisees. No Pharisee would object to Jesus
consorting with a repentant sinner. Borg thinks wrongly that as a
tax-collector, in rabbinic thinking, Zacchaeus would be permanently a sinner, and could never repent; consequently, according to
Borg the New Testament's picture of Zacchaeus as a repentant tax-
collector constitutes an attack on rabbinic thinking and a proof of
Jesus' opposition to the Pharisees. Here again, Borg is entirely
wrong. Zacchaeus' proposals for restitution are similar to those prescribed for robbers and tax-collectors in the rabbinic writings,
except that Zacchaeus proposes to give fourfold restitution to
known victims and also to give money to charity (presumably when
the victims were unknown).

Fourfold restitution is not required by the rabbis, and is a supererogatory expression of repentance probably based on Exod. 22.1
and 2 Sam. 12.6. The rabbis thought that most tax-collectors would
have robbed so many that they would have only hazy recollection
of whom exactly they had robbed (this comprised the chief obstacle
to restitution). This is why the rabbis prescribed contribution to

public works (in addition to reparation to known victims). Zacchaeus' method of giving to charity seems to have been an alternative way of dealing with the problem.

After Zacchaeus repented and made lavish reparations, what was the next step for him? Would he have to give up being a tax-collector? Given the conditions of the time, when tax-collectors were corrupt as a class, the answer is probably 'Yes.' Another answer is possible, however: Zacchaeus could remain a tax-collector if he determined to go against the grain and be an honest one, that is, one who exacted only the legal dues and did not seek to enrich himself by extorting extra sums. This possibility is envisaged in the rabbinic writings (*b. Bek.* 113a), and also in the New Testament (the case of the tax-collectors who approached John the Baptist, Luke 3.13).

The sum of the matter, then, is this: tax-collectors incurred disapproval on moral grounds, and could receive forgiveness by repentance, which had to include reparation, or at least attempts at reparation. In terms of ritual purity, they were exactly the same as all other Jews and had no special impurity as a class. The ideas that tax-collectors were unusually unclean and were regarded as incapable of repentance derive from misreadings of passages in the Mishnah and Talmud. These ideas sometimes form part of a general mistaken thesis (allegedly supported by anthropological research) that first-century Jewish society was riven by purity-based divisions. In fact, Jewish purity laws did not lead to social demarcation, since impurity was permitted except when entering the Temple, and purification, when required, was available to all, including tax-collectors. Disapproval of tax-collectors was on moral, not ritual purity, grounds, since they acted corruptly and oppressively. The case of the repentant tax-collector, Zacchaeus, and his offer of reparation can be fully understood through rabbinic parallels. The fact that Jesus consorted with tax-collectors (in the hope of inducing them to repent as Zacchaeus did of their dishonest and cruel practices) has no tendency whatever to prove the existence of a rift between Jesus and the Pharisees.

5

The Pharisees, the Poor and Authority

The Gospels locate the Pharisees among the rich. We are told that they battened on the poor and made huge profits from the poor: 'Woe unto you, scribes and Pharisees, hypocrites! for ye devour widows' houses, and for a pretence make long prayer: therefore ye shall receive the greater damnation' (Matt. 23.14; Luke 20.47; Mark 12.40, AV). This charge of oppression of widows could hardly be surpassed as a form of condemnation, since the Hebrew Bible makes such a continual point of the protection of widows and orphans as a central moral duty For example, Exod. 22.22–4, AV: 'Ye shall not afflict any widow, or fatherless child. If thou afflict them in any wise, and they cry at all unto me, I will surely hear their cry; And my wrath shall wax hot, and I will kill you with the sword; and your wives shall be widows, and your children fatherless.' See also Deut. 27.19, AV: 'Cursed be he that perverteth the judgment of the stranger, fatherless, and widow.'

This charge that the Pharisees callously flouted one of the most sacred principles of the Torah is hard to reconcile with other testimonies in the Gospels that the Pharisees were meticulous observers of the laws of the Torah. For example, 'For I say unto you, That except your righteousness shall exceed the righteousness of the scribes and Pharisees, ye shall in no case enter into the kingdom of heaven' (Matt. 5.20, AV). Here the Pharisees are being held up as an example of righteousness; otherwise, what would be the point of saying that Jesus' followers were to aim at exceeding their righteousness? If we take Matt. 23 seriously, this would be like saying that they could enter the kingdom of Heaven only if their righteousness exceeded that of Al Capone. In general, the New Testament's treatment of the Pharisees is full of the most extraordinary contradictions. On the one hand, they are vilified as hypocritical villains, utterly devoid of moral principle, and on the other, they are held up as showing the highest standard of virtue possible under the old dispensation of the Mosaic law.

But we are concerned in this chapter with the special charge that the Pharisees accumulated wealth at the expense of the poor. Is there any ground in other sources for this charge? Or is the evidence all the other way: that the Pharisees were themselves the champions of the poor, that they were almost all poor people themselves, and that, like Jesus, they opposed the oppressions of the rich? Here we must turn to the evidence of Josephus, of the intertestamental literature, and of the rabbinic writings (which have been dismissed groundlessly as too late to cast light on the first century, but in fact contain much evidence that is relevant). In addition, we must look at other evidence from the New Testament itself, which contradicts and refutes its own charge against the Pharisees as rich oppressors.

Josephus testifies to three things:

1. that the Pharisees were supported by the mass of the people; (*Antiquities* 17.1.15)
2. that the Pharisees, far from being powerful Establishment figures, were continually at odds with the rich Jewish Establishment and not infrequently suffered persecution from them; (*Antiquities* 13.10.298)
3. that the Pharisees provided the backbone of the Resistance to the Roman Occupation, even though, as a body, they preserved an officially uncommitted approach (*Antiquities* 18.1.23).

The rabbinic writings provide further evidence of the identification of the Pharisees with the poor. They show that many of the Pharisees, probably most of them, were themselves poor. Some of their greatest leaders made their living by the work of their hands (for example, Hillel was a manual labourer, Shammai was a carpenter). Some of them, who were rich, devoted themselves to charitable works. The movement, in fact, transcended the division between rich and poor. In the assembly of the rabbis, a rich rabbi and a poor rabbi had exactly one vote each, and counted as equals in discussion.

The New Testament itself, despite its vicious diatribes against the Pharisees, provides much evidence in their favour. For example, it stresses the popularity of Gamaliel with the people, though it neglects the fact that Gamaliel was not just a Pharisee, but the leader of the whole Pharisee movement. If the Pharisees were 'devourers of widows' houses' and in general hypocrites and oppressors, why was their most representative figure so loved by the people? We must conclude that there are two trends at work here, one of which seeks to blacken the Pharisees in every way, and the other of which portrays them sympathetically as popular religious leaders who were not regarded by the people as a sect, but as their guides in everyday religious practice and in fact as the guardians of normative Judaism against sectarian religion as practised by the Sadducees, Essenes, apocalyptic sects, Samaritans, and others. Their supreme reputation is grudgingly granted in the New Testament phrase, 'The Pharisees sit in Moses' seat' (Matt. 23.2, AV), though the sentence then continues in derogatory fashion. It is here granted that the Pharisees have an authority beyond that of all the sects that laid claim to have superseded them.

Yet there is here something of a paradox. For the New Testament also stresses that the Pharisees speak 'without authority' (in contrast to Jesus who speaks with such an air of authority that this is taken by the people, according to the authors of the Gospels, to be a sign of his divinity).

> And straightway on the sabbath day he entered into the synagogue, and taught. And they were astonished at his doctrine: for he taught them as one that had authority, and not as the scribes. (Mark 1.21–2, AV; see also Matt. 7.28–9)

This is an incident which must have puzzled many readers, for taken in conjunction with all the accusations against the scribes and Pharisees for their pride and their manifold issue of injunctions, how is it that we now find them described as people who did not claim authority? But in fact we here glimpse something that was true about the Pharisees: the modest claims they made for themselves. Though they 'sat in Moses' seat', they by no means claimed the authority of Moses or any other prophet. When one steps from the atmosphere of the New Testament to that of the rabbinic writings, one is struck by a huge difference. In the Gospels, there is really only one figure, that of Jesus, to whom all others are infinitely subordinate. If anyone disagrees with him, that can only be through malice, not from genuine difference of viewpoint. In the rabbinic writings, however, there is no dominant figure. All the rabbis are equal and constantly disagree with each other, in an amicable way. If a disagreement cannot be settled by argument, it is taken to the vote. Even when a ruling is pronounced, it is done in a non-authoritative way: there are no instances of 'thou shalt' or 'thou shalt not'; instead there is an impersonal statement of the decision – this is what 'one' does. The use of participles instead of imperatives in rabbinic literature has been much remarked on; but the ethos behind this usage has perhaps not been sufficiently noted. Here the rabbinic writings differ not only from the New Testament, but also from the Dead Sea Scrolls and all the other intertestamental writings which claimed 'authority' and in fact claimed to be part of the canon of Scripture.

For the Pharisees, the age of inspiration had ceased, and in its place had come an age of rational discourse, in which any qualified person could express an opinion, but no one could claim 'authority'. The inspiration of the Bible (that is, the Hebrew Scriptures) was unquestioned, but the interpretation of these Scriptures was open to discussion, and no one had unquestioned authority to state what exactly the meaning of any disputed passage was.

Several different attitudes could, and can, be taken towards this humble posture. One attitude is to take it as a degeneration, and many modern scholars have taken this view. R. H. Charles, the compiler of the intertestamental writings excluded from the rabbinic canon, saw the 'age of inspiration' as succeeded by an age of uninspired legalism, which found expression in the rabbinic writings. The stream of inspiration did not cease, however, but found expression in the Pseudepigraphic writings, such as Enoch, and finally regained its full force in the New Testament.

Another attitude is to see the rabbinic discussions and writings as a kind of rebellion against the divinely inspired Scriptures of the

Hebrew Bible. This attitude is found in the New Testament itself in the words attributed to Jesus, 'You have made God's law null and void out of respect for your tradition' (Matt. 15.6, NEB). This criticism of the Pharisees was actually characteristic of the chief opponents of the Pharisees, namely the Sadducees, who were opposed to all scriptural interpretation and believed that the words of Scripture were so perspicuous that they required no interpretation (an attitude revived later in the Christian Church by the Reformers rebelling against the manifold canons and interpretations of the Catholic Church). It is rather strange that Jesus is portrayed here as closer to the Sadducees than to the Pharisees, since the Sadducees were a highly reactionary party which objected to all the humane regulations characteristic of the Pharisees when such regulations seemed to tone down the literal harshness of scriptural commands.

This particular New Testament charge against the rabbinic movement as a kind of rebellion against Scripture is much beloved of modern-day antisemites. Certain rabbinic texts which assert the right of the rabbis, in the absence of prophetic inspiration, to make decisions by discussion and majority vote are constantly quoted in the antisemitic literature to show that the rabbis regarded themselves as having an authority superior to that of Scripture. These critics have overlooked a contradiction in their own proof-text in the New Testament, which declares that the 'scribes' unlike Jesus spoke ' without authority', yet does not regard this as inconsistent with the charge that they overrode the authority of Scripture.

As for the Pharisees themselves and their successors the rabbis, how did they regard their own disavowal of divine inspiration? Did they regard this loss of inspiration in a negative or in a positive light? The answer is 'both'. On the one hand, they deplored the cessation of the 'Holy Spirit' and looked forward to a time when it would be renewed. They referred frequently to the verse at the end of Malachi (which forms the concluding sentence of the Prophetic writings), which promised that at the end of days prophetic inspiration would be renewed through the return of Elijah, and also to other biblical verses which prophesied that at the end of days prophetic inspiration would actually be much greater in volume than ever before. But they accepted regretfully that their own days did not contain any prophets, even though some figures of the rabbinic age were regarded as worthy to be prophets (notably Hillel). Even the charismatic figures known as Chasidim, who were called 'men of deed' and were credited with high spiritual powers and miraculous gifts of rain-making and healing, were not regarded as prophets, and on occasion, when questioned, explicitly disavowed the gift of prophecy.

The rabbis were so insistent on their own lack of the prophetic gift that they couched all their writings in a deliberately low-key style (very much in contrast with the lofty apodictic tone of the Dead Sea Scrolls and Pseudepigrapha), and even for a time forbade the widespread publication of rabbinic writings in case they should be mistaken for additions to Scripture. Only when it became clear that the closure of the canon had been widely accepted by the Jewish people, was it permitted to publish the rabbinic writings in the form of the Mishnah and other tannaitic writings. As for the many writings of the Pseudepigrapha that claimed scriptural authority and thereby claimed the continuation of divine inspiration, the rabbis rejected all these as spurious and heretical, and thus rescued mainstream Judaism from many absurdities, especially the dualism by which Evil was elevated to a cosmic power rivalling God. Charles is quite correct, however, in saying that these pseudepigraphical writings fed into the New Testament, which shows the same dualism, though not on quite the same hysterical level.

On the other hand, there was also a positive side to the rabbis' acceptance of the cessation of prophecy. The prophets, after all, were passive recipients of divine inspiration (though the rabbis did not altogether rule out the possibility that each prophet had his own individuality which coloured the expression of his message). The rabbis, on the other hand, represented human faculties at work. The age of the rabbis was an age of reason and humanism, in which the human intellect was raised to a position of decision and arbitration. This was explicitly recognized in the rabbinic movement, and its writings contain some daring expressions of humanism as having a quality lacking in prophetism (it is these expressions of humanism that were seized on by Christian polemicists of the Middle Ages as implying insolent conviction on the part of the rabbis that their decisions and discussions were more important than Scripture).

Certain daring stories in the Talmud were particularly censured on this ground. Perhaps the most daring of all was the story previously mentioned that God once attempted to intervene in proceedings of a council of rabbis and was ruled out of order (upon which he laughed and said, 'My children have defeated me').[1]

Another daring story portrays God as taking part in a discussion in the Academy on High, members of which are the spirits of departed great rabbis; when a point was disputed, it was decided to send for the acknowledged expert on the subject, still on earth, Rabbi Nathan, so that he could give guidance to the Academy; it seems that God was not entitled to give an unequivocal decision even about his own Torah! Such stories were justified by the theory that though God had given the Torah, he had handed it over for discussion and development to the human race, to whom he had given the last word on how to interpret it. The council of rabbis, in which differing opinions were aired, and which reached its decisions when necessary by majority vote, was itself a God-given institution which God had undertaken not to subvert and by whose decisions he was ready to stand, right or wrong. As we have already seen (p. 22), there is an echo of this doctrine in the New Testament, in the charge of Jesus to Peter, 'What you bind on earth will be bound in heaven, and what you loose on earth will be loosed in heaven.' This is a true echo of Pharisee doctrine.[2]

Thus the Pharisees denied their own authority in one sense, yet asserted it in another. What they were really asserting was the validity and worth of the human intellect, which had been allowed no worth in the age of prophetism. And their contention was that God himself approved of this development. Like a good father, he was delighted to see that his children had become independent of him. The Written Law was the creation of God: but the Oral Law, built up over the years by interpretation of Scripture and by ordinances enacted by human authorities to cope with new situations, was largely (though not entirely, because a small part even of the Oral Torah was regarded as having been given by God to Moses on Mount Sinai) the creation of man. Yet all of it stemmed from God;

for all the discussions of the rabbis were attempts to understand God's written Scripture, and all the solutions were arrived at by express permission of God to engage in such discussion.

In one sense the rabbis could indeed be called great critics of Scripture; for they noticed every contradiction or even repetition in the text. If their contribution had been restricted to such perceptions, they would have given the impression that they regarded Scripture as a very self-contradictory and repetitious text. But the difficulties they were constantly raising were provided with solutions: the contradictions were reconciled and the repetitions were shown to provide indispensable nuances. Like modern scientists working on the chaotic material of nature, they worked to turn a comparatively shapeless body of material into shape and meaning. Yet, also like scientists, they did not ascribe finality to their own work, and were prepared to undergo criticism and disagreement among themselves, and even to scrap whole areas of theory in the light of new considerations. There is nothing among the rabbis corresponding to the Catholic idea of the infallibility of the Church. Thus the infallibility of Scripture, the rabbis' ruling concept, is something of a metaphysical idea: it is an ideal continually approached but never reached, because of the fallibility of the human intellects attempting to grasp it (see M. Fisch, *Rational Rabbis*).

Thus the shocked indictment made against the rabbis by Christian theologians is in a sense true: the rabbis did approach Scripture with a flexibility that is hard to reconcile with the notion of 'fundamentalism'.

But just like the Doctors of the Church, the rabbis were not mere exegetes. They were also the officiating officers of an ongoing institution, the Jewish community. This meant that they frequently had to make practical decisions depending on the exigencies of the moment, and these decisions might involve countering dangers to human life, or to overriding religious considerations. The rabbis might thus be called on to make emergency measures that involved temporary suspension of scriptural laws. The paradigm instance of this is the decision of Elijah (regarded here in his rabbinic rather than in his prophetic capacity) to offer sacrifices on Mount Carmel, in contravention of Deuteronomic laws forbidding the offering of

sacrifices outside the Jerusalem Temple. A national religious emergency, the need to set up a dramatic trial between God and Baal, led
to this daring decision. But it functions in rabbinic theory as the
germ of a principle that has particularly shocked some Christian
critics: that 'sometimes the decisions of the rabbis take precedence
over the decisions of Scripture'. Religion, in the rabbinic view,
should not be so rigid that it takes no account of emergency, and of
the human role in dealing with it. Less dramatic, but also evidence
of the power of the rabbis to engage in institutional activity, are the
setting-up of religious festivals or fasts not provided for in Scripture
(for example, Purim, Chanukah and Tisha B'av). The Christian
Church is fully familiar with such communal Church decision-
making, which is inevitable in the conduct, through the centuries,
of a functioning Church. At the time of the Reformation, indeed,
the new scripturalists, Luther and Calvin and others, revived
against Catholicism the same kind of criticism that had been
levelled against rabbinic Judaism; but as time went on, the new
Churches found it impossible to proceed without developing institutional frameworks for which no authority could be found in
Scripture. Yet this institutional activity is hard to justify unless the
religious theory itself sanctions it, by providing explicit scope for
human decisions independent of Scripture.

Thus the authority claimed by the Pharisees and their successors
the rabbis has been attacked for opposite reasons because it constitutes a kind of paradox that, to an uncomprehending or hostile
mind, seems like a contradiction. On the one hand, it comprises a
humility that made the Pharisees disclaim or discount all charismatic or sacerdotal authority, representing themselves as merely
laymen, whose qualifications came through education and were
available to all. On the other hand, it comprises a humanistic
confidence which made the Pharisees think that, in the full sway of
Council, they could rule God himself out of order. This breath-
taking claim is what lies at the root of the hatred against them that
informs the Gospels, which multiplies against them charges of
arrogance, hypocrisy and even corruption that clearly reflect deep
resentment of them by another movement for which only charismatic claims could be of any value. The hatred of the Pharisees that

pervades certain passages of the Gospels arises not from the overweening claims of the Pharisees but precisely from their lack of superhuman claims, and their substitution of human claims. This led to a multiplication of charges culminating in that of exploitation of the poor ('widows' houses') in only one passage – a charge so far removed from fact and so contradicted by every other source (including other New Testament sources) that it receives no elaboration even from those most hostile to the Pharisees.[3]

It would be wrong, on the other hand, to overestimate the Pharisees' valuation of their own importance in humanistic terms in the religious history of Judaism. Though they regarded the advent of rabbinism as having many positive aspects, they did not regard it as outranking the age of prophecy. After all, they regarded the age of rabbinism as a temporary interlude, after which the age of prophecy would resume. They were constantly on the lookout for the advent of the Messiah, who would be accompanied by a Prophet, the revived Elijah. When this finally happened, what would happen to the rabbis? They would become the judiciary of the messianic throne, and their relation to the Prophet would be that of rational administration to charismatic guidance. As a matter of fact, the relation between rabbis (organized in a Sanhedrin) and the Prophet in the Messianic Age was not fully worked out in rabbinic theory. To be sure, there was a model to be kept in mind: that of Moses and the Seventy, but that model was by no means perspicuous. What exactly had been the relationship between Moses and the Seventy who functioned under him as a Council? According to some indications in Scripture, the Seventy all had the status and inspiration of prophets themselves; but according to other indications, they were mere advisers or subordinate judges, taking from Moses much of the burden of administration which would have otherwise fallen on him. What would happen in messianic times to the right of majority vote that at present devolved on the rabbis? It would certainly survive in judicial situations, where a vote was required to decide a capital case. But would it ever be exercised to arrive at decisions on moot legal questions? In the presence of a Prophet, would there be any moot legal questions? There are indications that the right of the rabbis would still cover the power to vote on *taqanot*, that is, measures enacted not to settle disputed legal questions but to set up institutions required for public order. But what about measures enacted in the past by majority vote for which the inspired decision of the Prophet was now available? The case of Rabbi Eliezer, where an inspired view was overruled, is perhaps relevant, perhaps not. Eliezer did not have the status of a Prophet, even though he was able to call on divine support in this instance during a period of rabbinic authority. It seems likely that the majority decisions would stand even in the Messianic Age, since they had been arrived at in a constitutional manner; an indication of this is that certain disputed questions (which did not need an urgent decision) were postponed 'until the coming of Elijah' – this expression has many implications for the continuing validity of decisions made by not invoking such a principle.

More important than such speculations for our present topic is the fact, relevant to the time of Jesus, that the rabbis were constantly on the lookout for the coming of the Messiah and also for the coming of the Prophet (Elijah). So when the Gospels assert that people noticed that Jesus 'spoke with authority' unlike the rabbis, this does not imply that Jesus thereby incurred the enmity of the Pharisees. It all depends what is meant by 'authority'. It has been assumed in the history of New Testament exegesis that when Jesus 'spoke with authority', he was asserting his own divine status. If that had been the case, he would certainly have incurred the opposition of the Pharisees, who were loyal to the basic principle of Judaism that forbade divine worship of anyone in human shape. But there were other kinds of 'authority' (higher than rabbinic authority) which the Pharisees recognized, and which indeed they looked for eagerly. These were two: Messianic authority and Prophetic authority. The question that was put to Hanina ben Dosa, 'Are you a prophet?' (to which he answered, 'No') shows that there was constant expectation and hope that the age of prophecy would return. The defence of Peter and his companions by Gamaliel, urging that their claim of Jesus' messiahship should be treated with respect and hope (even though Jesus had been executed by the Romans) shows that Messianic authority was envisaged as a possibility even in the most unpromising circumstances.

If Jesus had been the Messiah or even a prophet, he would certainly have been entitled, on Pharisee principles, to speak with an individual 'authority' unclaimed by the Pharisees themselves, though they claimed high authority of a rational collective practical kind when they voted in the absence of a divinely-appointed guide.

Jesus began his public career by claiming, not to be the Messiah, but to be a prophet. Like John the Baptist, he proclaimed at first, 'Repent for the Kingdom of Heaven is at hand.' This amounted to a prediction of the coming of the Messiah, who would be a King and would rule on behalf of God. Jesus did not claim that the Messiah he was predicting was himself, any more than John the Baptist made this claim about himself. But later (after the Salutation of Peter) Jesus claimed to be the Messiah whom he had been prophesying. What was the attitude of the Pharisees to this sort of authority-claim, and how would they regard an individual who made such a claim? Would they regard him with hostility as someone who was challenging their own status, or would they regard him as coming within a category that formed part of their own thinking?

6

Jesus as Prophet and Messiah

Perhaps the most plausible line of argument to support the hostile Gospel picture of the Pharisees is that they resented Jesus' claims to prophetic and messianic status. After all, this was a considerable claim to superiority, and it seems plausible that the leaders of the people, who had the reverence of all ordinary folk who did not belong to the tiny minorities of the sects, should be annoyed by someone who said, in effect, 'I am far more important than you are.'

As far as the claim to prophetic status is concerned, a test case is that of John the Baptist. Even before Jesus, he claimed prophetic status and was actually accepted as a prophet by many of the people. Yet it is significant that the Gospels do not record any action taken against him by the Pharisees for this claim. Some people (not specified as Pharisees) seem to have regarded him as mad or possessed (Matt. 11.18). But on the whole, he seems to have come under the scope of the usual 'wait-and-see' policy of the Pharisees, as expressed by the Pharisee leader Gamaliel in Acts 5. The Pharisees cannot have disapproved of John's campaign of repentance, by which he aimed to raise the spiritual status of the people to a point where God would regard them as worthy to receive the Messiah who would bring with him 'the kingdom of God'. The rabbinic writings say many times that the only thing holding up the coming of the Messiah was lack of repentance on the part of the Jewish people. It is even said in one passage, 'If only the Jewish people would observe two Sabbaths properly, the Messiah would come' (*b. Shabb.* 118b). Another rabbi was told, 'The Messiah would come today, if only the people would repent' (*b. Sanh.* 98a). John's definition of repentance does not appear to have differed from that of the Pharisees, if we take as an example his rebuke of Herod Antipas (see below).

The Pharisees apparently did not regard John as slighting them by suggesting that they, like all other Jews, were in need of repentance. On the contrary, the attitude of the Pharisees was that, as leaders, they ought to set an example to the people by repenting for any shortcomings in their observance of God's commandments. The rabbinic writings are full of examples of rabbinic repentance, expressed usually through fasting and prayer.

There was nothing in the doctrine of the Pharisees that would require them to regard a prophetic claim as heretical. Their usual belief that the age of prophecy had ended with Malachi was by no means a dogma which had any power to cause them to reject prophetic claims. The end of prophecy was regarded by them, on the whole, with deep regret, though they did see compensating factors in the characteristics of the rabbinic age, and they saw some of these rabbinic features as destined to continue into the next prophetic age just as they had existed in previous prophetic times. Though they lived in a non-prophetic age, they were constantly on the lookout for the renewal of prophecy, and their hopes of this were not infrequently aroused. They even considered that one among their own ranks, Hillel, had all the personal qualities necessary for a prophet, but had not been granted by God the inspiration necessary to supplement these qualities – and the reason for this lay in the shortcomings of Hillel's contemporaries, not in any shortcomings of his own. A campaign to raise the general level was therefore very much in keeping with their thinking about how a prophetic age could be set in motion.

As sensible persons, the Pharisees would no doubt regard actual prophetic claims with some general scepticism; after all, such a claim could easily be made by a crank, or by someone genuinely and sincerely mistaken (as was the case with all the previous claimants who had raised the people's hopes of redemption and then unfortunately failed). But a priori scepticism could not possibly be formulated into a principle ('All prophetic and messianic claims are false'), for if so, how could the renewal of prophecy and the advent of the

Messianic Age to which they looked forward ever happen? In one Gospel story, Jesus asks the 'priests and scribes' what kind of authority they thought was possessed by John the Baptist, to which they answered, 'We cannot tell' (Matt. 21.23–7, AV). This is represented as a cunning answer intended to hide their total disbelief, which they wished to conceal from the people who regarded John as a prophet. Naturally, in the Gospels all Jewish religious authorities are evil and hate the good wherever they see it. But in fact, the answer given was an honest one. The special authority of both John and Jesus was an unknown quantity until it became clear that their announcement of the advent of the kingdom of God was correct. Meanwhile, both were regarded by the Pharisees as well-meaning, loyal and breathtakingly courageous Jews, making claims that had an honoured place in tradition and would some day be fulfilled, even if the present claimants, like so many before them, turned out to be disappointments.

It is significant, in this connection, that while the Gospels give a detailed account of how John the Baptist was persecuted and brought to his death, they do not involve the Pharisees to the slightest extent in this story of persecution. There are no stories about John the Baptist rousing the ire of the Pharisees by questioning their rulings or by proposing changes in the Jewish religion. On the contrary, John is portrayed as bringing persecution upon himself by behaviour that was typical of the Pharisees, and which would undoubtedly have had their full support. According to the Gospels, John aroused the resentment of the Herodian ruler by criticizing him for infringement of a halakhic point that formed part of Pharisee legislation, being derived from the legislation of the Torah. This was the rule that a man was not permitted to marry the widow of his brother (unless his brother had died childless, in which case he was actually enjoined to marry her under the levirate law). Herod Antipas had flouted this law by marrying his sister-in-law Herodias though she had produced offspring by his deceased brother Philip, and John, taking up the role of reproving prophet like Nathan to David, or Elijah to Ahab, denounced this breach of Torah-law.

This puts John into a very different light from the anti-authority Cynic wanderer beloved of the Crossan school; instead he becomes very much an Establishment figure himself, the representative of one arm of the threefold Constitution known in later times by the term 'the Three Crowns'. As Prophet, John saw himself as representative of the Crown of the Torah, as opposed to the other two Crowns, the Crown of Monarchy and the Crown of Priesthood.[1] When Elijah performed this role, Ahab unconstitutionally resisted and sought to kill him. In the same way Herod Antipas resisted the reproof of John, and this was historically typical of a pattern of conflict between two rival (yet equally authoritative) arms of the Jewish constitution. King David, on the other hand, is the pattern of the repentant subjection of the Crown of Monarchy (despite its possession of total power) to the authority of the powerless representative of the Torah, Nathan (2 Sam. 2.13).

The Pharisees, for a considerable time before the advent of John, had represented the Crown of the Torah and on many occasions took up the duty of reproving the power of the Crown, consequently not infrequently suffering persecution, as when they were massacred by Alexander Jannaeus. John the Baptist, by asserting his own status as a prophet was taking over this task of reproving the Monarch from the Pharisees. According to tradition, the prophet Isaiah had suffered death at the hands of the renegade King Menasseh, and John was now the latest in a history of prophetic martyrdom. He should be thought of, not as some eccentric sectarian in the mould of the Dead Sea Scroll sect, but as strongly ensconced in Jewish tradition and as a member of the party of tradition. John the Baptist, in other words, was a Pharisee, and this explains why the Gospels omit almost all mention of tension between him and the Pharisees, though their effort to identify John with Jesus (as precursor and hailer) might have led to their including him prominently in their picture of bitter Pharisee conflict with Jesus. Their omission to do so must be accounted one of the gaps in the Gospels' attack on the Pharisees – gaps glaring enough to betray the presence of an editorial campaign inserted by the Pauline Christian Church after the death of Jesus into what had originally been a pro-Pharisee narrative.

On the other hand, we are faced by the perplexing fact that the account given by Josephus of the execution of John by Herod

Antipas is very different from that given in the Gospels. Here the
figure of the reproving Prophet, championing the commandments
of the Torah against royal infringement is entirely missing. Instead,
we have a political account, in which Herod Antipas becomes
alarmed at the messianic aspect of John's message. By proclaiming
himself to be prophet, John, though he made no messianic claims
for himself, had awakened hopes in the people of the coming of the
kingly Messiah who would liberate the Jewish people from Roman
rule. According to Josephus, it was because John's campaign had
become dangerous in arousing these hopes that Antipas decided to
have him executed (*Antiquities* 18.5.117). Here again we do not
detect any hostility towards John on the part of the Pharisees, who
were well aware that a renewal of prophecy would, in Jewish traditional theory, be a prelude to the coming of the Messiah as liberator.

How does it come about that the story of the Gospels is so
different from that of Josephus? It seems likely that we have here a
difference of emphasis. It is Josephus that brings out Herod's
strongest motivation, which was political, and was directed against
any troublemaker who would render insecure his own position as
henchman of the Romans. No doubt, the Gospels' account of
religious tension between Herod and John on a halakhic matter is
historically correct, but for Herod this would be merely an added
provocation. On the other hand, the Gospels throughout are concerned to depoliticize the whole topic of the Messiah, whom they
wished to portray as a purely spiritual figure, not as a liberator. The
Gospel-writers therefore see danger in mentioning the political
aspect of John, because this may lead to the thought that Jesus too
had a political aspect which may have contributed towards his
death. In the Gospels, Jesus is handed over to the Romans for
execution, and on the face of it, this implied that Jesus' offence was
against the Romans. Indeed, the Gospels go so far as to acknowledge
that the offences with which Jesus was charged were against Rome,
but this was only a facade put up by the Jews, and his real offences
were against the Jewish religion. Thus the equivocal nature of the
charges against Jesus, and the general aim of depoliticization, are in
a sense echoed in the difference of emphasis found in the differing
accounts found in the Gospels and Josephus of the execution of

John. The Gospels have depoliticized John as part of their general aim of depoliticizing everything and everyone connected with Jesus (though in historical fact, John the Baptist was very little connected with Jesus, being the leader of a separate prophetic movement; it was only later Christian legend that portrayed John as subjecting himself to Jesus as his superior, and confining himself to the role of a precursor).

The main point here, however, is that the messianic aspects of the missions of both John and Jesus did not have the effect of alienating either of them from the Pharisees, any more that their prophetic claims had this effect. The Pharisees probably did not believe, except as a possibility, either that John was a prophet or that Jesus was the Messiah; the proof of this would lie in the outcome. But they also did not regard these claims as in any way blasphemous or contrary to the principles of Pharisaism.

It is particularly important to emphasize that a claim to Messiah-ship would not have been regarded as blasphemous by the Phari-sees, since this is a matter on which misunderstanding has been endemic. The Gospels themselves promote this misunderstanding, by their description of the behaviour of the High Priest at the alleged trial of Jesus (which in historical fact, as most scholars now agree, never actually took place). In this implausible account the High Priest is represented as tearing his clothes in horror when Jesus commits the blasphemy of admitting that he claims to be the Messiah, or Christ (Mark 14.61; Matt. 26.63). The whole trial, in Mark and Matthew, is represented as turning on this charge of blasphemy (though, confusingly enough, the actual initial charge in the trial is a different one, that Jesus had uttered threats against the Temple). Jesus is eventually condemned not on any charge brought against him by previously-summoned witnesses, but on the basis of a pronouncement made at the trial itself and witnessed by the members of the court; the account given in John, however, is entire-ly different and does not represent any kind of public trial. Yet it is not denied that the Jewish people lived in hope of the coming of the Messiah, or 'Christ', a word which is simply the Greek translation of 'Messiah'; and it is not explained how this could ever happen if anyone who came forward with such a claim were to be immediately charged with blasphemy. The premises of the 'trial' are riddled with illogicality, quite apart from substantive historical impossibilities with which it is replete, and the strong evidence from the Fourth Gospel that no Sanhedrin trial of Jesus took place (substituting for it a much more likely scenario: that Jesus was interrogated in the house of the High Priest with no members of the Sanhedrin present and no formal trial with witnesses).

What complicates the matter is that the word 'Messiah' (or its Greek equivalent 'Christ') means something different in Christianity from what it means in Judaism. Thus Jesus' assertion of his claim to be the Messiah is given a Christian connotation in the Christian concoction which comprises the Gospel account of his trial. Moreover, the title 'Son of God' (which is also brought into the account) has a meaning in Judaism that is very different from its meaning in Christianity (and in Hellenistic religion generally), which adds considerably to the confusion. All Jewish kings of the House of David had the title 'Son of God' (derived from explicit conferral of this title on King Solomon, 2 Sam. 7.14) and it did not imply divine status, but merely special exaltation among all the other children of God, that is, humanity. After all, even the New Testament accepts at one point that Adam, the first human, could be correctly described as 'son of God' (Luke 3.38), and thus that this title, in its Jewish origins, has no connotation of divinity.

If Jesus by declaring himself to be the Messiah or Son of God was thereby declaring himself to be a divine personage, this would indeed have been regarded as idolatry (not blasphemy, which means cursing the name of God). But by claiming to be the Messiah, Jesus was using a Jewish term that was well understood by his hearers (it would have been pointless to use it, as a surprising number of scholars have suggested, in a sense that was unintelligible to his hearers). Jesus meant that he was the Messiah in exactly the same sense as his ancestors David and Solomon were Messiahs, that is, kings. The word 'Messiah' in Hebrew means 'anointed one', and it was a title given to Jewish kings of the House of David, who were anointed with a special mixture of oils at the time of their coronation (this 'oil of anointing' was not used at the coronation of non-Davidic kings such as the Hasmoneans). A similar anointing was performed in only one other inauguration ceremony, that of the High Priest, who consequently had the title 'the Anointed Priest', or 'Christ Priest'). In a fully-functioning Jewish state, therefore, there were always two Messiahs, simultaneously in office, the King and the High Priest (this double-Messiah situation is found explicitly in the picture of the Last Days drawn up by the Dead Sea Scrolls sect). It is particularly ironic, therefore, that in the Gospels' fanciful account of Jesus' trial, it is the High Priest who expresses horror that anyone should dare to claim the title Messiah, since he himself was awarded this very same title on the day of his inauguration. The High Priests of this period were not renowned for their learning, but this at least they would be sure to know.

It is indeed worthy of remark that the antagonist of Jesus in the trial episode is not any of the Pharisees but the High Priest. Although throughout his career Jesus is alleged to have been criticized by the Pharisees, particularly on the question of Sabbath-healing (which in point of fact was not forbidden by Pharisee law), no Pharisee is represented as having appeared as a witness at Jesus' alleged trial to press these points, or to give expert advice on the question of whether a messianic claim was contrary to Jewish law. There is in fact no indication in any of the Gospels that the Pharisees regarded Jesus' messianic claim as 'blasphemous' or idolatrous. The most famous messianic claimant, apart from Jesus, was Bar Kokhba, who was a practising Pharisee and received full support from the leading Pharisee rabbi, Rabbi Akiva. The person who did certainly show himself horrified by this claim was the High Priest. The question that needs to be explored is, 'What were the motives of the High Priest in opposing Jesus' claim to be the Christ or Messiah?'

The High Priest was not a Pharisee. He was the leader of the Sadducee sect, which opposed the Pharisees and was regarded by them, and by the mass of the Jewish people who followed the Pharisees, as heretical. The Pharisees, strongly as they disapproved of the High Priest's religious views, were tolerant enough to think that these erroneous views did not disqualify him from functioning in the ceremonial High Priestly role as supervisor of the Temple and as Chairman of the Sanhedrin, in which the Sadducees were

usually the minority party (as the New Testament itself testifies
when it shows the Sadducees being outvoted by the Pharisees on
two occasion, the trials of Peter and of Paul). What qualified him for
this role was not any religious authority or beliefs that he possessed
but simply his descent from Aaron, the brother of Moses. In so far
as the High Priest had any kind of authority, it was political, not
religious. It came not from any Jewish party or body of voters, but
from the Romans. The High Priest was a henchman of Rome, and
was actually appointed to his position by the Romans, as Josephus
makes plain. This political nature of the High Priest's appointment
as quisling political authority (like Petain and Laval under the
Nazis) had been initiated by a Jewish ruler, Herod the Great, who
regarded the High Priesthood as reserved to his political sup-
porters.

   It is in the interest of the Gospels, however, to represent the High
Priest as chief religious authority among the Jews, who condemned
Jesus with the full weight of Judaism behind him. The erroneous
opinion that the High Priest was the Jewish Pope has existed in
Christian minds over the centuries (only being questioned by
Christian scholars of recent years), and this has contributed considerably to the general picture of Jesus as the victim of the intolerance of Judaism. Contributing to this error has been unawareness of
the dichotomy in Judaism between the priests and the rabbis, for in
Christianity no such dichotomy exists, and the Christian priesthood
combines both roles, being both ceremonial officials and religious
teachers. In Judaism, the teaching role (except in the eyes of the
small party of the Sadducees) belonged to the rabbis, from whom
guidance was sought on all doctrinal matters. One of the most
implausible features of the alleged Sanhedrin trial of Jesus is that in
it judgement is pronounced on Jesus' religious shortcomings by
someone who was regarded by the vast majority of the Jewish
people as himself a heretic. In the eyes of the vast majority of the
Jewish people, who supported the Pharisees, the disapproval shown
by the High Priest towards Jesus was a mark in Jesus' favour. It
would have been clear to all that the High Priest feared Jesus for the
same reason that Herod Antipas (in Josephus' version) feared John
the Baptist: because Jesus was raising hopes among the people of

rescue from the oppression of Roman rule – and this would have meant the end of the lucrative career of the High Priest as chief quisling supporter of the Roman Occupation.

I am not arguing (and never have argued) that Jesus was a Zealot. He did not concern himself with military or guerrilla tactics, as did the Zealots, the party of active Resistance against the Romans. The Zealot kind of messianic leader is typified in the first century by Judas of Galilee, who is mentioned in the book of Acts, and, in the second century, was exemplified by the heroic Bar Kokhba. Jesus, on the other hand, was the prophetic type of Messiah-figure, who relied on a miracle that would overthrow the Romans on the Mount of Olives, as prophesied by Zechariah. He is by no means the only example of this type: others were Theudas and the unnamed 'Egyptian' whose hopes were also centred on the Mount of Olives. Yet Jesus was fundamentally at one with the aims of the Zealots, in that he envisaged a new world which would no longer be dominated by the military power of Rome. This is probably why several of Jesus' closest followers were ex-Zealots (for example, Simon the Zealot, whose nickname makes him the most obvious example, though there are good reasons to suppose a similar background to at least three others).

The Zealots, like almost all the Messiah-movements, were Pharisees. The bulk of the Pharisees were too realistic to take part in movements that sought to overthrow the Roman Empire, but the enthusiasm for Judaism and the conviction of its future success came from the Pharisees and was always liable to throw off from them aspirants to messianic glory. Moreover, the popularity of the Pharisees and their hold over the masses of the Jewish people made any politico-religious movement stemming from them certain of widespread support.

In recent years (as pointed out briefly earlier, see pp. 1–3), a number of scholars have sought to combat the picture given in all the ancient sources of the Pharisees as the party of the masses. For a number of reasons this picture has proved very awkward to scholars; in particular, it conflicts with the Gospel picture of the Pharisees as dry-as-dust, pettifogging, cruel and corrupt hypocrites. How could such people be popular and revered? Yet the

Gospels themselves testify to the reverence in which the Pharisees were held by the vast majority of the people. The Gospels, together with the similar testimony of Josephus, are our chief source for the prominence of the Pharisees as far more than a sect, but on the contrary the representatives of normative Judaism, the grouping to which ordinary Jews automatically belonged. The Gospels are thus riven by a striking contradiction in relation to the Pharisees; reverent popularity on the one hand, and bitter unpopularity on the other.

Also quite unequivocal about the normative character of the Pharisees are the rabbinic writings, but they can always be dismissed as too late to be regarded as valid evidence. Further, a somewhat discreditable motivation has been attributed to them: namely, a desire to add to the authority of the rabbinic movement itself by tracing its origins to Temple times. If, however, the Pharisee movement was as insignificant as some modern scholars would like to think, the rabbis might be considered somewhat ill-advised to seek to derive authority from them.

Josephus describes a fundamentally threefold division of the Jewish people into Pharisees, Sadducees and Essenes (the Fourth Sect, the Zealots being a branch of the Pharisees), but Josephus (whose lifetime was during the period when these were all living movements) is quite certain that only the Pharisees were such a large-scale movement that they transcended the designation of a 'sect'. The Sadducees, their chief rivals, were a powerful sect, but not because they had popular adherence but because they comprised powerful people, that is, the rich landowners and the leading priestly families (the rank-and-file priestly families on the other hand mostly supported the Pharisees). The Essenes, on the other hand, were a small minority sect by choice, having adopted a way of life which deliberately marked them out from the populace.

One motivation of scholars deserves respect and sympathy: a desire to combat antisemitism. It is realized that antisemitism derives very substantially from the Gospel picture of the Pharisees. The very word 'Pharisee' exists in the English language, and other languages, as a synonym for everything contemptible, especially hypocrisy. English literature uses the word 'Pharisee' innumerable times in this sense, so that it is impossible for any English-speaking child to grow up without absorbing a strongly pejorative sense of the word. How desirable it would be to limit the meaning of the word 'Pharisee' to that of a minority sect that had no outstanding role in the religious life of Jesus' time! This motivation has perhaps played a part in the support given by certain Jewish scholars (Jacob Neusner, for example) to the scholarly campaign to play down the importance and normativeness of the Pharisees in the first century.

In reducing the Pharisees to a minority sect, certain modern scholars have explicitly denied that there was such a thing as normative Judaism in the first century. There were just a great number of 'Judaisms' – many more that Josephus is willing to admit. A vast proliferation of Judaisms has been obtained by taking every literary work that has been preserved (even those belonging patently to the same movement) as representing a 'Judaism' of its own.

Another motivation for this line of argument has been a desire to find Jewish roots for Christianity, a consideration very near to the heart of many New Testament scholars. If there were so many 'Judaisms' surely one of them could have given rise to Christianity! This renders obsolete the tendency of an earlier scholarship (such as that of Rudolf Bultmann or Richard Reitzentstein) to find affinities between the Christian ideas of Jesus as a descending-and-rising saviour God-sacrifice and Hellenistic cults which centred on what seemed similar myths. Although no one was able to find a precisely similar myth in any variety of Judaism, an endless profusion of Judaisms made it seem possible that one of them (as yet undiscovered) would turn out to have the appropriate characteristics.

E. P. Sanders opposed this tendency to multiply Judaisms, but without reinstating Pharisaism as normative Judaism. Instead he proposed that there was indeed such a thing as normative Judaism, which, however, transcended and united various varieties of Judaism. This he called 'covenantal nomism', or 'Common Judaism', that is, a belief in the validity of a divinely-given Law to which Jews were bound by a Covenant. Even varieties of Judaism as widely different as Pharisaism and the Dead Sea Scrolls sect agreed on this, and this differentiated them from sacrificial salvation-religions which depended on some kind of mystical union with a descending and rising god. In particular, Sanders thought, Paul had taken himself out of Judaism by his conception of salvation through the death of Jesus on the cross and by his nullification of the Torah as a means of salvation. Since the inclusion of Pauline Christianity in Jewish tradition was one of the chief concerns of the advocates of 'Judaisms', Sanders' view came into strong conflict with theirs. Sanders regarded Paul as the initiator of a form of religion that was definitely not Judaism. Paul, in Sanders' words, 'took himself out of Judaism'. However, Sanders still did not quite reinstate Pharisaism in the normative position that it occupies in the New Testament, Josephus and the rabbinic writings. Sanders in fact denied that the ordinary people looked to the Pharisee teachers primarily for guidance, and argued that the priests still had an important teaching role for the ordinary people in the first century, and not just for the Sadducees.

In more recent years, however, a new trend is discernible which goes beyond Sanders in asserting the existence of normative Judaism in the first century, and which actually goes back to identifying this normative Judaism with Pharisaism, in accordance with the copious ancient testimony to this effect, and in disregard of the motivations which impelled modern scholars to minimize the role of Pharisaism and to multiply 'Judaisms' almost without end.

A good formulation of this new–old point of view is by Roland Deines, whose work on Pharisaism outstrips all previous work in careful analysis of the sources. He says that Pharisaism was:

> a separate movement in the nation for the nation whose legitimacy was indeed accepted by large parts of the people, even though its requirements were not observed to an equal extent. This provides us in my opinion also with justification to consider Pharisaism also as normative Judaism, not because all lived according to Pharisaic halakhah, but because Pharisaism was by the majority acknowledged as legitimate and authentic interpretation of the divine will for the chosen nation.[2]

Deines denies altogether that the Pharisees were a sect, since they existed for the people as a whole and laid down no exclusive conditions of entry, as did, for example, the Dead Sea Scroll sect. A number of scholars have been influenced by this approach, though it seems likely that in the case of some of them, their departure from the standpoint of E. P. Sanders has been less motivated by their opposition to Sanders' particular concept of 'Common Judaism' than by opposition to his firm (and in my opinion entirely correct) conviction that Paul 'took himself out of Judaism'. Whether 'Common Judaism' is defined as 'covenantal nomism' or as Pharisaism, Pauline Christianity is an entirely different religion.

Deines has reaffirmed Josephus' picture of first-century Judaism as essentially threefold, consisting of one dominant and normative strand, Pharisaism, and two atypical sects, the exclusivist minority groups the Sadducees and the Essenes. Deines has also affirmed that this picture is, in essence, that of the New Testament too, and that it has been further attested by the MMT document of the Dead Sea Scrolls (see Chapter 11 note 1 on p. 210). So when we explore the topic of Jesus the Pharisee, we are enquiring into the quintessential Jewishness of Jesus. Jesus was no rebel or outsider. Though he aspired to an outstanding position in Judaism, as prophet and Messiah, this aspiration was itself a focal aspect of Judaism without which it would have lost its orientation to the future.

7

Were the Pharisees Hypocrites?

The history of the term 'Pharisee' contains a number of problems and uncertainties which must be taken into account in treating the central topic of this book. So far we have taken the word in its most usual meaning, as it is used invariably by Josephus; that is to say, as the name of a religious movement in the Jewish people. Josephus actually often gives the misleading impression that this movement is a sect, which can be put on the same level as such sects as the Essenes; it is generally agreed by scholars that Josephus does this in order to make the Jewish religious scene more intelligible to his non-Jewish readers. To this end, Josephus also misleadingly characterizes the Pharisees as having certain philosophical views: not that they did not have these views, but the impression given by Josephus is that, like groups familiar to the Greco-Roman public, they existed mainly to promulgate such views; whereas in fact the Pharisees saw themselves chiefly as exegetes and administrators of the Torah. Josephus, however, does correct his over-philosophical description of the Pharisees by stating that they had the backing of the masses of the people and that they were regarded as the chief experts in the 'traditions' of the popular religion. Thus by and large, Josephus does present a picture of the Pharisees not as just a sect or a philosophical group, but as the religious guides and leaders of the people as a whole.

When we examine the rabbinic literature, however, we find that the term 'Pharisees' is found very rarely, and when it does occur it may have several alternative meanings. The rabbinic movement did not call themselves 'Pharisees', and even more startlingly, very rarely call their predecessors 'Pharisees'; it would appear from rabbinic data that the Pharisees themselves did not call themselves

'Pharisees' except very occasionally. It was not the name they preferred for themselves. It seems very likely that it was a name conferred upon them by their antagonists the Sadducees; a name which
the Pharisees did not use amongst themselves but used only in
contexts when they wished to differentiate themselves from the
Sadducees. It was in fact originally an opprobrious or contemptuous name which, however, achieved a certain currency among the
very people it was intended to denigrate. An analogy in the history
of Christian religion is the name 'Puritans' which was invented with
opprobrious intent by their enemies, but eventually achieved such
currency that they used it, to some extent, among themselves.

In Hebrew, the word (transliterated by Josephus into Greek as
pharisaios) is *parush*, which means literally 'separated one'. When
first applied by the Sadducees to their opponents, it no doubt was
intended to convey the meaning 'heretics'. Indeed, even in the
rabbinic literature, the term sometimes retains this meaning. For
example, some early manuscripts show that the denunciation of
heretics later known as *birkhat ha-minim* which was included in the
Eighteen Blessings was in earlier times known as *birkhat ha-
perushim*. This was a prayer directed against heretics, and its wording was changed from time to time to apply to the leading heretical
threat of the time.

On the other hand, the rabbinic literature also contains the word
parush in an entirely different meaning, which still does not correspond to the usage 'Pharisee' found in Josephus and the New
Testament. In this sense, the word *parush* refers to a particularly
saintly, ascetic individual and corresponds to a large extent to the
word *chasid*, except that a *parush* lays more emphasis on observing
the strictest possible ritual purity, or (in some contexts) abstemious-
ness, rather than on the supererogatory acts of lovingkindness that
characterized the *chasid*. In this usage, the word *parush* does not
designate a religious sect or community but an individual, who has
devoted his life to a dedicated pattern of living not expected of ordinary people. Both the *chasid* and the *parush* (in this sense) were
regarded by the sages or rabbis with respect but also with certain
caution and qualifications. Their example was not recommended to
the average person, because they represented an exaggerated,

strained type of piety that might indeed result in true saintliness, but might equally lead to a breakdown of standards. The Chasid was suspected of overdoing his piety to the point of 'foolishness' (hence the expression found in rabbinic sources 'a foolish Chasid', see p. 34), the example being one who let a naked woman drown because he was too pious to risk seeing her nakedness by going to her rescue). The *parush*, on the other hand, was suspected of insincerity; we find passages in the rabbinic literature referring to various types of *parush* as putting on an exaggerated air of piety which did not accord with their inner character. Thus one passage refers to the 'bruised *parush*' (who breaks his head against a wall to avoid looking at a woman) and to the 'pestle *parush*' (whose head is bent in mock humility, like a pestle in a mortar): yet the same passage refers also to the 'God-loving *parush*', the only type that is genuine. The emphasis on an aspect of showing-off and self-display in the unsatisfactory types of *parush* ties in with the denunciations of 'Pharisees' by Jesus and suggests a historical connection between the two topoi, the rabbinic critique of the false *parush* and Jesus' denunciation of hypocritical 'Pharisees', but also suggests that Jesus' denunciation (in its original form) has to be seen not as the reaction of a lone critic but as belonging to an aspect of the Pharisaic or rabbinic movement itself.

In a well-known book, *A Hidden Revolution: The Pharisees' Search for the Kingdom Within*[1] (indeed a book that is essential reading on this subject) Ellis Rivkin considered the question of how to translate the word *parush* when it occurs in the rabbinic writings, taking into consideration its multiple meanings. Rivkin considered every instance of the occurrence of the word *parush*, and he came to the conclusion that we should be very wary of translating the word as 'Pharisee', and that there is no certainty that it has this meaning except in contexts when it is juxtaposed and contrasted with the term 'Sadducee'. In other contexts (especially when the word is found in the singular) it may well bear one of the other two meanings mentioned above: 'heretic' or 'individual devotee'. Even though both are represented in post-biblical Hebrew by the same word *parush*, they denote very different things. The root meaning, 'separated one' is multivalent, for there can be many different reasons for separation and a person who does not want to be separate may be stigmatized by an enemy as 'separate' simply because he represents ideas which the enemy wants to keep separate from himself, or which he regards as separate from the truth as he sees it.

Actually, in its literal meaning, the word *perushim* ('separated ones', the plural of *parush*) was a most unsuitable term for the religious movement which Josephus and the New Testament call the 'Pharisees'. For the watchword of these Pharisees was the saying of their most distinguished leader, Hillel, 'Do not separate yourself from the community' (*m. Avot* 2.42). As scholars have come to realize increasingly in recent years, the Pharisees were a movement that directed itself towards the people and existed to serve the people. It is unfortunate that they acquired a nickname (invented by their opponents) that seemed to imply the opposite. For this reason some attempts have been made from time to time to provided a different derivation for the word *perushim*, connecting it to a biblical word which means 'to explain'. On this theory the Pharisees were not separators but 'explainers', a word that certainly fits their historical role. Unfortunately, the linguistic and historical arguments against this translation are strong, and it is much more likely that the Pharisees acquired their name as a nickname given to them by their opponents who regarded them as 'seceders' or 'heretics'.

Rivkin's line of argument may be illustrated by the following extract from his work:

> R. Phineas ben Jair used to say: Purity leads to *perishut* and *perishut* leads to holiness. (M. Sot. 9.15).

> The categories enumerated are gradations of purity, not religious groupings or schools of thought. No *halakhah* confronts us here, only stages on the path to holiness. *perishut* [the abstract noun from *parush*], i.e. 'abstinence, restraint', continence, separation from sensuality,' is a prerequisite for attaining holiness, not the quality of being a Pharisee.

> 'When Rabban Gamaliel the Elder died, the glory of the Law ceased and purity and *perishut* died' (M. Sot. 9.15).

Are we to believe that the Mishnah is informing us that with the death of Rabban Gamaliel the Elder, Pharisaism died? Is it not obvious that a personal attribute of an individual is being referred to? Yet this seemingly unambiguous non-Pharisaic meaning of *perishut* did not restrain Danby from translating it 'the cleanness practised by the Pharisees'.

Rivkin also quotes many other instances of wrong translations of the same kind by a galaxy of translators (that is, cases where the word *parush* or some derivative has been wrongly translated as 'Pharisee' when it means something else). Some of these mistranslations (when the word in question has a derogatory meaning) tend to give credence to the New Testament's hostile picture of the Pharisee movement as a whole.

Some modern scholars (whose work is now fortunately outdated) have fallen into the trap set by the multiple meanings of the word *parush*. Jacob Neusner, in a series of writings, argued that the Pharisees were primarily a sect devoted to ritual purity. In this theory, the *perushim* are to be identified with the ritual-purity societies (known as *havurot*, whose members were known as *haverim*, and to whom the term *perushim* was sometimes applied). This approach makes an invalid identification between *haverim* (essentially members of societies) and *perushim* (individuals living a lonely saintly life, that is, when the word does not mean 'Pharisees') and utterly fails to explain the passages in rabbinic literature that employ the word *parush* in a deprecatory sense, while in other passages (though not many) the rabbinic literature refers to *perushim* as a title borne by their first-century predecessors who clashed with the Sadducees. Neusner's theory fails to take into account the multivalence of the word *parush*.

On the other hand, the multiple meanings of the word *parush* may provide some kind of explanation for the charge of 'hypocrisy' made so frequently in the Gospels (allegedly by Jesus himself) against the Pharisees. This is very probably a transfer of certain rabbinic diatribes and charges of hypocrisy originally made against individual would-be saints, who were designated by the term *parush*, to the whole movement which had received the nickname *perushim*, or

Pharisees. It is an ironic thought that the redactors of the Gospels made the same mistake as the modern scholar Jacob Neusner; they confused the various meanings of the word *parush*.

Nevertheless, in the present book I use the term 'Pharisees' always to mean the movement, not the individuals, to whom I allot their Hebrew designation *parush*. When I ask whether Jesus was a Pharisee, I am asking whether he was a member of the leading religious movement of his time, though I do not preclude that he was also a *hasid*, that is, an individualist saint, for the *hasidim*, despite their individualism, were also members of the Pharisee movement and were acknowledged by the whole movement as members of particular distinction, despite the reservations felt about some of them (the 'foolish *hasidim*'). A *hasid* such as Hanina ben Dosa or Honi the Circlemaker occupied a highly honoured position in the Pharisee movement, though they were not regarded as models for the ordinary person to try to follow.

Jesus, then, never spoke of the whole Pharisee movement as hypocritical, though he may well have criticized certain people, who had the name of *parush* (ascetic) as being hypocrites, since this charge was made against them in the literature of the rabbis which was indeed the literature of the Pharisees, as they were called chiefly by people outside the movement. To the rabbis who wrote the rabbinic literature, the Mishnah, for example, their predecessors, such as Hillel and Shammai, were not known as Pharisees but as sages or scribes. There is not one passage in the whole rabbinic literature in which Hillel, for example, is called a Pharisee; yet Josephus would have called him one, since Josephus was interested in labelling various religious factions, and when the aim was to differentiate personages like Hillel from the Sadducees, the name that tended to be used was the sectarian label Pharisees. Since the Pharisees themselves did not regard themselves as a sect, but as the whole Jewish people at prayer or study, they avoided using a self-designation that was a sect-label except when the context (controversy with the Sadducees) made this unavoidable.

Even the most devout believer in the historical truth of the Gospels would not assert that Jesus regarded Hillel or Gamaliel as hypocrites. Yet Hillel and Gamaliel are highly representative of the movement which so reluctantly acquired the sobriquet 'Pharisees'. It is only in the sense that Hillel and Gamaliel were Pharisees that Jesus himself, in the argument of this book, was a Pharisee. It is important to continue the use of this word, however inappropriate it may be in certain ways, because it has attained such general currency in the Western world for the movement as a whole and has illegitimately acquired the meaning 'hypocrite', thereby acting as a powerful ingredient in the formation of Western antisemitism. It has therefore become an important task of the scholar, as Paul Winter said, to clear the name of 'Pharisee' from the charge of hypocrisy and thereby to combat the woeful weight of antisemitism that has come down to us from the Christian ages of faith.

The Pharisees as a whole, in this sense, were a movement of conspicuous sincerity and freedom from hypocrisy, as becomes clear to any reader of Josephus and the rabbinic writings. The rabbis were well aware of the danger of hypocrisy and were constantly on their guard against it. Many rabbinic passages show their abhorrence of it. Their nomenclature in this regard is interesting. They use more than one designation to denote 'hypocrite', but a particularly interesting expression used for this purpose is 'someone whose inside is not like his outside'. In referring to hypocrites, the rabbis use many sayings which recall and echo the sayings recorded in the Gospels as used by Jesus. Here are some examples:

Woe unto him that has no court, but makes a gateway for his court! (*b. Yoma* 72b)

(Hypocrites are like) white pitchers full of ashes. (*b. Ber.* 28a)

They pretend to be able to read the Scriptures and the Mishnah, but they cannot: they wrap their prayer shawls around them; they put their phylacteries on their heads, and they oppress the poor. (*Ecc. Rab.* 4.1.1)

New Testament expressions similar to these readily spring to mind (for example, when Jesus refers to hypocrites as 'whited sepulchres' (Matt. 23.27, AV; see also Acts 23.3, 'whited wall'). Jesus also refers to hypocrites as flaunting their prayer-shawls and phylacteries

(Matt. 23.5), but directs this attack at the learned, not at those pretending to be learned. Probably, the saying about the pretended learned is the original version.

The main point, however, is that attacks on hypocrites were a familiar rabbinic topos, and Jesus is here treading well-trodden ground, though the editors of the Gospels, in their hatred of the Pharisees, extend these attacks to the whole Pharisee movement, rather than to individuals.

It ought to be added, however, that the rabbinic literature, unlike the New Testament, has room for the thought that, while outright hypocrisy should be roundly condemned, 100 per cent sincerity is something very rare, and is found only in the most saintly of persons. The majority of people, even the most estimable, have some motivations that are not entirely pure (ambition, for example, or desire for applause or glory), so that it is rare to find someone who pursues even the most admirable policies in life entirely for their own sake or for the love of God. The rabbis found this something of a problem, and after considering it carefully, came to the conclusion that it is better to do admirable things 'not for their own sake' than not to do them at all, because 'out of doing them not for their own sake, one may eventually come to do them for their own sake' (*b. Pesah.* 50b). Actually, this thought is itself part of the fight against hypocrisy; for to overestimate one's own or others' capability for complete sincerity is itself a kind of hypocrisy, or at least complacency.

A depth of psychological insight is illustrated in a rabbinic story (*b. Ber.* 28a). This story tells that Rabban Gamaliel (here is meant probably Rabban Gamaliel II) once issued an announcement to the students of his academy: 'Any of you whose inside is not like his outside should absent himself from the academy.' On the next day, hardly any students turned up for his class. This upset Rabban Gamaliel, who now felt that his proclamation was a mistake, since it was resulting in 'withholding Torah from Israel'. He was comforted by a dream which showed 'white pitchers full of ashes'. This symbolized hypocrites (that is, people whose 'inside was not like their outsides'), thus confirming his suspicion that many of his students came into this category. Nevertheless, he decided to rescind his proclamation; hypocrites were now to be allowed to attend his classes. As a result, his classes became well-attended again. The Talmud adds somewhat oddly that Gamaliel's dream should not be taken too seriously. It did not really mean that the students who absented themselves were hypocrites, though this is how Gamaliel understood the dream. It was sent to him merely to comfort him and ease his distress at the fear that he had made a mistake.

This story is an extraordinarily subtle essay on the subject of hypocrisy, and shows that this was a subject of deep meditation in the rabbinic movement. The most surprising aspect of the story is that when rabbinic students were accused of hypocrisy, that is, of 'putting on a front', their immediate response was to agree. Not one of them had the temerity to assert, 'I am just what I appear to be.' Here is an admission of hypocrisy that is itself the best possible answer to the charge of hypocrisy. It is an acknowledgement that some level of hypocrisy is the human condition; that only through suppressing or, better, sublimating (though never obliterating) the demands of the id, does the ego set up a civilized form of society.

But what of Rabban Gamaliel himself? Was he so complacent that he regarded himself as free of all hypocrisy, and therefore as entitled to demand the same total sincerity from his students? I think this interpretation would detract from the subtlety of the story, which is a description of a kind of social experiment which probably never happened, except in the mind of Rabban Gamaliel himself. The story is asking the question, 'Would it ever be possible to attain a state of society in which the human surface is entirely homogeneous with the interior of the human psyche?' The rabbinic movement was one of the most idealistic movements that have ever existed; but what (the question is being asked) is the meaning of idealism? Does it mean the total transformation of human nature? The answer given is, 'No'. The inside and the outside can be brought to live at peace with each other, but they can never be brought to identity; nor is it even even desirable that this should happen. We remember at this point rabbinic sayings that assert the value to the total personality of the energy of 'the evil inclination', when harnessed, or in Freud's phrase, 'sublimated'. Looked at from a certain superficial point of view, sublimation is hypocrisy; but it was a kind of hypocrisy which the Pharisees valued, and of which the New Testament appears to be unaware, because its hero is someone who is conceived as entirely perfect. In the whole of the rabbinic literature, there is no such figure, and even the most highly-estimated individual (beginning with Moses himself) is liable to be criticized at times.

To reinforce this interpretation we may ask the further question, 'Why did Rabban Gamaliel rescind his decree?' If he interpreted his dream to mean that the absentees were in fact all hypocrites, had he not been right to exclude them? So why did he now decide to take them back? The answer seems to be that Gamaliel now came to the conclusion that he had been wrong to expect too high a standard of sincerity from his pupils. The world could not continue without the Torah, and the Torah could be spread only by people who spent time in studying it, and if one were too scrupulous in examining the motives of such people, the world could not go on. This ties in with the rabbinic saying quoted above to the effect that it is better to do the right thing for the wrong motive than not to do the right thing at all. Perhaps the majority of Gamaliel's students had motives which did not bear much scrutiny. They wanted to study the Torah, but not for its own sake but for their own glory. They wanted to be highly-regarded scholars and cut a figure in the world. But Gamaliel came to understand that this was inevitable and must not be allowed to disrupt the progress of the world. True sincerity is a very rare commodity, and cannot be attained except through a long process at which insincerity is involved at every step. Gamaliel's students understood this better than he did himself. A striking aspect of the story is that they did not fool themselves; they knew their motives were impure. Yet they were honest enough to admit this to themselves, and out of their boundless admiration for Gamaliel, they did not wish to continue in a way of which he disapproved, even if this meant the end of their hopes and ambitions. The mixture of honesty, nobility, realism and insincerity that is portrayed in this story could be a subject for Henry James.

Thus when Jesus called the Pharisees 'hypocrites' he was not telling them something they did not know, even though, as portrayed in the Gospels, the accusation is crudely insulting, not an acknowledgement of the unbearable dilemma inseparable from all idealism, namely the temptation to complacency. Jesus (as portrayed) is a Gamaliel who did not progress into understanding and acceptance of human frailty, and of course the kind of hypocrisy which Jesus allegedly threw at the Pharisees was not a matter of scholarly motivation but of sheer criminal corruption, of a kind that was entirely alien to the Pharisee movement as whole.

8

Pharisees and Rabbis: The Continuity

The Pharisees were a religious grouping or rather a national movement that existed in Palestine in the period before the destruction
of the Temple by the Romans in 70 CE. As explained in the last
chapter, they did not actually call themselves Pharisees usually, this
being a name given to them by their opponents the Sadducees.
They preferred a non-sectarian designation that marked them out
as the teachers of the whole Jewish people: sages, or scribes.

Rabbis, on the other hand, did not object to being called rabbis,
since there was no danger that this would be mistaken for a
sectarian label. They existed after the destruction of the Temple,
when Judaism was re-constituting itself as a religion without
sacrificial rites and without a Temple. The rabbis instituted a system of prayers, or liturgy, which was performed in synagogues, or
meeting-places, where the study of the Torah took place, and sermons were delivered as well as prayer. Synagogues had existed even
when the Temple stood, especially in the Diaspora, but now the
synagogue became the centre of religion even in the Holy Land.
The various sects that had existed in Temple times (Sadducees,
Essenes and others) did not survive the destruction of the Temple.
Only one minority sect did survive, the Samaritans, who had never
recognized the Jerusalem Temple and had a Temple of their own on
Mount Gerizim. The Sadducess had made the Temple and the
priesthood the centre of their religious life to such an extent that its
demise left them without *raison d'être*; while the Essenes (or Dead
Sea Scrolls sect, if they were indeed identical with the Essenes) were
also Temple-centred and priest-centred, even though they had
seceded from the actual Temple as polluted by unacceptable practices. The Rabbis, however, though they mourned the end of the

Temple, had never made it the centre of their spiritual life and were able to continue without it. Moreover, the priesthood had never held a position of leadership among them. To the rabbis, learning and knowledge of the Torah and its interpretation (including the mass of traditional interpretations which they transmitted) was the criterion for leadership, not hereditary descent from Aaron. It was a rabbinic saying, 'A learned bastard takes precedence over an ignorant High Priest' (*m. Hor.* 3.8). The hereditary principle had no place in the rabbinic movement, and the highest places in it were open to people of the lowliest descent, provided that they showed the ability to master the body of rabbinic learning.

The rabbis considered themselves to be continuing the tradition of the sages ('Pharisees') of Temple times, whom they revered (Hillel for example) as their mentors and heroes. But serious doubt has been thrown in modern times on the genuineness of this link between Pharisees and Rabbis. It has been widely alleged that the link was actually invented by the rabbis, who wanted to give their movement some authority and history, whereas, in fact, they comprised a new movement which only began in post-Temple times. Plausibility was given to this approach by the fact that no writings of the Pharisees have survived. All information about the Pharisees comes from post-Temple writings: the historical writings of Josephus (about 90 CE), and the religious writings of the rabbis themselves, the earliest of which derive from the second century CE. Perhaps one piece of actual Pharisee writing has survived, a bare list of dates on which fasting was forbidden (*Megillat Ta'anit*) but this is very poor evidence for a movement of important influence. Yet many sayings of the Pharisees survive, but not in independent literary form: they are embedded in the rabbinic writings as sayings of Hillel, or Shammai or other Pharisaic teachers. It is always possible to argue that these sayings are not authentic and were attributed to the Pharisaic sages by rabbinic teachers of later date who wished to gain credence and respect for sayings that actually originated with themselves. We would certainly have to attribute, in this case, a large measure of cunning deception to the rabbis who compiled this corpus of purported Pharisaic sayings, and to believe in the existence of such a conspiracy may perhaps stretch the credence of the modern reader even more than the straightforward view that the rabbis were transmitting sayings that had been handed down to them.[1]

Josephus lived, during part of his life, at a time when the Pharisee movement was still flourishing, and his evidence is of great importance. He testifies that the Pharisees were much revered by the populace, that they were the guardians of ancient traditions of interpretation of Scripture, that they made decisions on topical matters and these decisions were generally accepted as authoritative, that they differed from the Sadducees in accepting the authority of oral tradition as well as that of Scripture. These are all important testimonies, which confirm the rabbinic view, expressed in the rabbinic writings, of the relation of themselves to the Pharisees. Nevertheless, ways were found by modern scholars (beginning with Morton Smith) to discount Josephus' evidence in this matter.

Certainly Josephus' testimony is very much lacking in the halakhic detail which is needed for full confirmation. Did the Pharisees actually initiate the legal system that is found so fully expounded in the Mishnah and other rabbinic writings? Josephus, however, is not entirely lacking in such detail. He confirms, for example, that the Pharisees differed from the Sadducees on the question of the water-libation which was offered during the festival of Tabernacles. Josephus even confirms the rabbinic story (*m. Sukkah* 4.9) that when a Sadducee High Priest attempted to flout this custom by pouring the water-libation on the ground instead of on the altar, he was pelted by the irate populace with their *'etrogim* (citrons – fruits which formed part of the rite) (*Antiquities* 13.13.372). This confirms not only the existence of a rabbinic law (the water-libation) in the Pharisee legal system, but also the contention of the rabbis that the Sadducee leaders in practice were forced by public opinion to conform with Pharisee law even when they disapproved of it. The story also confirms the existence of an Oral Torah which was affirmed by the Pharisees and denied by the Sadducees, for the water-libation has no support in the Written Torah.

My thesis in the present book that Jesus' religious orientation was Pharisaic depends on the view that the Pharisees were continuous with the rabbis, for my evidence is taken chiefly from the rabbinic writings. Moreover, I am taking the view that many sayings

attributed in the rabbinic writings to post-Destruction rabbis are
actually traditional sayings that existed long before the time of the
rabbis in whose name they are adduced. For many of the sayings
and attitudes which Jesus has in common with the rabbinic writings
are not even adduced there in the name of Pharisees, but in the
name of post-Destruction rabbis. However, this procedure is
always open to the objection that these sayings were actually initiated by Jesus, and then somehow found their way into the rabbinic
writings. We might end up with the proposition that Jesus was the
founder of the rabbinic movement, rather than that he was a member of it. This may seem a rather unlikely proposition, yet some
scholars, impressed by the strong similarity between Jesus' teaching
in many of its aspects and that of the rabbinic movement, have come
very near to asserting it. The corollary of this view, however, is that
the Pharisee or rabbinic movement of Jesus' own day was very
different from what it later became (under Jesus' influence). Thus
all the stories in the Gospels about the alleged horrid nature of the
Pharisees could be true, and this would not contradict the fact that
documentary evidence about the rabbis gives them no support.

This myth about Jesus' beneficent influence on the rabbinic
movement might seem a little too bizarre to command much support from scholars. Yet it is surprising how popular this theory has
in fact proved. An example is Jesus' use of parables. We find the
much-respected scholar Joachim Jeremias actually arguing that the
rabbis derived their propensity to tell parables from Jesus! If one
were able to take this suggestion seriously, it would, in a bizarre
way, actually strengthen the main thesis of the present book, since it
would tend to show that Jesus was not only a Pharisee but a leading
influence on the Pharisee movement.

Jeremias's actual words are as follows:

Jesus' parables are something entirely new. In all the rabbinic
literature, not one single parable has come down to us from the
period before Jesus; only two similes from Rabbi Hillel (c. 20 BC)
who jokingly compared the body with a statue, and the soul with
a guest (Lev. r. 34 on 25.35). It is among the sayings of Rabban
Johanan ben Zakkai (d. c. AD 80) that we first meet with a para-

ble . . . As its imagery resembles one of Jesus' parables, we may well ask whether Jesus' model (together with other factors, such as Greek animal fables) did not have an important influence on the rabbis' adopting parables as a narrative form.[2]

Why Hillel's 'similes' are dismissed as jokes is not explained. It is incorrect of Jeremias to use the title 'Rabbi Hillel', since Pharisee teachers of his period did not use the title 'Rabbi', and throughout the rabbinic literature he is referred to simply as 'Hillel'. It is strange that Jeremias dates Rabban Johanan ben Zakkai by his date of death rather than his date of birth. He was very long-lived, and was in fact a contemporary of Jesus (a fact which Jeremias appears to be trying to disguise), so it is just as likely that Jesus learnt how to compose parables from him, as he from Jesus. As it happens, the Talmud states that Rabban Johanan was an expert on parables (*b. B. Bat.* 134a), but that most of the parables stemming from him were later lost.

In any case, Jeremias himself points out, in a footnote on the same page, that elsewhere in the rabbinic literature (*m. Qohel.* 9.8), the same parable is attributed to Rabbi Judah I, who died in 217 CE. Jeremias judges that the ascription to Rabban Johanan is more probable, but he does not draw an important conclusion: that parables that stem from early rabbis may well be quoted in the name of later rabbis. This is simply because parables were, for a long period, handed down by word of mouth, so they tended to be attributed to the rabbi from whom one had heard it, even though it was in fact much older in origin. This destroys the whole basis of Jeremias's argument. For he is arguing that there were no parables among the Pharisees of the first century, since all the hundreds of parables found in the rabbinic literature (with the few exceptions he mentions) are quoted in the name of second-century rabbis. This proves nothing at all, for it was not until the second century that parables began to be recorded in writing, and they would naturally be recorded in the names of rabbis from whom they were heard, even though those rabbis had, in most cases, heard the parables in question from their teachers of the previous generation.

There was a great reluctance among the Pharisee teachers to put their views and decisions into writing in a 'published' form (that is, other than in note form) for the simple reason that the canon of Scripture had only just been completed and the rabbis did not want any writings of theirs to be included in the canon (this reluctance did not exist, of course, among the sectarians, who actively wanted their writings, the Dead Sea Scrolls and Pseudepigrapha, to be included in the canon of Scripture). The rabbis' reluctance to 'publish' their writings was even greater in the case of parables and animal-fables, which were regarded as mere preaching-material and were not preserved with any great diligence. It is said of Rabbi Meir, a second-century rabbi, for example, that he knew 300 animal-fables, and all but three of them had been lost (*b. Sanh.* 38b). These considerations, again, lessen the validity of Jeremias's remarks about the non-existence of parables before Jesus. The fact is that the period for which we have a wealth of written material, beginning with the second century, also contains a wealth of parables, showing that parables were a strong feature of the rabbinic movement in general as a method of preaching.

Now it is undoubtedly the case that there is a remarkable similarity between the parables told by Jesus and the many more numerous parables found in the rabbinic literature. The most immediately likely explanation of this is that Jesus was drawing on a tradition of parable-telling, and that this is a compelling indication that Jesus belonged to the parable-telling movement, the Pharisees. This kind of indication is more persuasive than any amount of similarity in moral sayings, for a movement is characterized by its atmosphere and the type of bonding and relationship which its leaders set up with its rank and file.

To the Pharisees/rabbis, parable-telling belonged to the aspect of rabbinic teaching that was known as *aggadah*, which means literally 'story-telling'. This existed alongside the more severely logical and intellectual aspect of rabbinic teaching, the *halakhah*, which comprised the vast structures of rabbinic law, with all its systems and hermeneutical principles.

We do not find parables in the Pseudepigrapha or in the Dead Sea Scrolls, but we do find them in profusion in the rabbinic writings, especially the Midrashim.

Some scholars, as we have seen, have argued that there is no evidence of the use of parables among the Pharisees of Jesus' day, and that the frequent parables of the second-century rabbis show that they were influenced in this aspect by Jesus himself. However, the likelihood is that the second-century rabbis were carrying on an established tradition of preaching in their use of parables. Part of the evidence for this is the fact that a rabbinic version of a parable can sometimes throw light on parables that appear in the Gospels in a version modified by the ideological aims of the Gospel redactor. The full range of the parable genre is, in fact, much better displayed in the rabbinic literature, which contains thousands of examples, than in the New Testament, which contains only 31. While the New Testament corpus of parables contains some incomparable examples of the genre (for example, the parable of the Prodigal Son), the range of topics employed is rather limited, being almost exclusively concerned with the imminent kingdom of God and the need for repentance in preparation for it. The rabbinic corpus, on the other hand, has a much wider range of topics.

An example of a rabbinic parable that is directly comparable with a New Testament parable is the parable of Rabban Johanan ben Zakkai already mentioned. This version of the parable is especially interesting because it points to solutions of the many problems arising in the New Testament version:

Rabban Johanan ben Zakkai said: This may be compared to a king who summoned his servants to a banquet without appointing a time. The wise ones adorned themselves and sat at the door of the palace. Said they, Is anything lacking in a royal palace? The fools went about their work, saying, Can there be a banquet without preparations? Suddenly the king desired [the presence of] his servants: the wise entered adorned, while the fools entered soiled. The king rejoiced at the wise but was angry with the fools. Those who adorned themselves for the banquet, ordered he, let them sit, eat and drink. But those who did not adorn themselves for the banquet, let them stand and watch. (*b. Shabb.* 153a, Soncino translation)

This parable shows affinities to two Gospel parables: that of the virgins (Matt. 25.1–12) and that of the wedding (Matt. 22.2–14; Luke 14.16–24, *Gospel of Thomas* 64.1–11). Since Rabban Johanan ben Zakkai, as we have seen, was a contemporary of Jesus, it is not at all impossible that the version recorded in his name in the Talmud is in fact an earlier and more authentic version than that found in the New Testament. Certain puzzling or redundant features in the Gospel versions suggest that the simpler Talmudic version is the earliest.

Let us look first at the Gospel parable that shows the closest similarity to Rabban Johanan's parable, that is, the wedding parable in Matthew, in order to judge which of the two versions would appear to be the earlier from internal evidence alone. This would appear to be a procedure that flies in the face of the scholarly method which relies on the principle that date of publication is the decisive factor; but we have reason to question this principle, not only on a priori grounds (see note 1), but on grounds of scholarly practice in other areas where 'publication' comes at the end of a long process of oral transmission. Recent research has confirmed the reliability in general of a long process of oral transmission, so it would not be surprising if a parable attributed to Rabban Johanan were to turn up in undamaged condition in a Talmudic text 400 years later.

Here is Matthew's version:

The kingdom of Heaven is like this. There was a king who prepared a feast for his son's wedding; but when he sent his servants to summon the guests he had invited, they would not come. He sent others again, telling them to say to the guests, 'See now! I have prepared this feast for you. I have had my bullocks and fatted beasts slaughtered; everything is ready; come to the wedding at once.' But they took no notice; one went off to his farm, another to his business, and the others seized the servants, attacked them brutally, and killed them. The king was furious; he sent troops to kill those murderers and set their town on fire. Then he said to his servants, 'The wedding-feast is ready; but the guests I invited did not deserve the honour. Go out to the main thoroughfares, and invite everyone you can find to the wedding.'

The servants went out into the streets, and collected all they could find, good and bad alike. So the hall was packed with guests.

When the king came to see the company at table, he observed one man who was not dressed for a wedding. 'My friend,' said the king, 'how do you come to be here without your wedding clothes?' He had nothing to say. The king then said to his attendants, 'Bind him hand and foot; turn him out into the dark, the place of wailing and grinding of teeth.' For though many are invited, few are chosen. (Matt. 22.2–14, NEB)

Immediately striking in this parable attributed to Jesus is a glaring contradiction. The king has just given orders to his servants to bring in people indiscriminately from the streets. Presumably most of them, if not all of them, would not be dressed for a wedding, and there is no instruction that they should be given time to go home and put on their best clothes. Yet the king is furiously angry with one of them for not being suitably dressed. How can we explain this? Then the final sentence adds further puzzlement: 'though many are invited, few are chosen'. This seems to contradict the previous trend of the story in which the emphasis is on the lack of choosiness in the inviting of the guests: 'good and bad alike'.

The parable, in fact, seems to fall into two sections which tell different stories and have different morals, while the final sentence expresses yet a third moral. We may pause to note that, if this example is anything to go by, some of the parables in the New Testament are in such a state of disarray that any light that can be thrown on them from some external source, however late, ought to be welcomed.

In the first section of the present patchwork of a parable, the concern is with the unwillingness of the invited guests to come to the wedding (the moral being presumably that people ought to be grateful, not churlish, when someone tries to bestow a benefit on them; this aspect indeed is the sole theme in the versions of the parable found in Luke and *Thomas*); while in the second section, the concern is with the unpreparedness of one of the guests who did come to the wedding (the moral being that people ought to be in a state of preparedness when a beneficial or honour-conferring turn of events is, to their knowledge, in the offing). The final moral, however, which by its placement seems to apply to the whole conglomerate, seems to fit neither section, for while the earlier sections stress the generosity of the invitations and censure the inadequate response by the guest, the final moral stresses that invitations, far from being generous, are mostly liable to cancellation by the host.

The parable quoted in the Talmud in the name of Rabban Johanan seems to correspond to the second section of the New Testament parable, since it is all about preparedness for a wedding. Again the wedding is arranged by a king, and again the king is angry when he finds that some of his guests have arrived in unsuitable clothes having failed to prepare themselves. In this case, however, the unpreparedness is clearly blameworthy, since the guests all had ample warning of the imminence of the wedding. Again, the king expresses his anger by punishing the unprepared ones, though far more mildly than in the New Testament story. There is no banishment to a place of darkness, where there is 'wailing and grinding of teeth' (an expression used elsewhere in the New Testament to signify hell), but merely the punishment of having to watch their better-prepared companions eat the delicious food provided.

Our first deduction, then, is that the New Testament story is actually not one parable but two, which have been confusedly put together. The second section was originally a parable on its own, on the theme of preparedness, and this section has its parallel in the Talmudic parable. Rabban Johanan's parable is not confused in the slightest. It sticks to a single theme, which it develops in a logical way. It therefore has first claim to be the authentic original version of the parable before it got into the hands of the New Testament redactor. This is no doubt very surprising, since the date of the Talmudic text is at least 400 years later than the date of the New Testament text, but this may lead us to pause and re-think questions of chronology when considering rabbinic influence on Jesus, and also when considering the question of continuity between the Pharisees and the rabbis. The fact that Rabban Johanan's parable had to undergo a long period of oral transmission before finding its way into writing may not be as important as many modern scholars have thought. A late text that displays qualities of clarity, simplicity and coherence may deserve preference over an early text character- ized by incoherence and confusion, when the factor of oral trans- mission is taken into account.

We may also note that the sections into which the New Testa- ment version falls differ also in respect of their claim to be a parable. The essence of a parable is that it is a story with a moral. If there is no moral, yet the story corresponds in various ways to some series of events in the outside world, then this is not a parable but an allegory. The New Testament story offers itself at the beginning as a parable: 'The kingdom of Heaven is like this.' The second section does indeed function as a parable illustrating the moral, 'Be prepared for the kingdom of Heaven, or you may miss it,' an important moral indeed. The first section, however, does not illustrate this moral, and it is doubtful whether it illustrates any other. It simply tells a story about a king who had disobedient and rebellious subjects who angered him to such a point that he punished them severely. Surely this could not be intended to illustrate such a crude moral as 'Do not be a disobedient and rebellious subject.' It certainly does not illus- trate the moral that was announced at the beginning: 'The kingdom of Heaven is like this.' It would seem appropriate, therefore, to say that the first section is not a parable at all, but an allegory, and the events which it allegorizes are the disobedience and rebelliousness of the Jewish people, who have been punished for their refusal to accept Jesus as Messiah by having their capital city, Jerusalem, destroyed. (It should be noted that in the versions of Luke and *Thomas*, the messengers are not ill-treated, as in Matthew, but the invitation is simply treated with contempt; this really constitutes a third version of the parable, in which the guests are not merely unprepared, but contemptuous of the invitation. This, too, prob- ably has an allegorical overtone of Jewish rejection of Jesus, but not so hostile and condemnatory as the version in Matthew, which por- trays the Jews as showing continual violence, not merely contempt.) In the allegory, the king is God, and the son is Jesus; his wedding is the founding of the Christian Church to which all the Jews were invited. But they churlishly refused the invitation and persecuted God's messengers (here there is also an allusion to the accusation that the Jews in previous ages had persecuted the prophets whom God sent to them). Finally, the king 'set their town on fire' (Matt. 22.7, NEB. This makes little sense within the parameters of the story itself, because the town belonged to the king, so he would be destroying his own property. But it makes perfect sense as an allegory of the destruction of Jerusalem, for this (in Christian theory) amounted to the repudiation of the Jews as God's people and his transfer of his affections to the Christian Church, so that he no longer regarded Jerusalem as his city. This aspect too is contained in the allegory plainly enough: 'the guests I invited [i.e., the Jews] did not deserve the honour. Go out to the main thoroughfares and invite everyone you can find to the wedding.' In other words, invite the Gentiles to form my new Church. The servants then collected 'good and bad alike', an allusion to the Pauline Christian doctrine that salvation was not a matter of merit, but of grace.[3]

So what here purports to be a parable about preparedness for the kingdom of Heaven is diverted into an allegory of the supplanting of the Jews by the Christian Church. This section, therefore, dates from a time after the destruction of the Temple and Jerusalem (70 CE) and cannot be an authentic utterance of Jesus. Only after this anti-Jewish digression has ended do we begin to encounter the genuine words of Jesus in a parable which does in fact point a moral about preparedness for the kingdom of Heaven.

If we now compare this genuine parable with that recorded in the Talmud in the name of Jesus' contemporary Rabban Johanan ben Zakkai, we notice many similarities, but also one important difference. The moral of Rabban Johanan's parable does not have messianic reference. It does not refer to the approaching kingdom of heaven, but points a moral that applies to every day of ordinary life: namely, the importance of daily repentance as a preparation for death. This must have been the form in which the parable reached Jesus. His originality lay in giving this parable, well-known in Pharisee circles, a messianic reference.

We may find further light by considering another New Testament parable which is unequivocally on the subject of preparedness:

The kingdom of Heaven will be like this. There were ten girls, who took their lamps and went out to meet the bridegroom. Five of them were foolish, and five prudent; when the foolish ones took their lamps, they took no oil with them, but the others took flasks of oil with their lamps. As the bridegroom was late in coming they all dozed off to sleep. But at midnight a cry was heard: 'Here is the bridegroom! Come out to meet him!' With that the girls all got up and trimmed their lamps. The foolish said to the prudent, 'Our lamps are going out; give us some of your oil.' 'No,' they said, 'there will never be enough for all of us. You had better go to the shop and buy some for yourselves.' While they were away the bridegroom arrived; those who were ready went in with him to the wedding; and the door was shut. And then the other five came back. 'Sir, sir,' they cried, 'open the door for us.' But he answered, 'I declare, I do not know you.' Keep awake, then, for you never know the day or the hour. (Matt. 25.1–13, NEB)

This parable is much more like that of Rabban Johanan ben Zakkai in being unequivocally on the subject of preparedness for a wedding. The foolish girls (or 'virgins' in the well-known AV version) all fail to be properly prepared, and their punishment is to be excluded from the wedding. The parable however suffers from various defects compared with Rabban Johanan's very straightforward and intelligible version. Why do there have to be ten virgins at a wedding? Is one of them the bride and the others bridesmaids? Or are they all bridesmaids? This is not explained; one might almost think that a multiple wedding is about to take place (the Catholic practice of referring to nuns as 'brides of Christ' might point to this interpretation). Why is it necessary for them all to have functioning lamps? If some of them have lamps which provide light, surely the others could simply follow them? Or is there some reason why the bridegroom must have virgins with functioning lamps? We seem to have here another example of a mangled parable; something must be missing that would explain the difficulties. Again, we conclude that while Jesus is portrayed as a teacher who is fond of telling parables, the process of transmission by which these parables have reached the printed page is often flawed, and any evidence from other sources of the original form of the parables is to be welcomed. In this particular case, there is no helpful evidence from rabbinic sources of a wedding parable involving ten virgins, so the parable must remain problematic. All we can say is that Rabban Johanan ben Zakkai's parable shows that the theme of unpreparedness was a favourite one in rabbinic preaching. At least we can be thankful that the parable of the ten virgins has not been contaminated by anti-Jewish propaganda.

It is unfortunate, however, that not only are many of the New Testament parables presented in mangled form, but the whole topic of parable-telling has been debased in the Gospels by the suggestion that Jesus told parables not to enlighten people but to obfuscate them. This theory is expressed in the following passage:

> When he was alone, the Twelve and others who were round him questioned him about the parables. He replied, 'To you the secret of the kingdom of God has been given; but to those who are outside everything comes by way of parables, so that (as Scripture says) they may look and look, but see nothing; they may hear and hear, but understand nothing; otherwise, they might turn to God and be forgiven.' (Mark 4.11, NEB; see also Matt.13.13; Luke 8.10)

According to this passage, the purpose of the parables is to act as riddles, hiding their meaning from those who are not given the key. These are the people who are 'outside', and Jesus declares his intention to keep them outside permanently, not even allowing them an opportunity to repent and be forgiven. There could hardly be a more unattractive way of presenting Jesus' aim in presenting his message in parables. In order to justify it, he cites a biblical passage from the Hebrew Bible, (Isa. 6.10), a bitter, ironic reproof, which, however, ends with a message of hope. These passages in the Gospels are part of the recurring message that there is no more hope for the Jews, who have forfeited God's love by their history of evil, which, in Rosemary Ruether's phrase, is 'a trail of crimes'. Even when Jesus preaches to them, he does so not to enlighten them (which is impossible) but to put them even further into the dark.

This is expressed more crudely in Mark than in Matthew, for in Mark it is said that the parables are told 'in order that' (*hina*) they may look and look and see nothing, while in Matthew the particle used is *hoti* which means 'because'. In other words, Mark represents Jesus as deliberately misleading the Jews by his use of parables, while Matthew's version is that Jesus was so convinced that the Jews were beyond all persuasion or betterment that he did not trouble to make himself intelligible. Which of these versions is morally preferable, however, is debatable.

Yet nothing is more certain than that Jesus did not have either of these aims when he preached to his fellow-Jews in parables. The Gospels' presentation of Jesus' purpose is a reflection of a period after Jesus' death, when the Jews had been written off by the Christian Church as an incorrigible, reprobate people. Nothing could illustrate more clearly that when we read the Gospels, we are sometimes reading the authentic words of Jesus, a Jew who loved and supported his people, and sometimes we are reading words of hate, emanating from enemies of the Jews.

When we consider those parables of Jesus that have survived in undistorted form, it is obvious enough that Jesus did not intend them as riddles, hiding the truth, but on the contrary as modes of teaching by which his message could be purveyed in charming and intelligible form, appealing to the understanding of even the simplest of his hearers. And this is precisely the way the rabbis and their predecessors the Pharisees used parables in their preaching. The kinship of Jesus and the Pharisees is nowhere more perspicuous than in their use of parables to win the hearts of their audience and especially to bring them to repentance. Yet the passages we have been considering (particularly that of Mark) actually state that the purpose of the parables was to *prevent* Jesus' hearers from repenting!

We may now consider more closely the rabbinic use of parables, in order to derive from this source further insight into the kinship between the Pharisees and Jesus, and also to derive further information about the continuity between the Pharisees and their successors of post-Temple times, the rabbis.

9

Continuity: Further Considerations

Jesus' main mission was to preach the coming of the kingdom of God, and for this purpose he set out on a campaign to bring the Jews to repentance, for it was a well-established principle among the Pharisees/rabbis that full repentance by the Jewish people would bring about the coming of the Messiah, who would redeem Israel by rescuing them from the domination of foreigners and restoring the kingdom described in the Torah. This kingdom was an earthly kingdom, but it was called 'the kingdom of God' (equivalent to 'kingdom of Heaven', since 'Heaven' was one of the names of God) because it was to be a theocracy. Its earthly ruler, however, would be the Messiah himself, a descendant of the House of David, who would sit on the throne of his ancestor in Jerusalem and rule over the twelve tribes (the lost tribes being restored from exile). This vision is not merely national or patriotic, however, for the prophecies of the Hebrew Bible also envision a change in the character of the whole world at this time, when swords would be beaten into ploughshares, and the whole world would enjoy peace and prosperity. Jerusalem would be the spiritual centre of the world, to which all nations would come in pilgrimage. This pilgrimage of the future is described by the prophet Zechariah (ch. 12), and there is much evidence that Jesus was influenced in his messianic mission particularly by this prophet (for example, he entered Jerusalem at the time of the Triumphal Entry, mounted on a donkey, as prophesied by Zechariah, as a sign of the humility expected of a Jewish king, who was commanded not to allow his heart to be lifted up above his brothers (Deut. 17.20). Further, Jesus, at the culmination of his messianic effort, stationed himself on the Mount of Olives, where, in Zechariah's vision, the final triumph of the Messiah over foreign occupiers of the Holy Land would take place.

Jesus began his mission as a prophet, not as a messianic claimant. Like John the Baptist, he prophesied the coming of the Messiah and prepared for his coming by a campaign of repentance. Only at a later stage, under the prompting of Peter (at the Salutation) did Jesus decide that he himself was the Messiah whom he had been prophesying, and from that point on he behaved as a kingly figure. At no point did Jesus conceive of himself as a divine figure whose mission was to die on a Roman cross, thereby bringing salvation (that is, rescue from hell) to humankind. This was a view of Jesus' mission that developed after his death, largely under the influence of Paul, whose upbringing in Tarsus disposed him to views similar to those of the mystery religions. The authentic Jewish concept of messianic redemption as an earthly kingdom appears many times in the Gospels, overlaid, however, by the later Pauline doctrine of Jesus as a divine sacrifice who would bring immortality to his devotees.

Throughout Jewish history, messianic campaigns (of which there were many) were accompanied by campaigns of repentance. Jesus, therefore, was treading a well-trodden path in preaching repentance as an accompaniment to his messianic campaign. His use of parables in the course of this campaign was only to be expected. Many rabbinic parables deal with the theme of repentance. A simple example is the following:

A king's son was at a distance of a hundred-days' journey from his father. Said his friends to him, 'Return to your father.' He said to them, 'I cannot. The way is too far.' The father sent to him and said, 'Go as far as you are able, and I shall come the rest of the way to you.' Thus the Holy One, blessed be He, said to Israel, 'Return unto Me, and I will return unto you' [Mal. 3.7] (Midrash, *Pesiq. Rab.* 44.9)

Pharisee parables were often tied to the exegesis of a biblical text. It is probable, as Graves and Podro have argued,[1] that many of Jesus' sayings and parables were originally tied to texts in the same way.

Perhaps the finest example of Jesus' repentance preaching is the

parable of the Prodigal Son (Luke 15.11–32). The moral of the
parable introduces it (as a second example): 'I say unto you, that
likewise joy shall be in heaven over one sinner that repenteth, more
than over ninety and nine just persons, which need no repentance'
(Luke 15.7, AV). This is similar to the Talmudic saying: 'Where the
repentant sinners stand in the World to Come the perfectly righteous are not permitted to stand' (*b. Ber.* 34b). Thus Jesus put into
the form of a parable a truth which was current in the movement to
which he belonged, the Pharisees. I am not suggesting that Jesus
lacked originality. On the contrary, the genre of the parable gave
free rein to the artistic originality of the Pharisee teachers. In
general, the Pharisee/rabbinic movement was one in which individuality was encouraged in many different ways. The names of many
hundreds of rabbis are known to us, and each of them had some
special traits; some of them were positively eccentric. Amicable disagreement is the norm in the rabbinic writings; every page contains
some disagreement between rabbis. But there were ground-rules
and accepted genres for canalizing creativity, and the parable was
one of them.

For the Prodigal Son who returned to his father in repentance the
fatted calf was killed; and when the faithful son protested, his father
replied, 'Son, thou art ever with me, and all that I have is thine. It is
meet that we should make merry, and be glad: for this thy brother
was dead, and is alive again; and was lost, and is found' (Luke
15.31–2, AV). With this kind of parable, Jesus assured the sinful and
despairing that it was not too late for them to turn back to God: that
even though the 'day of the Lord' was close at hand it was possible
for them to enter the kingdom of God at the last minute if they truly
repented; more, that their place in the kingdom would be higher
than those who had never sinned, for 'the last shall be first', and the
last-hired labourers (to cite another parable) would receive their
penny before those 'which have borne the burden and heat of the
day' (Matt. 20.12, AV).

This last-mentioned parable (about the last-hired labourers,
Matt. 20.1–16) has an analogue in the Talmud not in the form of a
parable but in the form of a story (the relationship between parables
and stories will be discussed shortly):

It was said of Rabbi Eleazar ben Dordai that he did not omit having intercourse with any prostitute in the world. Once he heard that there was a certain prostitute in a sea-port who accepted a purse of denarii for payment. So he took a purse of denarii, and he crossed seven rivers to reach her.

As he was beginning intercourse with her, she farted. Upon this, she commented, 'Just as this fart will never return to its place so Eleazer ben Dordai will never return to God and be accepted.'

He went and sat between two mountain-ranges, and said, 'Mountain-ranges, plead with God to have mercy on me.' Said the mountain-ranges 'Before we pray for you, we should pray for ourselves, for Scripture says, "For the mountains shall depart and the hills be removed" [Isa. 54.10].'

He said, 'Heavens and Earth, ask God to have mercy on me.'

Said the Heavens and Earth, 'Before we pray for you, we should pray for ourselves, for Scripture says, "For the heavens shall vanish away like smoke, and the earth shall wax old like a garment" [Isa. 51.6].'

He said, 'Sun and Moon, ask God to have mercy on me.'

Said the Sun and Moon, 'Before we pray for you, we should pray for ourselves, for Scripture says, "Then the moon shall be confounded and the sun ashamed" [Isa. 24.23].'

He said, 'Stars and Constellations, ask God for mercy on me.'

Said the Stars and Constellations, 'Before we pray for you, we should pray for ourselves, for Scripture says, "And all the hosts of heaven shall moulder away" [Isa. 34.4].'

He said, 'Then the thing depends on me alone.' He put his head between his knees, and groaned and wept until his soul departed. Then a heavenly voice went forth and said, 'Rabbi Eleazar ben Dordai has been summoned to the life of the World to Come.'

Rabbi Judah the Prince, when he heard of this, wept, and said, 'There are those who gain the World to Come by the toil of many years: and there are those who gain the World to Come in one hour.'

And he added, 'It is not enough for those who repent that they are accepted: they are called "Rabbi" too!' (*b. Avod. Zar.* 17a)

This is a story not a parable, since it is about a real person, and purports to be an event that actually happened, while a parable is always presented as a fictional narrative. But a story, like a parable, can have a moral, and the moral of this story is the same as that of the New Testament parable of the last-hired labourers, that it is never too late to repent. As it happens, it is not always easy to distinguish between a parable and a story; for example, the 'parable' of the Good Samaritan in the Gospels always strikes me as a narrative of something that actually happened.

The Talmudic story just cited contains an earthy element that distinguishes it from any of the Gospel parables or stories. One cannot imagine Jesus telling a narrative which contained a prostitute's fart. This is certainly an instance of an element in the Talmud that marks it off from the Gospels; for the rabbis are all very human, while Jesus is too superhuman to be depicted in any way that might detract from his dignity. The rabbis of the Talmud defecate and urinate and discuss problems of women's menstruation. There is a rough, Rabelaisian quality there at times, and the prostitute's fart is a good example of it. Yet, paradoxically, it is this same prostitute who brings the rabbi to repentance by her remark, so acquiring a human dignity as the instrument of redemption. The story contains a strange mixture of registers, ranging from the squalid to the sublime. It has the added dimension that the repentant sinner was once a distinguished rabbi, who has gone to the bad. As against the sordidness of the prostitute's fart, there is the grandeur of Eleazar's appeals to the mountain ranges, the Heavens and Earth, the Sun and Moon, the Stars and Constellations, placing the story in a cosmic setting. Yet all these noble entities can do nothing to bring about repentance and forgiveness. All depends on the individual himself, whose massive effort of repentance actually brings about his death, and finally his salvation. Then in the end, there is an almost comic touch, as Rabbi Judah the Prince, after a lifetime of arduous endeavour, weeps ruefully to see that the World to Come can be gained in an hour, and that moreover the repentant sinner is treated with special honour. He is like the older, blameless son in the parable of the Prodigal Son, who was so rueful that his years of faithful service were, in the end, set below the sudden glory of his scapegrace brother's repentance. This complex Talmudic story, is, in my opinion, more subtle in its dizzy changes of mood than the charming Gospel narrative, but it clearly belongs to the same spiritual milieu, even though the personalities involved belong to the second century.

While dealing with the difference between a parable and a story, I cannot resist citing another rabbinic story which has a nuance that many people will find very unexpected, and which will afford an example of the wide range of moral lessons in the stories of rabbinic literature. This is a story not about repentance, but about another virtue – honour to parents:

> R. Abbahu said: His disciples asked R. Eliezer the Great, 'Wherein consists the honour of father and mother?' [i.e., how far does it extend?] He replied,
> 'Go and see what Dama b. Netina did.'
> Our Rabbis say that he was a Gentile of Ashkalon. Some of our wise men came to him to buy a precious stone in the place of one which had been lost from the breastplate of the High Priest.
> They agreed with him to give a thousand gold pieces for the stone. He went in, and found his father asleep with his leg stretched out upon the box which contained the jewel: he would not disturb him, and came back without it.
> When the wise men perceived this, they thought that he wanted more money, and they offered ten thousand gold pieces. When his father woke up, he went in, and brought out the jewel. The wise men offered him the ten thousand pieces, but he replied: 'Far be it from me to make a profit from honouring my father! I will take only the thousand which we had agreed.'
> (*b. Avod. Zar.* 23b; *y. Pe'ah* 1.1)

What is remarkable about this story is that when R. Eliezer is requested to give an example of the exercise of the virtue of honour-ing a parent, his example is not a Jew, but a Gentile, and, as another passage makes clear, an idolatrous one. This invites comparison with the Gospel story ('parable') of the Good Samaritan, in which Jesus gives a Samaritan as the exemplar of the virtue of being a good neighbour. The Samaritans were despised as heretics (especially because they did not recognize the Jerusalem Temple, but had a Temple of their own on Mount Gerizim), but they were acknowledged to be Jews and monotheists. The rabbinic story of Dama ben Netina thus goes even further than the Good Samaritan story in the unexpectedness of its exemplar of virtue, who is a worshipper of idols. It is especially remarkable that the story is told by Rabbi Eliezer, of all people, a rabbi particularly known for his strict adherence to Jewish tradition.

It should be noted that the Good Samaritan story has nothing to do with the topic of ritual purity, as some scholars have asserted, but is solely about the question with which it opens, which is, 'Who is a good neighbour?' It is not correct to explain the bad behaviour of the priest and the levite on the ground that they were afraid of incurring ritual impurity by coming to the help of the wounded man, who might die and thus infect them with corpse-impurity. Priests were forbidden to incur corpse-impurity, but levites were not; and even priests were enjoined, by rabbinic law, to regard all considerations of ritual purity as unimportant compared with the duty of saving life. Even lesser considerations overrode ritual purity for priests: it was regarded as the duty of a priest who came upon an unburied corpse to busy himself with giving it decent burial (*met mitzvah*) even if this meant handling the corpse; so in the case under consideration, the priest was doubly obligated to 'turn aside' to help the wounded man, firstly to try to save his life, and secondly to give him burial if he should die. Why then did the priest and the levite not 'turn aside' to help the wounded man? Simply because they fell short of love of neighbour (the theme of the whole story), being afraid that the bandits who had attacked the man might be still in the vicinity. The ritual purity considerations have been imported into the story by modern scholars despite the fact that the text itself does not even mention ritual purity. This is not an uncommon procedure among scholars who wish to convict the Judaism of the time with undue preoccupation with matters of ritual purity. What was wrong with the priest and the levite was not that they were preoccupied by ritual purity, but that they failed in their duty to their neighbour in his hour of need. The moral of the story is that a good person should be assessed not by his rank in society, but by his actual behaviour. The priest and the levite, being of high rank might have been expected to show a good example, but they did not. The Samaritan, being of lowly rank, might have been expected to show a low standard of virtue, but instead he proved a good neighbour.

This story has been taken to be a criticism of the Judaism of Jesus' time, but in fact it is an example of a genre which is typically rabbinic: stories which aim to shame the Jewish people into behaving, as they ought, as a holy people, by pointing out that others of whom not so much is expected behave better than they do. The story of Dama ben Netina is an example of this same genre. A similar mode of rebuke can be found in the Hebrew Bible itself: 'From furthest east to furthest west my name is great among the nations. Everywhere fragrant sacrifice and pure gifts are offered in my name: for my name is great among the nations, says the Lord of Hosts. But you profane it . . .' (Mal. 1.11–12, NEB).

It is interesting that the two stories (the Good Samaritan and the story of Dama ben Netina) are even similar in structure. Both start with a question. The question that introduces the Good Samaritan story is, in substance, 'What is meant by being a good neighbour?', while the question introducing the rabbinic story is, 'What constitutes honouring one's parents?' In both cases, the answer is given by recounting an incident involving someone who is not (at least in the full sense) a Jew. In both cases, I suggest, we have a narrative that is not fictional but recounts something that actually happened. So, once more, we find in the Good Samaritan story, an expression on the part of Jesus that unites him with the Pharisees, and does not, as is generally thought, set him apart from them.

Parables and stories of the above kind are excellent indications of affinity between Jesus and the rabbinic movement because they are so idiosyncratic in character. Even more than similarities in unadorned moral and legal teachings, they are evidence of a similar approach and psychological structure. But other kinds of evidence exist that point strongly to the same empathy and kindred spirit.

The Lord's Prayer

A prominent example of affinity between Jesus and the rabbinic movement is the prayer which Jesus composed, known as 'the Lord's Prayer'. There is scarcely a single phrase in this prayer that does not have its parallel in rabbinic sources.[2] The Lord's Prayer was composed by Jesus in response to a request from his disciples to provide them with a prayer 'as John also taught his disciples' (Luke 11.1, AV). Rabbis often composed a prayer for their disciples, not to supersede the regular daily prayers, but as an addition to them. Neither John nor Jesus wanted to abolish the regular prayers consisting mainly of the Shema (the affirmation of the Unity of God and the command to love Him), which was prized by Jesus (Matt. 22.37), and the Amidah, or Eighteen Blessings (a series of prayers, couched as blessings, composed, according to tradition, by the Great Assembly, the founding body of the Pharisees). It was only in the later Church that the Lord's Prayer was given liturgical centrality.

Some scholars, noting parallels between rabbinic prayer and the Lord's Prayer, conclude that Jesus had an influence on the rabbis, rather than the reverse (see above, on parables). This, however, is to ignore the communal nature of rabbinic thinking, by which patterns of creativity derive from mutual exchange and tradition, rather than from an individual. Each rabbi had his own measure of creativity and originality, set within a framework of societal patterning. It is highly unlikely that Jesus invented new patterns which were then adopted by the rabbis; much more likely that he exercised his own individuality within existing patterns, just as they did.

Modes of expression

The use of parables by both Jesus and the rabbis is, as we have seen, strong evidence of their affinity, especially as parables are not found in any of the sectarian movements such as the Dead Sea Scrolls sects. Further, parables are not found in the Gospel of John, the least rabbinic of the Gospels, which shows in many other ways its departure from the portrayal, found in the Synoptic Gospels, of

Jesus as a typical rabbi. Parables, therefore, can be regarded as a kind of fingerprinting by which Jesus' religious affiliation can be deduced. But there are even stronger kinds of fingerprinting: these are actual modes of expression. If we can find in Jesus' reported utterances strong affinities to rabbinic style of expression, as found in the Talmud and other rabbinic literature, we shall be justified in postulating that Jesus moved in a milieu that was saturated with rabbinic culture.

Examples may be found in Jesus' use of metaphor and hyperbole. When he says that it is easier for a camel to go through the eye of needle than for a rich man to enter heaven (Matt 19.24), this extravagant turn of phrase is typically rabbinic. Indeed, the parallel rabbinic phrase expressing impossibility is even more extravagant, involving an elephant and a needle (*b. Ber.* 55b; *b. B. Metzi'a* 38b). In another passage, the animal is indeed a camel, but instead of going through the eye of a needle, dances in a tiny area (*b. Yevam.* 45a). Exegetes who have tried to reduce the extravagance of Jesus' simile (by saying that the 'camel' means 'rope', or that the 'needle' was the name of a gate in Jerusalem), are failing to appreciate the authentically exuberant rabbinic idiom of Jesus' saying.

Similarly, Jesus' sayings on hypocrites have a genuinely rabbinic air. He says (Matt. 7.5, AV), 'Thou hypocrite, first cast out the beam out of thine own eye; and then shalt thou see clearly to cast out the mote out of thy brother's eye.' The rabbinic parallel runs, 'Rabbi Tarfon said, I wonder if anyone in this generation knows how to accept reproof. If anyone says to him, Take the splinter from between your eyes, he replies, Take the beam from between *your* eyes' (*b. Arak.* 16b). Here the charge of hypocrisy is made in order to avoid a just reproof. Yet, despite the somewhat broader context, the metaphor for hypocrisy is almost identical.

Similarly, Jesus refers to hypocrites as 'whited sepulchres, which indeed appear beautiful outward, but are within full of dead men's bones, and of all uncleanness' (Matt. 23.27, AV). The rabbis used very similar imagery, as is shown by the dream of Rabban Gamaliel in which he saw 'white pitchers full of ashes'. This, as we saw above, was in a context where he had issued a proclamation, 'No disciple may enter the House of Learning unless his inside is like his outside' (*b. Ber.* 28a). Thus not only was the similarity one of theme, but also one of mode of expression.

Modes of thinking

But also very significant are the similarities on modes of thinking, especially halakhic thinking, that exist between Jesus and the rabbis. These similarities have far-reaching implications: not only do they point to Jesus' membership of the rabbinic movement; they also give the lie to the cherished hypothesis of scholars that rabbinic modes of thinking did not exist before the second century, and that the rabbinic movement was only pretending to have antecedents in the period of the Second Temple. The sayings of Jesus provide evidence not only of his membership of the rabbinic movement, but cast invaluable light on the history of that movement. This is a line of thought that has been much neglected by scholars, and deserves careful examination.

The affinity between the sayings and stories of Jesus and those of the rabbis as recorded in the rabbinic writings is very striking to anyone who has engaged in rabbinic studies in any sort of depth. Yet this affinity is customarily dismissed by scholars as having little significance with relation to the aims and personality of Jesus himself, since the rabbinic writings are so late and the chief personalities mentioned in the earliest of them belong to the second century, not to the first (and even those that belong to the first century, such as Hillel, are written off as unreliable evidence on the ground that their sayings are recorded in writings of a later date). I have endeavoured to argue that this dismissal of rabbinic evidence is invalid, and that if Jesus appears to a student of the rabbinic writings very much as a typical rabbinic figure, this is for the very simple reason that he *was* a typical rabbinic figure. I am now, however, going to turn the argument round, and put forward the thesis that the rabbinic-like character of Jesus itself throws light on the topic, so important in all New Testament studies, of the continuity (or alleged non-continuity) between the Pharisees and the rabbis.

On the face of it, it seems plausible to deny such continuity, simply on chronological grounds, and on the basis of lack of Pharisee writings to confirm such continuity directly. But I contend that there are indeed writings which confirm the continuity directly – and these writings are the Gospels! In these writings we have a detailed (though heavily edited) account of the thinking and self-expression of one first-century personality who shows the utmost continuity with the rabbis of the second century. True, this person, Jesus, is represented not as a Pharisee, but as an anti-Pharisee, but this is part of an anti-Pharisee campaign or polemic that is being conducted by the editors of the Gospels (see next chapter), for easily-discerned political reasons. When the bias of the editors is removed, Jesus stands as the best possible evidence of the continuity of Pharisaism and rabbinism.

I have concentrated on Jesus' idiosyncrasies (telling of parables, modes of expression, idiomatic phrases) rather than on his explicit endorsement of the Pharisees, whom he described as 'sitting in Moses' seat', because such finger-printing is more telling as evidence than any explicit self-explanation. It is the unconscious and unselfconscious behaviour of a person that proclaims his identity more than any form of self-explanation. Moreover, this idiosyncratic aspect is less open to the ploy, often in use in New Testament studies, of resorting to the notion of 're-Judaization'. This ploy consists of explaining every sign of normative Judaism in Jesus' teachings as a later importation into the text by 're-Judaizers', that is, members of the Jesus movement who, immediately after Jesus' death, fell back weakly into the practice of normative Judaism, contrary to the teaching of Jesus himself. Whole communities of Jesus-followers are alleged to have lapsed into this 're-Judaization'; even whole books of the New Testament have been described as written specifically for the requirements of these 're-Judaizing' communities. The Gospel of Matthew has been especially singled out as a 're-Judaizing' document, because it contains so many testimonies to Jesus' loyalty to normative Judaism; though some scholars, notably E. P. Sanders, have demurred strongly from this judgement, on the ground that Matthew is also the most anti-Jewish of the Gospels.

But, from the standpoint of consideration of the continuity question, it appears to have escaped the notice of the advocates of 're-Judaization' that their ploy is invalid, because the 're-Judaizing' communities postulated were themselves living in the first century, not the second century. Even if we were to accept that Jesus himself did not utter the endorsements of normative Judaism attributed to him in the Gospels, and that these endorsements were actually inserted to please 're-Judaizing' communities, we would have to date these endorsements to the first century, the period of the Pharisees; and these very same 're-Judaizing' utterances would provide incontrovertible evidence of the continuity between first-century Pharisaism and second-century rabbinism. What we are looking for is evidence of a strong link between the Pharisaic movement and the rabbinic movement, and here, on any reckoning, we have it. In the first century, we have documents (the Synoptic Gospels) that declare that not one jot or tittle of the Law will ever pass away, and that the Pharisees sit in Moses' seat, and this proof of continuity is valid whether Jesus actually uttered it or not. In hundreds of ways, the Gospels provide the proof of this continuity, which the rabbis themselves asserted, but which is so awkward for scholars who wish to take the Gospel denunciations of the Pharisees at face value, despite the rabbinic evidence that Pharisee thinking was similar to that of the rabbis themselves – compassionate, rational, and totally free of corruption or dishonest legalism. Scholars have long given up the attempt (once undertaken by Emil Schürer, Ferdinand Weber and others) to show that rabbinic thinking and behaviour were open to the same condemnation that the Gospels assert against the Pharisees; their refuge however has been the doctrine of discontinuity; the rabbis, after the death of Jesus, as one Christian scholar put it to me in conversation, 'pulled their socks up'. But the Gospels themselves are the best refutation of this asserted discontinuity.

Another point that appears to have been neglected is that so many of the second-century rabbis who formed the rabbinic movement had their early education and even their early career in a first-century, that is, Pharisaic, setting. The prime example, of course, is Rabban Johanan ben Zakkai, the leader of the reconstituted movement in Yavneh after the disaster of the Jewish War against Rome. He was a pupil of the great Hillel, and was an actual contemporary of Jesus. He, more than anyone else, set the tone of the rabbinic movement after the War, when he was already an elderly man. He alone is sufficient to refute the fantasy that the rabbinic movement had no continuity with Pharisaism.

But many other second-century rabbis had personal links with the Pharisees. The following famous rabbis, who flourished mainly in the second century, are some of those who had their education and early career in a Pharisaic setting: Rabbi Eliezer ben Hyrcanus, Rabbi Joshua ben Hananiah, Rabbi Akaviah ben Mahalalel, Rabbi Zadok, Rabbi Eliezer ben Jacob, Rabbi Nahum ben Gimzo, the teacher of Rabbi Akiva. It is no wonder that the authors of the rabbinic writings took it for granted that the rabbinic movement was the direct continuation of the Pharisee movement, even though it was acknowledged that many adjustments had to be made to the new situation of a Judaism without a Temple. The Pharisees, however, had shown their adaptability to many crises before, so even this was not completely without precedent.

In general, the dogma of discontinuity should not be allowed to hamper the study of the New Testament, which itself provides much evidence against it. The vicious campaign against the Pharisees in the Gospels, which unhistorically shows them as persecuting Jesus, should be recognized for what it is, rather than obscured by attempts to isolate the Pharisees of Jesus' time from the general course of rabbinic Judaism.

Emil Schürer and Ferdinand Weber (as pointed out above) attempted to substantiate the Gospel criticisms of Pharisees by adducing alleged testimony from the rabbinic writings, not doubting the continuity between Pharisaism and rabbinism. Other Christian writers, however, took a very different line; they set about the rehabilitation of the Pharisees (in contradiction to the Gospel denunciations) in the light of the rabbinic evidence: these writers too did not doubt the continuity between the Pharisees and the rabbis. Prominent among these pro-Pharisee writers were R. Travers Herford, George Foot Moore and James Parkes, whose valuable works remain a monument to Christian ability to appreciate the good qualities of rabbinism and to withstand the slurs cast on Pharisaic Judaism by the Gospels. In more recent times, their work has been continued by E. P. Sanders in his monumental work, *Paul and Palestinian Judaism*.[3]

10

Jesus and the Polemic against the Pharisees

In the Gospels, the Pharisees are not only attacked on personal grounds of hypocrisy, corruption and murderousness, but stigmatized as reactionary and static in their views, refusing to admit the possibility of reform in the Jewish laws. Jesus, on the contrary, is portrayed as the advocate of reform, wishing for example to allow healing on the Sabbath, which the Pharisees are alleged to regard as totally forbidden. An examination of these 'reforms' proposed by Jesus, however, shows a very different situation. The reforms already existed in Pharisaic thinking, and Jesus is advocating measures which had already been enacted in the Pharisaic movement. Jesus is represented as combating Pharisaism by using arguments which were familiar and accepted in the Pharisee movement; instead of being the anti-Pharisee portrayed, he emerges as a typical Pharisee. The whole picture, therefore, is one of anti-Pharisee polemic on the part of the Gospel-writers, seeking to blacken the Pharisees through a conflict with Jesus which never took place. We are left with a problem to solve: what is the motive of this polemic against the Pharisees? Why are the Gospel-writers so anxious to bend the truth that they misrepresent everything that Pharisaism stood for?

The Gospel-writers were working with material which had come originally from the Jerusalem Church, which was not anti-Pharisee; so the polemic against the Pharisees is the result of a process of editing existing material, not the creation of an entirely new narrative. As in the case of all editing, traces of the original text remain, since editing is never a perfectly performed operation.

This process of re-editing is not just a hypothesis; it can be plainly seen within the Gospels by comparing the way in which the

various Gospels treat the same incident. The fact that there are four
Gospels, instead of just one, makes the task of reconstructing the
original story much easier, especially when one bears in mind the
results of modern scholarship, which have shown in what order
the Gospels were written. According to the most firmly based
scholarship, Mark is the earliest Gospel, so we can often be enlight-
ened just by comparing the version of Mark with that of any later
Gospel.

To give just one preliminary example, we find in Mark an
account of a conversation between Jesus and a certain lawyer (a term
used as an alternative to Pharisee both in the Gospels and in later
Christian literature):

> Then one of the lawyers, who had been listening to these discus-
> sions and had noted how well he answered, came forward and
> asked him, 'Which commandment is first of all?' Jesus answered,
> 'The first is, "Hear O Israel: the Lord our God is the only Lord;
> love the Lord your God with all your heart, with all your soul,
> with all your mind, and with all your strength." The second is
> this: "Love your neighbour as yourself." There is no other com-
> mandment greater than these.' The lawyer said to him, 'Well
> said, Master. You are right in saying that God is one and beside
> him there is no other. And to love him with all your heart, all your
> understanding, and all your strength, and to love your neighbour
> as yourself – that is far more than any burnt offerings or
> sacrifices.' When Jesus saw how sensibly he answered, he said to
> him, 'You are not far from the kingdom of God.' (Mark
> 12.28–34, NEB)

The version of this story found in the later Gospel, Matthew, is as
follows:

> Hearing that he had silenced the Sadducees, the Pharisees met
> together; and one of their number tested him with this question:
> 'Master, which is the greatest commandment in the Law?' He
> answered, '"Love the Lord your God with all your heart, with all
> your soul, with all your mind." That is the greatest command-

ment. It comes first. The second is like it: "Love your neighbour as yourself." Everything in the Law and the prophets hangs on these two commandments.' (Matt. 22.34–40, NEB)

In this second version of the story, the friendliness of the exchange has been obliterated. The Pharisee questioner is not motivated by admiration, as in the first version, but merely wishes to 'test' Jesus, that is, try to catch him out. In the first version, the Pharisee questioner is given a lengthy reply to Jesus, praising him and adding a remark of his own about the superiority of love to sacrifices, and to this Jesus replies with courteous respect, saying that his questioner is not far from the kingdom of God. All this is omitted in the second version, which is just one more story about an envious Pharisee being silenced by the superior wisdom of Jesus.

It should be noted, too, that Jesus' singling out of these two verses from the Hebrew Bible (one from Deuteronomy and the other from Leviticus) as the greatest of the commandments was not an original idea of his own, but an established part of Pharisee thinking. The central feature of the liturgy created by the Pharisees (and still used by Jews today) is what is called the Shema, which is the very passage from Deuteronomy cited by Jesus: 'Hear O Israel: the Lord our God is only Lord; love the Lord your God with all your heart, with all your soul, and with all your strength.' This injunction was regarded by the Pharisees as so important that they declared that merely to recite these verses twice a day was sufficient to discharge the basic duty of prayer (*b. Ber.* 13b). Interestingly, too, in view of Jesus' final comment to the 'lawyer', the rabbis regarded these verses as having a strong connection with the 'kingdom of God' (a phrase not coined by Jesus, but part of Pharisaic phraseology). They declared that to recite these verses comprised 'the acceptance of the yoke of the kingdom of God'. It should be noted that in Pharisaic thinking, the kingdom of God had two meanings: it meant the present kingdom or reign of God, or it could mean the future reign of God over the whole world in the Messianic Age. It is possible to discern in Jesus' frequent use of the same expression the same twofold meaning: sometimes he means a future state of affairs which he has come to prophesy (for example, 'Repent, for the

kingdom of God is near', and sometimes he is referring to the present kingship of God, which every mortal is obliged to acknowledge
(for example, 'The kingdom of God is among you'). In the present
passage, it seems to be the second meaning that is paramount. The
other verse quoted by Jesus from Leviticus, 'Love your neighbour
as yourself' ,was also regarded by the Pharisees as of central importance, and was treated by the two greatest figures of Pharisaism,
Hillel[1] and Rabbi Akiba[2], as the great principle of Judaism on which
everything else depended. This did not mean, of course, that the
rest of the Law was to be ignored or swept away, just because this
was the most important principle of it; on the contrary, the Law was
regarded as the working out and practical implementation of the
principle of love of neighbour, giving guidance about how love of
neighbour could be expressed in the complexities of daily life; a
principle without such elaboration would be as much use as the
axioms of Euclid without the propositions. Later Christian writers,
misunderstanding this point, thought that, when Jesus singled out
love of God and love of neighbour, he was thereby dismissing the
rest of the Torah. There is no reason whatever to think that this was
Jesus' meaning, especially as he was in such cordial agreement with
the Pharisee lawyer (at least in the earlier and more authentic
account of Mark).

The apparently disparaging remark of the 'lawyer' about the
sacrifices should also not be misunderstood. He did not mean that
he thought that sacrifices or the Temple worship in general should
be abolished, only that the words of the Hebrew prophets should be
borne in mind, continually warning against regarding the sacrifices
as a magical means of producing atonement, rather than as symbols
of true repentance and reconciliation with God. The most awesome
day of the Jewish year was the Day of Atonement, when sacrifices
were offered in the Temple and the scapegoat was sent into the
wilderness; yet it was Pharisee doctrine that none of these awe-
inspiring ceremonies had any effect unless true repentance had
occurred and restitution had been made for any harm done to one's
fellow man. So the Pharisee was not opposing the offering of
sacrifices (which were prescribed in Holy Writ), but putting them
into their proper place, just as the Pharisees in general supported

the Temple worship and the priesthood in their duties, but strongly opposed any tendency to regard all this as the be-all and end-all of Jewish religion, as the Sadducees tended to do. Here again, there is no reason whatever to suppose that Jesus' attitude towards the Temple worship was any different.

The analysis of this incident about Jesus and the 'lawyer' thus shows two things: that there was no disagreement between Jesus and the Pharisees, and that there is a process of editing going on in the Gospels to make it appear that there was. For the later Gospel version turns an amicable conversation into a hostile confrontation. This does not mean that we may turn to the Gospel of Mark, the earliest Gospel, for an unbiased picture of the Pharisees; on the contrary, the Gospel of Mark is full of bias against the Pharisees, but, as the earliest Gospel, it has not carried through the process of anti-Pharisee re-editing with quite such thoroughness as the succeeding Gospels, so that more of the original story is still apparent.

Here we hit upon an important principle of interpretation of the Gospels: when we come across a passage that goes against the grain of the narrative, we may be confident that this is part of the original, authentic narrative that has survived the operations of the censor (for a fuller explanation of *tendenz* criticism, see Chapter 12, p. 157). Since the general trend is anti-Pharisee, so that the narrative becomes more and more anti-Pharisee as it is successively re-edited, any passages friendly to the Pharisees cannot be late additions to the text (for the motivation of the editor is to cut out such passages, not to add to them); instead they must be survivals that have escaped the eye of the editor. This does not mean that a later Gospel must always, and in relation to every incident, be more thoroughly edited and less authentic than an earlier Gospel, for the various Gospels are not presenting the same material taken from only one source. Each Gospel contains material for which it is not indebted to a previous Gospel and which it is handling as a first-time editor; these different sources of material have been labelled by modern scholars with capital letters such as Q, L and the like. Consequently, when such an independent source is in question, a later Gospel may retain authentic early material not contained in an earlier Gospel. Any scientific study of the Gospels must always bear the above considerations in mind. It follows that, when we speak of a later Gospel taking the bias or tendency further, we mean that this occurs when both Gospels are handling material taken from the same source. This is the case in the example given above, where it is clear that the report of the incident of Jesus and the 'lawyer' occurs first in Mark, and when it later occurs in Matthew, it is an adapted version produced by the author of Matthew on the basis of the report in Mark, which the author of Matthew had before him when he wrote his Gospel.

This is, of course, only a preliminary example. Now follows a more extended argument to show that Jesus was no antagonist of Pharisaism, but was himself a Pharisee.

An important ground of conflict between Jesus and the Pharisees, according to the Gospels, was Jesus' insistence on healing on the Sabbath, which was allegedly against Pharisee law. The Gospels allege that the Pharisees not only criticized Jesus for healing on the Sabbath, but schemed to bring about his death for this reason (Mark 3.6; Matt. 12.14). Jesus is also credited with certain arguments which he put to the Pharisees to defend his practice of Sabbath healing: for example, that since circumcision was permitted on the Sabbath, why should healing be forbidden (John 7.23)? It is an amazing fact that, when we consult the Pharisee law books to find out what the Pharisees actually taught about healing on the Sabbath, we find that they did *not* forbid it, and they even used the very same arguments that Jesus used to show that it was permitted. Moreover, Jesus' celebrated saying, 'The Sabbath was made for man, not man for the Sabbath', which has been hailed so many times as an epoch-making new insight proclaimed by Jesus, is found almost word for word in a rabbinic source (*Mekhilta Shabbeta* 1, on Exod. 31.13), where it is used to support the Pharisee doctrine that the saving of life has precedence over the law of the Sabbath. So it seems that whoever it was that Jesus was arguing against when he defended his Sabbath healing, it cannot have been the Pharisees.

An indication of who these opponents really were can be found in one of the Sabbath stories. Here it is stated that, in anger at Jesus' Sabbath healing, the Pharisees 'began plotting against him with the partisans of Herod to see how they could make away with him'

(Mark 3.6, NEB). The partisans of Herod (that is, Herod Antipas, ruler, by Roman appointment, of Galilee) were the most Hellenized of all the Jews and the most politicized, in the sense that their motivation was not in the least religious, but was actuated only by considerations of power. An alliance between the Pharisees (who were the centre of opposition to the Roman Occupation) and the Herodians is quite impossible. But an alliance between the Herodians and the Sadducees was not only possible but actual. The Sadducees, as explained above, though ostensibly a religious party, were so concerned to preserve the status quo that they had become henchmen of Rome, their leader, the High Priest, being a Roman appointee, entrusted with the task of serving the interests of the Occupation. It seems most probable, then, that, by an editorial intervention, the name 'Pharisees' was substituted here for the original 'Sadducees', and this is probably the case, too, in the other stories in which Jesus is inexplicably arguing a Pharisee viewpoint about the Sabbath *against* the Pharisees. The Sadducees, we know, had a stricter viewpoint about the Sabbath than the Pharisees, and (though this cannot be documented, since no Sadducee documents have survived) it may well be that, unlike the Pharisees, they forbade healing on the Sabbath. This, at any rate, is a hypothesis that makes sense, whereas the stories as they stand, with Pharisees wishing to kill Jesus for preaching Pharisee doctrine, make no sense.

Since Jesus certainly came into conflict with the High Priest of his day, who was a Sadducee, it would be quite natural for stories to be preserved in which Jesus figures as an opponent of Sadducee religious doctrines, even though, as we shall see, the *chief* point of conflict between Jesus and the Sadducees was political rather than religious. In the Pharisee literature many stories are found about Pharisee teachers who engaged in argument with Sadducees. A frequent topic of these debates was the question of the resurrection of the dead, in which the Pharisees believed, and the Sadducees disbelieved. As it happens, such a story has been preserved in the Gospels about Jesus (Mark 12.18–27 and parallels). The answers given to the Sadducees by Jesus are typical of those given by Pharisees in their debates. Even among non-Jews it was too well known that the Pharisees believed in resurrection for these stories to be re-edited as confrontations between Jesus and the Pharisees, so they were left unaltered – interesting evidence of the status of Jesus as a Pharisee, though, of course, the Gospels represent Jesus as arguing, not as a Pharisee, but simply as one whose views happened for once to coincide with those of the Pharisees.

What was the motive for the re-editing of stories about conflict between Jesus and the Sadducees so that he was portrayed as in conflict with the Pharisees instead? The reason is simple. The Pharisees were known to be the chief religious authorities of the Jews, not the Sadducees. In fact, at the time that the Gospels were edited, the Sadducees had lost any small religious importance that they had once had, and the Pharisees were the sole repository of religious authority. As we shall see shortly in more detail, it was of the utmost importance to the Gospel editors to represent Jesus as having been a rebel against Jewish religion, not against the Roman Occupation. The wholesale re-editing of the material in order to give a picture of conflict between Jesus and the Pharisees was thus essential. Also, since it was known that the Sadducees were collaborators with Rome, any substantial picture of opposition by Jesus to the Sadducees, even on purely religious grounds, would have given an impression of Jesus as an opponent of Rome – just the impression that the Gospel editors wished to avoid. That there was in reality no conflict between Jesus and the Pharisees is shown by certain telltale features which have been allowed to remain in the narrative. An important example is: 'At that time a number of Pharisees came to him and said, "You should leave this place and go on your way; Herod is out to kill you"' (Luke 13.31, NEB). This passage has puzzled all the commentators. Why should the Pharisees, who, in previous stories, have been represented as longing for Jesus' death because of his Sabbath healings, come forward to give him a warning intended to save his life? Some pious Christian commentators, anxious to preserve the picture of malevolent Pharisees, have concocted an elaborate scenario in which the Pharisees were playing a double game: knowing that there was more danger for Jesus in Jerusalem than in Galilee, they gave Jesus a spurious warning about Herod in order to induce him to flee to his death in Jerusalem. Apart from the fact that this is mere fantasy, it is hardly likely that, if the

Pharisees had previously shown themselves to be Jesus' deadly enemies, they could expect Jesus to accept a message from them as actuated by the friendliest of motives.

This story indeed is valuable evidence of friendly relations between Jesus and the Pharisees; to give such a warning, the Pharisees must have regarded Jesus as one of their own. The very fact that this story is so inconsistent with the general picture of Jesus' relations with the Pharisees in the Gospels guarantees its historical truth; such a story could not have been added at a late stage in the editing of the material, but must be a survival from an early stage, which by some oversight was not edited out.

An important indication that the stories about Pharisee opposition to Jesus on the question of Sabbath healing are not to be taken at face value is the fact that there is no mention of this charge at Jesus' trial. If Jesus, as the Gospels represent, actually incurred a capital charge in Pharisee eyes because of his Sabbath activities, why was this not brought against him at a time when he was on trial for his life? Why, in fact, is there no mention of *any* charges brought specifically by the Pharisees at Jesus' trial? Jesus' indictment (I do not say 'trial' for there are good reasons, as we shall see, for claiming that he never had a Sanhedrin trial) was not on religious charges at all, but on political charges, though the Gospels, pursuing their general aim of de-politicizing Jesus' aims, try to give the political charges a religious flavour. Yet, if there really was a trial and it was a religious one, who better than the Pharisees, the alleged bitter religious enemies of Jesus, to play the most prominent part in the proceedings? The question really ought to be shifted to the opposite extreme and put in this form: why was it that the Pharisees did not defend Jesus at his trial, in the same way that Gamaliel, the leader of the Pharisees, defended Jesus' disciple Peter when the latter was put on trial before the religious Sanhedrin? (Acts 5). The answer is that the Pharisees were not even present at Jesus' 'trial', which was not before the religious Sanhedrin, but before an interrogation in the house of the High Priest, as representative and henchman of the Romans, as stated quite plainly in the Gospel of John.

If the matter of Sabbath healing cannot be substantiated as a ground of conflict between Jesus and the Pharisees, what about the other features of Jesus' teaching which the Gospels represent as revolutionary and offensive to the Jewish religious authorities of the time?

What about Jesus' claim to be the Messiah? Was not this blasphemous in the eyes of the Pharisees? What about Jesus' threat to destroy the Temple – an allegation brought against him at his 'trial'? What about his aspiration to reform or even abrogate the Law of Moses? The answer is that none of these matters constituted any threat to the religious view of the Pharisees, and on examination we shall find that on all these matters Jesus' view was pure Pharisaism and one that confirms that he was himself a member of the Pharisee movement.

Jesus' claim to be the Messiah was not in any way blasphemous in the eyes of the Pharisees or, indeed, of any other Jews, for the title 'Messiah' carried no connotation of deity or divinity.[3] The word 'Messiah' simply means 'anointed one', and it is a title of kingship; every Jewish king of the Davidic dynasty had this title. To claim to be the Messiah meant simply to claim the throne of Israel, and while this was a reckless and foolhardy thing to do when the Romans had abolished the Jewish monarchy, it did not constitute any offence in Jewish law. On the contrary, the Jews all lived in hope of the coming of the Messiah, who would rescue them from the oppression of foreign occupation and restore to them their national independence. Anyone who claimed to be the promised Messiah (prophesied by the prophets of the Hebrew Bible) who would restore the beloved dynasty of David would be sure of a sympathetic following. Jesus was by no means the only person during this period to make a messianic claim, and not one of these claimants was accused of blasphemy. These messianic claimants were not all of the same type: some were warriors, like Bar Kokhba or Judas of Galilee, while some were non-militarist enthusiasts, like Theudas or 'the Egyptian' (both mentioned in the New Testament as well as in Josephus),[4] who gathered a crowd of believers and waited confidently for a miracle by which the Romans would be overthrown. Jesus was of the latter type, as I have argued in full elsewhere; like 'the Egyptian', he expected the great miracle to take place on the Mount of Olives, as prophesied by Zechariah.[5] Some Messiahs had the limited aim of merely liberating the Jews from Rome, while others, of whom Jesus was one, expected this liberation to be the precursor of an era of peace and liberation for the whole world, when, in the words of the prophets, the swords would be beaten into ploughshares, and the wolf would lie down with the lamb. But none of these aspirations had any tinge of blasphemy; on the contrary, they were an integral part of Judaism, in which the Messianic hope was the logical outcome of belief in the One God, whose reign would one day extend over all humanity.

In later Christianity, however, after the death of Jesus, the Greek translation of the Hebrew word 'Messiah' (that is, 'Christ') had come to mean a deity or divine being. Consequently, Christians reading this meaning back into Jesus' lifetime, found it easy to believe that Jesus' claim to Messiahship would have shocked his fellow Jews and made him subject to a charge of blasphemy. The Gospels, indeed, credit Jesus with a concept of his own Messiahship that was different from that of his fellow Jews; but even if this were the case, since he used the word 'Messiah' about himself, his fellow Jews would have no reason to believe that he meant anything abnormal by it, especially as, according to the Gospels, he was so reticent about the alleged special meaning that he attached to this word that even his own disciples did not understand his meaning. Consequently, no charge of blasphemy could arise from a concept that was never divulged. In historical scholarship, however, the idea of an undivulged messianic concept ('the messianic secret') is merely an attempt by later Christians to attribute to Jesus an idea that in reality did not arise until after his death.

It is interesting, again, that in the Synoptic Gospels it is never the Pharisees who accuse Jesus of blasphemy on messianic grounds, but only the High Priest. This indicates that the charge against Jesus for claiming to be the Messiah was not a religious charge at all, but a political one. It was no infringement of Pharisee law to claim to be the Messiah, but since 'Messiah' means 'king', and since the Romans had abolished the Jewish monarchy, anyone who claimed to be the Messiah was acting subversively towards the Roman Occupation, and, as the Roman-appointed quisling whose task was to guard against anti-Roman activities, the High Priest would be bound to take an interest in any messianic claimants with a view to handing them over to the Romans for punishment. The Gospels, however, in pursuance of their policy of representing Jesus as a rebel against Jewish religion, depict the High Priest as concerned about blasphemy rather than rebellion.

Similarly, the charge against Jesus that he threatened to destroy the Temple and rebuild it was brought against him only at his trial, and the Pharisees are not associated with this charge. This is indeed a political, not a religious charge, for the Temple built by Herod was not expected by the Pharisees to last into the Messianic Age. Jesus very probably did declare his intention of destroying the Temple and rebuilding it, for this is just what anyone seriously claiming to be the Messiah would do. The Pharisees had no superstitious veneration for the Temple, and would not be horrified at the idea that Jesus intended to build a new one, like his ancestor Solomon.

The only people who would be seriously upset by such an intention would be the High Priest and his entourage, who could expect to see themselves swept away by the projected messianic regime. Indeed, at the time of the Jewish War in 66 CE, the first thing that the rebels against Rome did was to dismiss the High Priest and appoint a new one from a family uncontaminated by collaboration with Rome. Yet again, this charge is represented in the Gospels as a religious charge of blasphemy instead of as a political charge of rebellion against the status quo, in which the High Priest and the Temple were instruments of Rome.

As for the alleged reforms of Judaism which Jesus is represented as advocating, none of these, on examination, proves to be in breach of Pharisee ideas. Thus we are told that Jesus opposed the concept of 'an eye for an eye', found in the legal code of the Hebrew Bible, substituting the law of love for the law of revenge. This is a travesty of the situation in Pharisaism. The Pharisees did not regard the expression 'an eye for an eye' as a literal legal prescription. They poured scorn on such an idea as quaint and uncivilized (asking, for example, 'What happens if a one-eyed man knocks out someone's eye?'). They regarded the expression 'an eye for an eye' as meaning that in principle any injury perpetrated against one's fellow man should be compensated for in accordance with the seriousness of the injury. Indeed, the legal code of the Hebrew Bible itself provides for such compensation, when it states that loss of employment and doctor's bills must be paid for by the person responsible for an injury (Exod. 21.19). So clearly the Pharisees were not putting any strained interpretation on the Hebrew Bible when they understood the expression 'an eye for an eye' to refer to monetary compensation rather than savage retribution. As for Jesus' further recommendation that one should not seek compensation if injured, but should offer the other cheek, he certainly did not extend this idea to freedom from any obligation to compensate for injuries that one may have committed. As a counsel of perfection (not as a practical law), the idea of refusing to receive compensation was an option in Pharisaic thought too; but this did not mean that injuries could be committed with impunity without any remedy in law; on the contrary, the very person who was ready to waive his own legal right to compensation would be the first to uphold the right of others, especially if he himself had injured them. This is an area in which confusion of thought is rife, and Jesus is credited with upholding a definition of the 'law of love' which is mere nonsense, and would result in a society in which oppression and violence would reign unchecked. The Pharisees too believed in the 'law of love', as is shown by their doctrine that love of God and love of fellow man are the basic principles of the Torah; but love of one's fellow man is shown more by a determination to secure his rights than by a blanket abolition of all rights. There is no reason to suppose that Jesus held such a foolish doctrine, or that his views were different from those of other Pharisees.

As for Jesus' individual 'reforms' of Jewish laws, these were non-existent. We find in Mark 7.19 an expression which has been translated (NEB) to mean that Jesus 'declared all foods clean', but this translation has been much disputed, and many scholars regard the phrase as an editorial addition anyway. In another passage, we find Jesus explicitly endorsing the Jewish laws of purity, when he tells the leper he has cured, 'Go and show yourself to the priest, and make the offering laid down by Moses for your cleansing' (Mark 1.43, NEB).

True, we find Jesus speaking in the tone of a reformer in the

Sermon on the Mount, when he says, 'You have learned that our forefathers were told . . . But what I tell you is this.' Here he seems to assume a tone of authority and an independence of previous teaching which would justify the description of a 'reformer'. However, since the whole episode of the Sermon on the Mount is Matthew's invention (the sayings being found scattered over various episodes in the other Gospels, except in Luke (6.17), where the sermon is transferred to a plain and the grandiose note of authority is missing), the simplest explanation is that the reformer's tone has been imported into the story by later Christian editors, to whom the idea that Jesus taught with the same kind of authority as other Pharisee teachers was unpalatable.

An interesting episode that seems to support the picture of Jesus as a ruthless reformer of the Torah and as unconcerned with the observance of its laws is the corn-plucking incident, which first occurs in Mark 2:

> One Sabbath he was going through the cornfields; and his disciples, as they went, began to pluck ears of corn. The Pharisees said to him, 'Look, why are they doing what is forbidden on the Sabbath?' He answered, 'Have you never read what David did when he and his men were hungry and had nothing to eat? He went into the House of God, in the time of Abiathar the High Priest, and ate the sacred bread, though no one but a priest is allowed to eat it, and even gave it to his men.'
>
> He also said to them, 'The Sabbath is made for the sake of man and not man for the Sabbath: therefore the Son of Man is sovereign even over the Sabbath.' (Mark 2.23–8, NEB)

This incident cannot be explained as having been originally an altercation with the Sadducees, for the Pharisees did indeed forbid the plucking of corn on the Sabbath, together with all other forms of agricultural labour. So Jesus, by allowing his disciples to pluck ears of corn on the Sabbath, was flouting a clear Pharisee law, or so it appears.

An indication that all is not as it appears, however, is Jesus' saying at the end: 'The Sabbath is made for the sake of man and not man for the Sabbath.' This is a Pharisee maxim, and it gives the key to the whole incident. For the Pharisees used this maxim to show that *in circumstances of danger to human life* the Sabbath laws could be, and had to be, ignored. In the story as it stands, there was no danger to human life to excuse the disciples from ignoring the Sabbath law; but, as we examine the story further, we find more and more indications that the circumstances did indeed involve extreme danger.

Jesus in his explanation to the Pharisees cites, in true Pharisee fashion, an episode from Scripture as the ground of his attitude to the corn-plucking. This is the case of David and his violation of the sanctity of the shewbread; and this case is explained in the Pharisee literature (with good support from the actual text) as having been one of extreme danger to life, since David and his men were dying of starvation in their flight from King Saul. That is why, in Pharisee theory, David and his men were justified in eating the holy shew-bread, though in circumstances where there was no danger to human life this was regarded as a heinous sin. Since the case of David was one of extreme emergency, it would seem to be an absurd instance for Jesus to give unless the circumstances of himself and his disciples were equally desperate at the time of the corn-plucking incident. If, as the narrative seems to indicate, they were engaged merely in a leisurely stroll through the cornfields on the Sabbath, and the disciples idly plucked and munched the corn for want of anything better to do, the David incident would have been quite irrelevant (apart from having nothing to do with the Sabbath). If we restore the element of emergency to the narrative, however, it suddenly makes perfect sense.

Jesus and his followers, in flight from Herod Antipas and the Romans, at the last extremity of exhaustion and hunger arrive at a cornfield. It is the Sabbath day, but Jesus, judging the situation to be, like the case of David, an emergency in which all ritual observances, whether of the Sabbath or the Temple, are abrogated by Pharisee law, allows his disciples to satisfy their hunger by plucking corn. Later, when questioned about the incident by some Pharisee friends, he explains how he came to rule that the Sabbath law should be broken.

This explanation also throws light on another puzzling point. To pluck ears of corn from a field was not only a breach of the Sabbath law, but also a breach of the law against theft. Some scholars have tried to cover this point by referring to the law in Deut. 23.25, AV: 'When thou comest into the standing corn of thy neighbour, then thou mayest pluck the ears with thine hand.' This, however, as the Pharisee literature shows (for example, *m. B. Metzi'a* 7.2) applies only to workmen who are working in a field for the owner; life would soon become impossible for farmers if every casual passer-by were allowed to take his fill of corn. But in cases of danger to life, the laws of theft were regarded as null and void – in fact, Pharisee law regards it as a duty to steal in order to save life. Jesus, therefore, was quite entitled, in Pharisee thinking, to disregard the law of theft as well as the law of the Sabbath in such circumstances.

Why then, was the element of emergency removed from the story as we have it in the Gospels, thus reducing the whole episode to nonsense? The answer is: for the same reason that the element of emergency has been removed from the whole of the Gospels, which portray Judaea and Galilee as peaceful areas under benign Roman rule, instead of what they were in historical reality at this time, areas of bitter unrest and constant rebellion against the savage oppression of the Romans and the depredations of the tax-farmers (or publicans). If the sense of emergency had been retained in the story, not only would it have to be revealed that Jesus was not flouting Pharisee law but also that he was a hunted man, wanted by Herod and the Romans, and in rebellion against them.

Thus the corn-plucking incident, so far from telling against the view that Jesus was a Pharisee, cannot be understood except on the hypothesis that Jesus was one. His use of biblical precedent and of a Pharisee maxim in order to establish that exceptional circumstances warranted a breach of the law are entirely in accordance with Pharisee practice and principles, and do not justify an interpretation in terms of rebellion against the law. Jesus' final remark, 'therefore the Son of Man is sovereign even over the Sabbath', is generally held to mean that Jesus was declaring his lofty independence from Jewish law and his right to abrogate its provisions at will. This, however, is not necessarily the meaning of the sentence. The expression 'son of man' in Aramaic simply means 'man' or 'human being'. The meaning could therefore be, 'Human beings are more important than the Sabbath', a sentiment with which all Pharisees would agree. Many of the puzzling 'Son of Man' sayings in the New Testament can be explained on similar lines, though a residue remains in which Jesus uses the expression 'Son of Man' as a title expressive of his own role. As a title, it by no means implies divine status, but rather prophetic status; it is used throughout the book of Ezekiel in this sense.

The alleged conflict between Jesus and the Pharisees on the question of his association with 'publicans and sinners' has been dealt with earlier (see pp. 44–6) where it is shown that this matter had nothing to do with 'ritual purity'. Jesus' attempt to reclaim 'the sinners of the house of Israel' was quite in accordance with the behaviour expected of a would-be Messiah.

It should be remembered that Jesus would have been a most unusual Pharisee if he had never disagreed with other Pharisees. Amicable disagreement was an essential ingredient in Pharisaism, and the Pharisee literature is full of disagreements between the various sages of the movement. In some cases, the New Testament has created conflict between Jesus and the Pharisees, not by altering 'Sadducees' to 'Pharisees' or by removing some essential element from the story, but simply by turning what was originally a friendly argument into a hostile confrontation.

The existence of conflicts of various kinds within the Jewish community has been used by some scholars to explain the vilification of the Pharisees found in the Gospels. Thus, there was undoubtedly a strong conflict between the Pharisees and the Sadducees, and the Dead Sea Scrolls sect was at odds with all other Jewish movements. Thus it seems plausible to attribute the Gospels attacks on the Pharisees to 'intra-Jewish conflict', a well-attested phenomenon. This explanation, however, is hopelessly inadequate. The venom of the anti-Pharisee polemic in the Gospels goes far beyond any example of 'intra-Jewish conflict', which could be bitter at times, but never reaches anything like the tone found, say, in Matt. 23, where the Pharisees are characterized as the greatest villains in all history. Moreover, in the Gospels there is another ingredient that raises the indictment to a height never approached in other conflicts: the accusation of Christ-murder, a charge of mythical stature that leads inevitably in later years to the demonization of the Jews, with the Pharisees as their most hated representatives.

Thus in various ways, Jesus has been isolated in the Gospels from the movement to which he belonged, the Pharisees. Yet, despite every effort to turn him into an isolated figure, his identity as a Pharisee remains indelibly stamped on him by his style of preaching. His use of parables (often thought by people unfamiliar with Pharisee literature to be a mark of his uniqueness) was typical of Pharisee preaching; and even his quaint expressions such as 'a camel going through the eye of a needle', or 'take the beam out of your own eye' are Pharisee locutions found in the Talmud. This is true, of course, only of the Jesus found in the Synoptic Gospels (Mark, Matthew and Luke). In the Fourth Gospel, that of John, Jesus has become unrecognizable. He uses no parables, nor any idiosyncratic rabbinical expressions; instead he spouts grandiose Hellenistic mysticism and proclaims himself a divine personage. Here the authentic Jesus has been lost in the post-Jesus myth. It is not here that we find the genuine Jesus, rooted in the Jewish religion of his time, and pursuing aims that were intelligible to his fellow Jews.

We may ask finally, 'Why are the Pharisees given such a hostile portrayal in the Gospels?' This is a different question from 'Why are the Pharisees portrayed as so hostile to Jesus?', a question that can be answered by the simple explanation that they were not, since Jesus' alleged deviations from Pharisee doctrine are spurious. What needs explanation is why the Gospels are at pains to blacken the Pharisees as deceitful, hypocritical, corrupt and even murderous, and also as stick-in-the-mud reactionaries – a picture that is so distant from the facts that this ranks among one of the most unscrupulous hate-campaigns in history, one which has made a sad contribution to later Christian antisemitism. The answer, as adumbrated above, is basically political. The Gospels were written at a time when the Jews were in very bad odour with the Roman authorities, having engaged in a desperate attempt to achieve their freedom from Roman rule in the Jewish War of 66–70 CE. All the

Gospels were written in the period immediately succeeding the Jewish War. The Gentile Christian Church was much concerned to deny any connection with the rebellious Jews; yet they had a difficult task, for their object of worship, Jesus, was a Jew and had died on a Roman cross and therefore was under the presumption of having participated in rebellion against Rome (since crucifixion was the regular punishment for rebels). The strategy adopted by the Gentile Christians (but not by the Jewish Christians, who continued to be Jewish patriots) was to aver that Jesus had never rebelled against Roman authority, being an other-worldly pacifist. Why then had he died on a Roman cross? Not for rebelling against Rome, but for rebelling against Judaism. The Jews, it was alleged, wanted him dead because of this rebellion, and so misrepresented him to the Roman authorities as a rebel against Rome. Though Pilate, the Roman governor, had had strong doubts about this, he had succumbed to Jewish pressure and executed Jesus as one who had unlawfully claimed to be King of the Jews, an illegal and rebellious claim in Roman eyes.

It was therefore of the utmost importance to the Gentile Christian Church (for whom the Gospels were written) to substantiate the claim that Jesus was a rebel against the Jewish religion, not against Rome. The chief representatives of the Jewish religion were the Pharisees, and this political aim is the underlying ground for the campaign of denigration undertaken against the Pharisees. It could not be hidden that the religious figure who actually handed Jesus over to the Romans was not the Pharisee leader, Gamaliel, but the High Priest (who was a Sadducee, an anti-Pharisee and a pro-Roman quisling), but the religious differences between the High Priest and the Pharisees were sedulously covered up in the Gospels, and the High Priest was ridiculously portrayed as chief representative of Jewish religion, even though, in historical fact, he was regarded by the majority of the Jews, who were followers of the Pharisees, as a heretical Sadducee and as a person who could in no way stand as representative of Judaism.

Another way in which the Gospels attempt to rebut the charge that Jesus was anti-Roman is to adopt a strongly pro-Roman stance. The Gospels are pro-Roman and anti-Jewish (especially anti-

Pharisee) documents, which whitewash the Romans in every possible way. Pilate, the Roman governor who gave the order for Jesus'
death, is known from other sources to have been a bloodthirsty and
corrupt administrator; but the Gospels give him such a favourable
portrayal that he appears at the worst as weak, and at the best as
positively righteous (in the Ethiopian Church he was later made
into a saint, while before the commentary of Origen he was not even
regarded as weak). Not one word in the Gospels hints that the
Roman Occupation of Judaea was cruel and oppressive. Even the
centurion who presided over Jesus' crucifixion is given a favourable
portrayal, as the person who first recognizes Jesus' divinity.

The Gospels are thus not to be trusted in their portrayal of the
relations between Jesus and the Pharisee movement. They are
engaged in a politically-motivated polemic, of which the Pharisees
are the chief victims.

Jesus in the Talmud

The question has often been raised in recent years whether rabbinic Judaism of the kind familiar to us from the rabbinic writings from the Mishnah onwards existed at all in the Second Temple period (see Chapter 9). The alternative is that the Pharisees, whom the rabbis claimed as their predecessors, actually had a type of Judaism that was very different from rabbinic Judaism. The fact that no document similar to the Mishnah was discovered from the Second Temple period seemed to confirm this; and the writings of the authors who claimed to have been Pharisees, at least at one time, Paul and Josephus, showed little similarity to rabbinic writings. The library of the Dead Sea Scrolls sect contained, it was thought, nothing confirming the existence of a movement similar to that of the post-Destruction rabbis.

The authorized publication of the MMT document in 1995 has somewhat tempered this view, however.[1] Here is a document which, while not itself rabbinic, seems to be combating views that are known to have been held by the post-Destruction rabbis; they therefore constitute evidence that these views were not a creation of the post-Destruction period. The MMT document is in fact a powerful argument for continuity between the Pharisees and the rabbis, though its scope is limited. Some scholars have held that the Dead Sea Scrolls are not the production of a single sect, the Essenes, but actually constitute a library, brought to the caves from Jerusalem, of the whole pre-Destruction period. These scholars (Norman Golb for instance) are faced with the problem that this library contains no Pharisee documents. Thus either there were no Pharisee documents at the time, or the library (if that is what it is) is less comprehensive than Golb thinks. As for the MMT document,

Golb is reduced to denying that it is directed against the Pharisees, and argues, very unconvincingly, that on the contrary it is itself a proto-Pharisee document, showing how different Pharisaism was from the later rabbinism.

My own view is that the Dead Sea Scrolls are indeed a Jerusalem library, not a production of a single sect, whether Essene or otherwise. However, the reason why it contains no Pharisee documents (if such documents existed) is that it is the library of the High Priest who was a Sadducee and would have regarded Pharisee documents as heretical (this is a view that was put forward by K. H. Rengstorf in 1960[2] and is due for revival). Where then should we look for evidence of the existence of rabbinic/Pharisee doctrines in the pre-Destruction period?

The natural place to look, one might think, is in the writings of Paul. Here are the writings of a person who proclaimed his Pharisee affiliation and even claimed to have held, at one time, a prominent position in the Pharisee movement. Some modern scholars, indeed, have professed to find strong affinities between Paul's writings and those of the rabbis, the most sustained effort in this direction being W. D. Davies' book *Paul and Rabbinic Judaism*.[3] This kind of effort, however, has now been given up, since it is generally agreed that there is very little in common between Paul's views and modes of expression and those of rabbinism. If we have to look to Paul for the character of Pharisaism, then it was indeed a movement that had little in common with rabbinism, and the rabbis' claim to continuity with the Pharisees is a sham.

There is indeed very little written evidence of the activity of the Pharisees. One written work, *Megillat Ta'anit*, appears to derive from them, but it is very short and consists of a mere list of days on which fasting was prohibited because some happy event had occurred (this gives the work some historical value). Apart from this, there is evidence that certain elements in the Targums (Aramaic translations of the Hebrew Bible) derive from the Pharisees, since they contain laws that differ slightly from later rabbinic laws and thus show signs of earlier legal development, though in the same general style (development was always a characteristic of rabbinic law). But in general, as explained earlier, the

Pharisees did not build up a literature, but confined their thoughts to perishable notes; for they were concerned not to add to the canon of Scripture, and this is perhaps the chief explanation for the lack of a Pharisee body of literature.

Yet, as argued in Chapter 9, there is one source from which we can derive much information about the Pharisee movement, including confirmation of its continuity with the later rabbinic movement – and that is the New Testament, and especially the sayings of Jesus. It is an extraordinary fact that while Jesus is portrayed in the Gospels as a strong opponent of the Pharisees, he himself is the most recognizable Pharisee in the whole of first-century Jewish literature. As we have seen, his style of preaching (with parables) and even his modes of expression are so consonant with the style of the rabbinic literature that they alone constitute evidence that rabbinic modes of thought did not begin in the second century (as many would like to think) but already existed in the first century, and that therefore the constant claim of the rabbis that their spiritual roots lay with the Pharisees of the first century has much to recommend it. However, there is also much more evidence than this.

Let us now take one piece of halakhic evidence which shows Jesus wielding the Jewish rabbinic law in true rabbinic style. When arguing that healing on the Sabbath was permitted, Jesus uses the following argument: 'If circumcisions are permitted on the Sabbath, an operation that affects only one part of the body, surely healing the whole body should be permitted!' This is an argument that appears in identical form in the rabbinic literature, and this proves a number of things. First, it proves that, contrary to whole passages of the Gospels, the rabbis did not forbid healing on the Sabbath; for if the argument about circumcision was already known to Jesus, it must be reckoned a first-century argument, not a second-century argument, which it would otherwise undoubtedly be called. Secondly, the whole method of argument is typically rabbinic. Where, except in the rabbinic literature, is the halakhic question mooted: what should happen if a circumcision is due to take place on the Sabbath?

Here is a question about conflict of duties that is typical of rabbinic Judaism. On the one hand, making incisions (if not for medical purposes) is forbidden on the Sabbath as a form of 'work'. On the other hand, the Torah states explicitly that circumcision should take place on the eighth day. Which of these two duties should have priority? The rabbinic decision, as recorded in the Mishnah, is that circumcision should have priority – not an obvious decision, since one might have thought that circumcision could be postponed to the ninth day in deference to the sanctity of the Sabbath (as it happens, the rabbis were not averse to postponing circumcisions for other causes, namely medical causes, if the child were suffering from jaundice for example).

But the important point is that Jesus takes it for granted that everyone knows that the halakhah in this case sanctions the breaking of the Sabbath in favour of circumcision. He clearly lived in a milieu where this fact was widely known or even taken for granted (John 7.22, NEB: '... you circumcise on the Sabbath'). In other words he lived in a rabbinic milieu, which in the first century has to be described as a Pharisaic milieu. We have here clear evidence of rabbinic practice in the first century, not instituted by Jesus, but assumed by him. The continuity between the Pharisees and the rabbis, so often denied, is proved by no less a person than Jesus.

There is further evidence of rabbinic thinking in Jesus' very mode of arguing which is by a fortiori argument, known in rabbinic sources as the *qal va-homer* argument, the chief weapon of rabbinic logic. If something is true in a weaker case, *surely* it is true in a stronger case. Here, Jesus argues, 'Breaking the Sabbath is permitted where only one part of the body is concerned' (the weaker case), then *surely* it is permitted where the whole body is concerned (the stronger case). There could not be a more characteristically rabbinic style of argument. In fact, it has been claimed that the rabbis were unique in using the a fortiori argument not as a mere device of rhetoric (as in Greek literature) but as a form of strict logic, the rules of which they worked out in an exact form.

But did not Jesus declare that the Law was at an end? Why then is he here arguing like a typical rabbi? It will be necessary to quote some familiar passages which show Jesus asserting very emphatically that the Law was not at an end, and that its Pharisaic interpretation ought to be regarded as authoritative. We will also consider some of the arguments which have been used to discount these very outright and specific passages. I postpone full discussion of these passages, however, to the next chapter.

Meanwhile, it may be asked, 'If Jesus was indeed a Pharisee teacher, one of the sages (as they were called) and if there is continuity between the Pharisee sages and the post-Destruction rabbis, why is it that none of Jesus' sayings appear in the writings of the second-century rabbis?' After all, many Pharisee sages (for example, Hillel and Gamaliel) are mentioned by name in the Mishnah and Talmud, and their sayings are copiously recorded as treasures of the rabbinic movement itself. It is no answer to say that Jesus was primarily a messianic claimant rather than a teacher, for it is clear from the Gospels that he was indeed a teacher as well as a messianic claimant. Here he differed from other messianic claimants, such as Bar Kokhba, who never claimed to be teachers, and whose sayings therefore quite understandably do not appear in the literature.

The main answer, of course, is that since Jesus (quite beyond his own intention) gave rise to a new religion which abrogated the Torah and produced anti-Pharisee writings, the name 'Jesus' undeservedly fell into bad repute among the members of the rabbinic movement, and any sayings of his that had survived were erased from the tradition.

However, this is not the whole story. One of Jesus' rabbinic dicta does indeed appear in the rabbinic literature, a curious relic of what was once probably a considerable body of dicta. For when, at the beginning of the second century, the Jesus movement of the Jerusalem Church was declared by the rabbis to be heretical (having been earlier accepted as an acceptable form of Judaism, unlike the Pauline Gentile Church which had always been regarded as outside Judaism altogether, and therefore as not even heretical), Jesus himself lost his status as a rabbi of authority and his sayings were almost all suppressed. A similar case was Elisha ben Avuyah, who was regarded at one time as a highly-respected rabbi, but turned to heresy and was excommunicated in his lifetime: his sayings were, on the whole, suppressed, though some of them were preserved in the rabbinic writings. In Jesus' case, where he became regarded some time after his death as the founder of a whole heretical movement, the suppression was more thorough, which makes it all the more interesting that one saying of his, in his capacity of Pharisee rabbi, was preserved, though the content of the saying is not very remarkable in itself, and may have been imperfectly preserved.

This rare saying is found in the Babylonian Talmud, and also in some other rabbinic sources. It is related that Rabbi Eliezer ben Hyrcanus, one of the most eminent of the rabbis, was arrested by the Roman authorities on suspicion of being a Christian (this was at a time of Roman persecution of the Christians, probably during the reign of Trajan). Eliezer, however, was found innocent and released, but was very upset at having undergone this unpleasant experience, thinking that this must be because of some sin he had committed of which this was a punishment. His pupil, Rabbi Akiva, attempting to put his mind at rest by locating the cause of his teacher's tribulation, said to him, 'Perhaps someone once quoted a saying of some heretic to you, and you received it with pleasure instead of repudiating it?' To this Eliezer replied that indeed something of the sort had happened. He had once met a disciple of Jesus called Jacob of Kefar Sakhnaya in a street in Sepphoris. They had a conversation, in the course of which, Jacob reported a saying of Jesus which was a halakhic interpretation of a verse in Micah: 'For she gathered it of the hire of an harlot, and they shall return to the hire of an harlot' (Mic. 1.7, AV). Jesus interpreted this to mean that since the money originated in a place of filth, it could be applied without conscientious scruple to a place of filth. Therefore, if the hire of a harlot were consecrated to the Temple, it should not be entirely rejected as unworthy, but should be used for the purpose of building a privy for the High Priest. Rabbi Eliezer reported that he found this interpretation pleasing; but afterwards, when he underwent certain sufferings, he blamed himself for having given the teaching of a heretic such a good reception and thought his suffering was a punishment for this (*b. Avod. Zar.* 16b).

This incident reflects a period when the Jesus movement had become heretical in the eyes of rabbinic Jews, but the rabbinic character of Jesus himself had not yet been totally forgotten. The incident is thus historically very significant. At first, the Jesus movement was regarded without animosity as a harmless variety of Judaism: this phase is seen in the New Testament itself in the re-action of the Pharisee leader Gamaliel to Peter and his companions (Acts 5). At this time, the insistence of the Jesus movement that Jesus was still alive and would shortly be returning to resume his career as king-messiah was not regarded as contradicting any prin-ciple of Judaism: Gamaliel's reaction was simply, 'Let's wait and see. Perhaps they are right.' As time went on, however, and Jesus did not return, the persistence of the Jesus movement began to arouse opposition. Moreover, the growth of a Gentile movement dedicated to Jesus as a deified figure (under the influence of Paul) perhaps tended to turn Jewish opinion even against the Jewish Christians who still regarded Jesus as a human king: a movement that could have such deplorable consequences (including the publi-cation of anti-Jewish literature in the shape of the Gospels) could hardly be regarded with favour. Yet the Jewish Christians were still not banished altogether from the Jewish fold. They were re-garded not as idolaters (like the Pauline Christians) but as heretical Jews.

Furthering this development was the continuing reverence of the Jewish Christians for Jesus as their teacher. His sayings circulated among them as superior to the pronouncements of the rabbinic sages. In fact, the Jewish Christians cut themselves off from the rabbinic developments in Judaism which took place after the destruction of the Temple. It was essential to rabbinic orthodoxy to accept the authority of rabbinic decisions, even though these were often arrived at by majority vote and were not regarded as infallible. To stand outside this process of law-making was to be like citizens of a democratic state who declared themselves unbound by the decisions of Parliament.

It seems also that though Jesus was not worshipped by the Jewish Christians as God (in the Pauline style), he was given a magical status that offended against rabbinic thinking. It seems from certain rabbinic passages that amulets circulated among the Jewish Christ-ians inscribed with the name of Jesus, and these amulets were held to be efficacious as remedies for illness. This smacked of sorcery, and gave further offence.

Consequently, Jesus himself began to be held responsible for these aberrations, and instead of being regarded as merely another failed messiah, who could be honoured as a martyr in the cause of Judaism, he began to be regarded as a heresiarch. It was not until much later, however, that he began to be regarded as an idolater; the passages in the Talmud that portray him as having abandoned Judaism for idolatry and as having been condemned to death by the Sanhedrin belong to a much later period (about 200 CE) when the historical Jesus had faded entirely from the Jewish memory, and Talmudic comments at this time were merely responses to intensive Christian missionary activity. At an even later period, a whole mythology of an idolatrous Jesus was worked up into the anti-Christian propaganda known as *Toledot Yeshu*.

It was not until the Middle Ages that Jewish scholars began to recover something of the historical Jesus by study of the Christian Gospels, which revealed to them, in the Synoptic Gospels, the outlines of the historical Jesus as a rabbinic/Pharisaic figure (these Jewish medieval students of the New Testament, especially Profiat Duran, were the real founders of the scientific study of the New Testament). These studies led to a picture of Jesus as a truly Jewish figure who had been misrepresented in many parts of the Gospels as hostile to Pharisaic Judaism. Thus arose what has been called 'the Jewish view of Jesus', which has given rise to many books by Jewish authors, the present book being only the latest of them.

The story before us about Rabbi Eliezer gives us a rare, perhaps unique, glimpse of a period when Jesus had not yet lost his rabbinic character in the eyes of members of the rabbinic movement. At this time (about 100 CE), Jesus was thought of as a rabbi who had gone to the bad, like Elisha ben Avuya – someone whose ideas had once been sound, and whose sayings, dating from his early period might be quotable and even admirable.

It is significant that the conversation between Rabbi Eliezer and Jacob of Kefar Sakhnayim took place at all. Jacob was well known to be a disciple of Jesus of Nazareth, yet Rabbi Eliezer did not scruple to stop in the street to have a conversation with him. He certainly regretted this afterwards, but the very fact that the conversation occurred shows that the status of the Jesus movement was still somewhat equivocal in the eyes of rabbinic Jews and had not yet been totally outlawed. It is probable that it was only at some time after this conversation that further stages of rejection of the Jesus movement took place, so that Rabbi Eliezer, casting back in his mind for some sin he may have committed that would account for his present misfortune, now retrospectively regarded his affability to Jacob as culpable.

Let us examine a little further the halakhic insight here attributed to Jesus. The Torah states, 'You shall not allow a common prostitute's fee, or the pay of a male prostitute [or the price of a dog: AV] to be brought into the house of the Lord your God in fulfilment of any vow, for both of them are abominable to the Lord your God' (Deut. 23.18, NEB). In Jesus' day, the second clause would be regarded as meaning 'the price of a dog', since the Hebrew word concerned does mean literally 'dog', and it is only a theory of modern scholarship (probably correct) that understands the word to be meant metaphorically to signify a male prostitute. In any case, Jesus' comment is applied to the first phrase 'the hire of a common prostitute'.

The Talmud understands this to mean that if a person gave a prostitute a sheep in payment for her services, it was forbidden for her or anyone else to bring that sheep to the Temple as a sacrifice. Jesus, however, seems to be interpreting the phrase to refer to money earned by a prostitute, and he is using another biblical text to suggest that, while such money must not be used to pay for the offering of a sacrifice, it might be used to pay for a base but useful service to the Temple. The verse that he uses to prove this is from the prophetic book of Micah. The verse is part of a prophecy of the destruction of Samaria for its sins of idolatry: 'And all the graven images thereof shall be beaten to pieces, and all the hires thereof shall be burnt with the fire, and all the idols thereof will I lay desolate: for she gathered it of the hire of an harlot, and they shall return to the hire of an harlot' (Mic. 1.7, AV). It is hard to see how this verse can serve to produce the halakhic conclusion which Jesus draws from it; yet there must be some rationale in his argument or Rabbi Eliezer would not have been so pleased with his reasoning.

The reasoning is perhaps based, in the first instance, on a similarity of phraseology. The expression used for 'hire of an harlot' (*etnan ṣonah*) is identical in Deuteronomy and Micah, and this seems to invite the inference that some cross-reference is intended (this is the rabbinic hermeneutical principle of *gezerah shavah*). By using the same distinctive phrase as Deuteronomy (found rarely in Scripture), what is the verse in Micah trying to tell us about the verse in Deuteronomy? This use of the *gezerah shavah* hermeneutic principle is itself a characteristically rabbinic feature of Jesus' insight.

Jesus is saying that the movement of the verse suggests that something base may have its own natural cycle. Similar is the verse, 'For dust thou art, and unto dust shalt thou return' (Gen. 3.19, AV). When a human being returns to the earth as dust, he is not entirely useless; he may serve to fertilize the ground. Similarly, suggests Jesus, the 'hire of an harlot', though despised and banned from all honourable purposes in the Temple, such as providing sacrifices or holy vessels, could serve some lowly purpose; and he suggests that this might be the provision of a privy for the High Priest. The graven images which were gathered of the hire of a harlot may still 'return' in some way that is as low in the scale of things as 'the hire of an harlot' itself, but serves a useful purpose. Jesus is looking for some meaning that he can attach to the positive word 'return', used by Micah, which might otherwise seem inappropriate.

It has been suggested that Jesus' contribution here may reflect his kindly attitude towards prostitutes as shown in certain passages of the New Testament. He regarded them as capable of repentance and retrieval; but here he goes even further and suggests that even their earnings as prostitutes are capable of a kind of reclamation from utter ignominy.

The important point, however, from the standpoint of the present study, is that Jesus appears here for a brief moment as a fully-fledged member of the rabbinic movement known in his day as the Pharisees. He puts forward a thought that might well have formed part of a discussion in a rabbinic academy. Even though this fleeting memory is already tinged with hostility because of the conflict that developed between the Jesus movement and the rabbinic movement, it retains something of the flavour of a period when no such hostility existed, and the Jesus movement was an active participant in rabbinic intellectual, legal and moral activity.

It may be objected, however, 'How do we know that we can attach any historical authenticity to the story of the conversation in the street between Rabbi Eliezer and Jacob of Kefar Sakhnayin, the disciple of Jesus?' This story appears in the Talmud in a text which was redacted at about 500 CE, that is, about 400 years after the event it purports to describe.

I would suggest that the story is, in its kernel, very historically reliable. Much of the Talmud consists of traditions, handed down by word of mouth until finally put into writing, and recent research has confirmed the extraordinary durability and reliability of many such oral traditions. This particular tradition however is especially reliable because it goes so much against the grain. It depicts a Jesus totally at variance with the Jesus portrayed elsewhere in the Talmud as a non-rabbinic sorcerer and idolater. On the well-known principle of literary research, *lectio difficilis melior*, 'the more difficult reading is better', we have to regard this story as a survival from a time when the outlines of the true, historical Jesus were still, to a considerable extent, remembered. No one could have invented this story at a later period, when the prevailing picture of Jesus was so different, because of Christian missionary activity, which told the Jews that Jesus had been an opponent of the Jewish Law, the Torah, and a self-idolater, who put himself forward as a deity through whom alone mankind could be saved. Jews at this later period took Christian missionaries at their word, and concluded that Jesus, being guilty of idolatry, had been rightly condemned to death by the highest Jewish tribunal, the Sanhedrin. The Jews even came to believe that the Sanhedrin carried out Jesus' execution themselves, even though the Christian Scriptures themselves did not claim this, retaining the historical truth that Jesus was executed by the Roman authorities as a threat to Roman power.

This is not to say, however, that the actual details of the story are not subject to challenge. First, is it credible that Rabbi Eliezer, a prominent rabbi, should have been arrested on suspicion of being a Christian? He seems the last person on earth to have to face such a charge (some Christian scholars have seized on the story with delight to show that Christianity could indeed be attractive to even such an entrenched rabbi as Eliezer, and have been inclined to think that the charge may have had some substance in it). Secondly, as a rabbi, Eliezer had the reputation of being of a very conservative cast of mind, and most disinclined to accept new theories or new inter- pretation of biblical laws, yet here we find him listening without impatience to an entirely new interpretation of a biblical law. Thirdly, the type of argument attributed to Jesus is not very typical, for it uses a verse in the book of Micah, very loosely interpreted, to reach a halakhic modification of a law of the Torah. Such modifi- cations (which were indeed quite commonly made by the more innovative rabbis) were usually made on the basis of a new interpre- tation of some verse in the Torah (Pentateuch), not on the basis of a book like Micah, which belonged to the section of Scripture known as 'the Prophets' which were regarded as of lesser inspiration than the Torah.

So the details of the story require further examination. As for the arrest of Eliezer as a Christian, it has been plausibly suggested by Travers Herford that this occurred during a persecution of Christians that took place during the reign of Emperor Trajan in 109 CE (see Eusebius, quoting Hegesippus, *Ecclesiastical History* 3.32). This persecution seems to have been political, rather than religious (since during it Simeon, the Christian leader was crucified as a descendant of David, and therefore a claimant to the Jewish throne). Eliezer may have been suspected of subversive political leanings, rather than of sympathy with Christianity as a religion; after all, since Jesus himself was executed for political reasons (even according to the Gospels, which, however, represent this as a false charge), it is not surprising that his successor in the Jerusalem Church (a relative of Jesus, as were all the leaders of the monarchi- cal 'Jerusalem Church') was similarly regarded as a subversive. Eliezer, as a survivor of the period of the Jewish War against Rome, might well have been on a Roman list of possible rebels and thus came to be mistakenly identified as a member of the Jesus movement.

As for the halakhic argument attributed to Jesus, there exists a more credible version of it in another source. Here Jesus' conversation with Eliezer is reported as follows:

> He [Jacob] said, 'It is written in your Torah, "Thou shalt not bring, etc." What of these?' I [Eliezer] said to him, 'They are forbidden.' He said to me, 'They are forbidden as an offering: it is permitted to destroy them.' I said to him, 'In that case, what should one do with them?' He said to me, 'He shall make with them bathhouses and latrines.' I said to him, 'Thou has well said.' And the halakhah was concealed from me for the moment. When he saw that I agreed with his words, he said to me, 'Thus has Jesus taught me, They come from filth and they go to filth, as it is said [Mic. 1.7] "For the hire of a harlot, etc." They shall make seats for the public. And it pleased me.' (Midrash, *Qohelet Rab.*, on 1.8)

This version of Jesus' teaching is much more credible and also much more in true rabbinic style. Jesus here is not deriving his halakhic teaching directly from a verse in Micah, but from close examination of the Torah text itself (using the Micah text just as corroboration), which forbids the use of the 'hire of a harlot', but confines this prohibition to its use as an 'offering' in the Temple. Jesus thus argues that this does not forbid all use, but rather suggests that some permissible use is being hinted at. This, he suggests, is some base but useful use. Note that in this version, he does not suggest use of the despised funds for the construction of a privy in the Temple, but of a privy for public use. This again is more plausible, since even the construction of a privy in the Temple might be regarded as some kind of 'offering'.

To the objection that Rabbi Eliezer was a very conservative kind of rabbi, who would not be likely to listen patiently to any kind of halakhic innovation, even if not proffered in the name of Jesus, it may be replied that Rabbi Eliezer was not quite so conservative as the Talmud (and Rabbi Eliezer himself) represents, and examples can be given of his accepting innovations if based on sound argument. He himself, however, tries to apologize for this aspect, when he says, in the above-quoted version, 'The halakhah was concealed from me for a moment.' He is suggesting that he was misled by an aberration of mind for which he was not wholly responsible.

However, whatever the individual details of the story may be, the salient point remains that Jesus is still remembered here as a halakhah-minded rabbi – a picture of Jesus quite alien to his portrayal in later sources which portray him as a sorcerer and idolater.[4] The essential fact is that at some period it was possible to tell such a story about Jesus, and this must have been a period before he was relegated to the status of an idolater, and was still remembered as a Pharisee, even though a Pharisee of bad repute.

12

Jesus' Support for Pharisaism

Not only do Jesus' preaching and teaching show strong Pharisaic traits, but he is actually on record as giving explicit support to the Pharisee movement. The fact that the following remarks have been preserved is remarkable in view of the determined efforts of the Gospel writers to portray Jesus as implacably anti-Pharisee:

> For verily I say unto you, Till heaven and earth pass, one jot or one tittle shall in no wise pass from the law, till all be fulfilled. Whosoever therefore shall break one of these least commandments, and shall teach men so, he shall be called the least in the kingdom of heaven: but whosoever shall do and teach them, the same shall be called great in the kingdom of heaven. For I say unto you, That except your righteousness shall exceed the righteousness of the scribes and Pharisees, you shall in no case enter into the kingdom of heaven (Matt. 5.18–20, AV).

We see hear that the Pharisees are being held up as providing the standard of righteousness which Jesus' followers are to attempt to emulate, and if possible even surpass. Some commentators have attempted to reduce the startling degree to which this passage shows Jesus' respect for the Pharisees by interpreting it to mean, 'The Pharisees have a pretty low standard, so you must do better than that'; this is the effect of the NEB translation: 'Unless you show yourselves far better men than the Pharisees . . .'. The Greek, however, (*pleion*) does not sustain the translation 'far more', but simply means 'more', so this is a prime example of mistranslation in the interests of making Jesus as scornful of the Pharisees as usual. In any case, even if we adopt this wrong translation, the result is hardly cogent, if the Pharisees are taken to be unrighteous: it would be like saying, 'Unless you show yourselves far more righteous than Al Capone, you will not enter the kingdom of heaven' – a statement that would leave plenty of room for wrongdoing. As it stands, in its correct translation, the statement is a definite tribute to the Pharisees as providing the criterion of righteousness.

And what about the verses that lead up to the tribute to the Pharisees? These verses show Jesus as the very opposite of the rebel against Judaism that he is so often represented to be. He says that not one iota of the Law will ever pass away; and he winds up by endorsing the Pharisees as the people who are best qualified to interpret the meaning of the Law.

These verses have always been a stumbling-block to the traditional picture of Jesus as abolishing the Law. Interpreters have fastened on the words, 'till all be fulfilled' as providing the escape route. Jesus is saying that the Law remains in force until the Eschaton, when it will cease to have force, since all things will then have been fulfilled; or, as many Christian interpreters prefer, until the advent of the Christian Church, which will take over the function hitherto discharged by the administrators of the Jewish Law. But this is a very doubtful interpretation. The phrase seems rather to echo the earlier phrase 'till heaven and earth pass' – in other words, the Torah will last until the end of the universe, when, according to the prophet Isaiah, God will reign alone.

In another passage in Matthew, the following occurs:

> Then spake Jesus to the multitude, and to his disciples, Saying, The scribes and the Pharisees sit in Moses' seat: All therefore whatsoever they bid you observe, that observe and do; but do not ye after their works: for they say, and do not. (Matthew 23.1–2, AV)

This is rather typical of the Gospel of Matthew which contains some of the bitterest diatribes against the Pharisees in the New Testament, yet at the same time contains the most pro-Pharisee and pro-Law passages too. We shall examine the reason for this paradoxical mixture soon, but at present I want to point out that the above passage actually pays the highest tribute possible to the authority of the Pharisees. Even though they are called hypocrites, their teachings are wholeheartedly endorsed. Those modern scholars who would like to relegate the Pharisees to a minor role in the Second Temple period are here very thoroughly contradicted. Jesus himself declares them to be not some sect, but the arbiters of the Law for the whole nation. The chain of tradition which opens the tractate *Avot* in the Mishnah, tracing the authority of the rabbis generation by generation in a succession stemming from Moses himself, is here given a rousing endorsement. Since Jesus is here recommending his listeners to follow the teachings of the Pharisees in every detail, we can safely conclude that he did this himself and that he was therefore a practising member of the Pharisee movement.

In another passage, Jesus, despite all the denunciations of the Pharisees attributed to him, acknowledges clearly that the Pharisees are blameless:

> And it came to pass, as Jesus sat at meat in the house, behold, many publicans and sinners came and sat down with him and his disciples.
> And when the Pharisees saw it, they said unto his disciples, Why eateth your Master with publicans and sinners?
> But when Jesus heard that, he said unto them, They that be whole need not a physician, but they that are sick.
> But go ye and learn what that meaneth, I will have mercy, and not sacrifice: for I am not come to call the righteous, but sinners to repentance. (Matt. 9.10–13, AV).

Here the Pharisees play the role of the Elder Brother in the Lukan parable of the Prodigal Son. They may be rather less colourful than the sinful characters to whom Jesus gives his full attention, but they are given credit for being 'whole' and 'righteous'. They do not need Jesus' attention because they have done nothing wrong – a very different picture from that which prevails in the New Testament, of Pharisees who are corrupt and slimily self-serving.

It hardly needs to be said that the passage just quoted has nothing whatever to do with ritual purity, though many scholars (until recently) have tried to introduce this topic. The Pharisees are not criticizing Jesus for consorting with publicans (that is, tax-gatherers) and sinners because they are ritually unclean; no such consideration is mentioned in the passage. There was nothing sinful about being ritually unclean; this was simply a condition in which most people were most of the time, except when ritual purity was required, for example for entering the Temple at festival times. The tax-gatherers were gangsters (as Philo graphically describes them), and the 'sinners' were real sinners, not just unwashed people, that is, thieves, robbers, cheats of every description. Jesus, on his mission to 'the lost sheep of the house of Israel' hoped to bring these lost souls to repentance; and the Pharisees expressed some natural scepticism about whether such a heroic feat of reclamation was possible; but the point is that the Pharisees themselves were, on the evidence of this passage at least, not guilty of any such crimes and not in need of Jesus' devoted efforts, not being included in 'the lost sheep'. This meant that the Pharisees could not rise to the high status that could be attained only by repentant sinners, but they were blameless, useful people to whom the saying of the father in the parable of the Prodigal Son was applicable, 'You are always with me' (Luke 15.32, NEB).

We now turn to the problem of why the Gospels, which are usually so prejudiced against the Pharisees and against their Torah-teaching, yet contain passages of exactly the opposite import, prais-ing and reverencing the Pharisees and declaring that the Torah, so far from being abrogated by the advent of Jesus, is eternally valid. The explanation that was offered at one time was straightforward. These passages belong to an earlier version of the Gospels and have survived the extensive re-editing to which the Gospels have been subjected. Since these passages go so much against the grain of the Gospels as a whole, they could not have been added at a late stage of editing, but must belong to the earliest and most authentic layer. The Gospels are documents which derive, in their core, from the Jewish Christians of the Jerusalem Church; and we know that these Jewish Christians, led by James and Peter, were staunch adherents of the Torah and totally observant Jews. They were, in fact, Pharisees. Consequently, wherever they have left their traces on the Gospels as they now stand, they testify to the Jewishness and Pharisaic character of the earliest strand of the Jesus movement, including, of course, Jesus himself. That is why pro-Pharisee passages stand out like islands in the text of the New Testament, all relics of an earlier document that was pro-Pharisaic and indeed Pharisaic. They are Freudian slips, betraying the underlying truth under layers of deception and defence.

This type of explanation is an example of what is known as *tendenz* criticism, that is, examination of an ancient document (many of which have gone through a process of editing) in the light of the general motives or propaganda purposes in the interests of which it has been edited. Where some passage (usually short) is found to contradict this general motivation, or *tendenz*, it is considered to be specially illuminating, for it represents the character of the document before the work of editing began. This is an instance of an even more far-reaching principle of criticism, which applies to the restoration and correction of ancient texts in general, *lectio difficilis melior* (see p. 149). This means that when a scholar, comparing two manuscripts of the same work, finds a reading of a sentence or phrase in one manuscript that is plain and obvious, while in the other manuscript the reading of the same sentence or phrase is obscure or unexpected, it is the latter reading that is probably authentic, since it is more likely that some editor would smooth down a difficult passage to make it more intelligible than that he would deliberately take an easy passage and make it more difficult.

On the principles of *tendenz* criticism, then, the pro-Pharisee passages of the New Testament are the most authentic parts of the whole work. This conclusion, however, was most unpalatable to scholars who were either Christian believers or, even if agnostic, retained Christian predilections. The picture of Jesus as a rebel against the Pharisee establishment (as it was seen, though in fact the Pharisees never formed an Establishment and were themselves always opponents of established power) was too beloved to be given up without a struggle.

There arose then a most ingenious way of turning the matter on its head. It began to be argued that the pro-Pharisee and pro-Torah

passages of the Gospels were not the earliest but the latest elements
in these documents. This conclusion was reached through a more
generalized theory known as form criticism, which proposed that
large portions of the Gospels were written, shortly after the lifetime
of Jesus, to meet the doctrinal and communal needs of various
Christian communities. Words were put into Jesus' mouth that
suited the needs of these communities. Now some of these communities were what were called 're-Judaizers', that is, communities
that could not face the radical revisions of Judaism which Jesus had
demanded, and wished to return to a more Jewish way of life in
accordance with the Torah – while still declaring their adherence
to Jesus as the Messiah and still cutting themselves off from the
general body of Jewish believers. It was these 're-Judaizers' who
were responsible for the introduction of pro-Jewish passages into
the Gospels which made Jesus seem a much more Jewish figure than
he actually was. At the same time, these 're-Judaizers' were also
anxious not to relapse into Judaism itself, so they cherished their
differences from normative Judaism, especially their belief in Jesus
as a divine Messiah. In fact, their anxiety not to relapse into Judaism
became even more intense because of their 're-Judaization' of the
figure of Jesus, and this accounts for the bitterness towards Judaism
and especially Pharisaism shown in their writings. This is an
instance, it was argued, of the bitterness of 'intra-Jewish rivalry',
which can be seen elsewhere in the diatribes of the Dead Sea Scrolls
cult against their fellow-Jews. We thus have a theory that not only
restores Jesus to his role as a rebel against Judaism, but accounts for
the strange mixture of pro-Jewishness and anti-Jewishness found
in the Gospels. This 're-Judaizing' theory was held to apply particularly to the Gospel of Matthew, which, it was suggested, was
written specifically for a community with strong tendencies towards
the retention of Jewish observances.

But the theory of form criticism, to which the theory of 're-
Judaization' belongs, also has much wider applications and implications. It was used to cast doubt on the historical truth of many other
aspects of the Gospel stories, which were held to have been inserted
to meet the needs of various types of Christian communities.
Indeed, in the hands of its most ruthless exponents, such as Rudolf

Bultmann, very little was left in the Gospel accounts that could be trusted as reliable truth about the life of Jesus. The quest for the 'historical Jesus' was held to be a chimera, and should be abandoned. Christianity, Bultmann held (at least in his earliest, most radical writings), was based not on the historical Jesus but on the 'risen Jesus', whom Bultmann (who still counted himself a Christian believer) did not hesitate to call 'mythical'. Religion was not a matter of historical fact, but of myth, and the best religion was the one that had the best myth, and this was Christianity. Myth was a way of expressing spiritual truth, and the process of understanding myth was the way to understanding the deepest elements in Christianity. This process was named by Bultmann 'de-mythologizing', by which he had no intention of connoting 'debunking', but rather a process of illumination. This understanding of myth as the code of truth was taken up by enthusiastic Bultmannites such as Joseph Campbell, who applied the method to the whole corpus of world mythology, with the Christian myth at its apex.

Yet a study of the actual stages through which the method of New Testament form criticism passed (having begun its career in relation to Old Testament studies with the work of Hermann Gunkel on the Psalms) shows that the desire to expel the 'Jewish Jesus' was a powerful early motivation. This is stated in surprisingly explicit form by one of the founders of form criticism (even before Bultmann began his work), namely Max Müller.

While form criticism still retains some hold on New Testament studies, it has now acquired a much modified form. The abolition of the quest for the historical Jesus has been rescinded, and recent New Testament studies have explicitly renewed the quest, including the acknowledgement that Jesus was a very Jewish figure. However, the aspects of his character that were so unpalatable to Christian scholars of the past – that is, those aspects that show him as sympathetic to Pharisaism – remain out of bounds. Jesus is Jewish, yes, but not in any sense that would identify him with the normative Judaism of his day. He remains a rebel against any form of official Judaism and against the entire Jewish Establishment, to which the Pharisees are still held to belong. The fact that the Pharisees were themselves anti-Establishment figures, or as Josephus called them 'continual trouble-makers to those in authority', is still a well-kept secret. Jesus is Jewish, but only in some non-political sense. He could not have called himself 'the Messiah', because (as this is now at least appreciated) this is a term shot through with political implications. He had no ambitions to overthrow the Roman Occupation of his native land, because he was indifferent to patriotism and thought one form of government no better than another. He was a wandering peasant philosopher, interested in communicating with peasants like himself, and having a message to communicate that nullified all forms of societal hierarchy or plans for organized reform. In fact, he was a Jewish Diogenes.

How then, on this view, are we to explain the passages in which Jesus pays tribute to the Pharisees and to the Torah and declares himself an adherent of traditional Judaism? It seems that for these passages the expedient of 're-Judaization' is still held to work. The historical Jesus could never have uttered these passages. They were put into his mouth by some editor who still revered the Torah, yet at the same time hated its chief exponents, the Pharisees. Alternatively, Jesus' commendatory remarks about the Pharisees themselves are explained away in various ways; the chief one being that they were intended ironically. Thus when Jesus told the Pharisees that he was associating with sinners because his mission was to the sick not to the whole, he did not really mean that he regarded the Pharisees as whole, but rather that he regarded them as so convinced of their wholeness that it was hopeless to try to put a dent into their complacency; better results could come from administering to the spiritual needs of those who were sinners and knew that they were sinners. When Jesus said (Matt. 5.19) that not one jot or tittle of the Torah would ever pass away, he meant that certain fundamental truths enshrined in the Torah, such as love of neighbour, were eternal and would survive the passing of the inessentials. When he said 'not one jot or tittle', his mode of expression was mere hyperbole arising from the enthusiasm of the moment. Every little detail was linked in some way with the central truths, so even in their dying-away they would in some sense survive.

Another expedient is to return to a medieval way of thinking, that of allegorization. In the Middle Ages, it was held that every word in the so-called Old Testament was truth, but not literal truth; all the passages which the simple-minded Jews took literally should be interpreted symbolically. On this basis, Jesus could have said that not one jot or tittle of the old Scriptures would ever pass away, for their symbolic truth remained even after their literal meaning had become outmoded by the advent of Christianity. This method of interpreting Jesus' saying (apart from its inherent implausibility) meets with difficulty because of Jesus' use of the word 'commandments': 'whoever sets aside one of the least of these commandments and teaches others to do so shall be called least in the kingdom of heaven; but whoever keeps them and teaches others to keep them shall be called great in the kingdom of heaven' (Matt. 5.19, my translation) 'Setting aside commandments' and 'keeping commandments' are expressions that do not lend themselves readily to symbolic interpretation. Either one keeps a commandment by actually acting in accordance with it, or one does not.

It is interesting to see how Francis Wright Beare, in his well-known commentary on Matthew, deals with the difficulties raised by this saying of Jesus. He points out that the saying is indeed very puzzling, especially as it is immediately contradicted by the succeeding sayings in the same chapter. After saying that the Law will never pass away, Jesus immediately begins to contradict the Law, saying, 'Moses said that, but I say this . . .'. Beare concludes that the saying under discussion derives from the Jerusalem Church, which continued to insist on the validity of the Mosaic Law, despite their acceptance of Jesus as the Messiah. Matthew himself, however, did not belong to the Jerusalem Church but to the body of believers who regarded the authority of the Mosaic Law as having been abrogated by Jesus. Why then did Matthew include in his Gospel a doctrine of the Jerusalem Church in which he himself did not believe? All that Beare has to say about this is: 'Matthew felt no obligation to reproduce everything that he found in his sources, and we must suppose that he did not find this saying so completely incompatible with the pronouncements of Jesus which follow, as it seems to us.' In other words, a total contradiction just did not register on Matthew's mind.

This rather condescending 'explanation' is, however, less

important for our enquiry than Beare's conception of the conflict between the Jerusalem Church, or Jewish Christians, and the Gentile Christians, to whom he assumes that Matthew belongs. He sees this conflict as existing between two contemporaneous schools of thought about Jesus, each of which had its idiosyncratic view of what Jesus had to say. The Jerusalem Church thought of Jesus as an observant Jew who wished to retain the Mosaic Law, while the Gentile Christians, on an equal footing, thought differently. It does not appear to occur to Beare that the Jerusalem Church had better evidence in this matter than the Gentile Church. The Jerusalem Church was led by persons who had had long personal acquaintance with Jesus himself, and were surely in a better position to understand his viewpoints than persons to whom Jesus was someone in the past whom they had never met. Even the leading personality to whom the Gentile Church looked with awe, Paul, never met Jesus in the flesh, and relied entirely, for his version of Jesus' opinions, on visionary experiences in which he met and talked to the heavenly Jesus (of course, in Paul's view and that of his adherents, this made his account of Jesus' views more, not less, reliable than the account given by persons who merely derived their views from Jesus' own earthly mouth). To a modern scientific enquirer, however, it seems perverse to put the tradition of the Jerusalem Church on a dead level with the Paul-derived conception of Jesus that was current in the Gentile Church. What the Jerusalem Church thought was what Jesus himself thought. To attribute the views of the Jerusalem Church to a post-Jesus 're-Judaization' (a view held even by the revolutionary thinker F. C. Baur) is incredible. That Jesus' own brother, James and his chief confidant, Peter, would fundamentally falsify Jesus' views immediately after his death stretches credulity to breaking-point. If the Jerusalem Church reported Jesus as saying that not one jot or tittle of the Law would ever pass away, that was because this is what Jesus actually said.

Why then, it may still be asked, did Matthew include in his Gospel a saying that was so opposed to everything that he himself thought about the message of Jesus? Why did he not simply suppress this saying, as did Mark (Luke, however, did include it in a qualified, watered-down form, see Luke 16.16–17; John, of course, contains no trace of it). The answer must be that this saying was so well attested that Matthew's nerve failed him. While he did not scruple to suppress sayings of Jesus that did not suit his own way of thinking in many other instances, here he could not persuade himself that such ruthless editing was justified. We may conclude, therefore, that of the sayings of Jesus recorded in the Gospels, this is the most reliable and authentic of all – so authentic that even Matthew could not bring himself to excise it.

This conclusion is the exact opposite of that of the Jesus Seminar which puts the whole passage under discussion into black type (signifying inauthentic) and remarks,

> The complex Matt. 5:17–19 reflects a controversy in the early Christian community over whether the Law was still binding on Christians. Matthew's position is that the most trivial regulation . . . must be observed. Matthew thereby nullifies Jesus' relaxed attitude towards the Law, the centrality of the love commandment in Jesus' teaching and Jesus' repeated distinction between the qualitative fulfillment of God's will and the formal observance of the Law, especially the ritual Law. These statements even contradict the antithetical statements that follow in 5:21–48 . . . This effort to retain the validity of the Law is of Judean-Christian inspiration, which must have arisen already in the Q community, but had grown in intensity in Matthew's time. Words such as those found in Matt. 5:17–20 could readily have been put on the lips of Jesus because the early Christian community thought that the risen Jesus continued to speak to it. [This] is a pronouncement, so to speak, of the risen Jesus.[1]

One could hardly imagine a more wrong-headed judgement than this. The person who was claiming to receive pronouncements from the risen Jesus was Paul, whose reports of the views of the risen Jesus were the direct opposite of the sentiments expressed in Matt. 5.17–19. As for Matthew, it is clear that his own opinions were in accordance with Matt. 5.21–48, not with Matt. 5.17–20, which sticks out from his Gospel like a sore thumb. As for 'Judean-Christian inspiration' it apparently does not occur to the members of the Jesus Seminar that this might be especially reliable, since it came from people who had consorted daily with Jesus himself in the flesh. The Jesus Seminar claims to be applying new objective standards to the assessment of New Testament texts, but its standpoint is actually traditionally Christian. It is a prime exponent of what I call 'pious scepticism'; that is, readiness to doubt and jettison New Testament texts if they conflict in any way with traditional pious views. Its use of the 're-Judaization' theory goes even further than most in attributing 're-Judaization' not to inertia (by which Christian communities fell back supinely into Jewish ways of thinking) but to claimed divine revelation. It refuses utterly to connect alleged 're-Judaization' with the testimony of the apostles James, Peter and John, who reported views which they had personally heard coming from Jesus' mouth.

Here we must turn our attention to a topic that has been much neglected by scholars: the polemic in the Gospels against the Jerusalem Church. The reasons why modern scholars, such as members of the Jesus Seminar, are so reluctant to grant any authority to the leaders of the Jerusalem Church, and so willing to assign opinions which could be very naturally and plausibly attributed to them in their role of direct disciples and tradents of Jesus to an extraneous and deplorable 're-Judaization' tendency instead, can be traced ultimately to a campaign of denigration of these same leaders in the New Testament itself.

13

The Polemic against the Jerusalem Church

It is taken for granted by most New Testament scholars that the twelve disciples, or apostles, of Jesus did not understand him fully, or even adequately. What is not recognized, however, is that this 'lack of understanding' is carefully planted in the Gospels (and Acts) themselves, and forms a major element in a programme of indoctrination that was historically of the utmost importance in the early Church.

The early Church had two aims which were equally important, but were not fully reconcilable. One was to promulgate the view of Jesus (chiefly derived from Paul) as a divine figure who had abrogated the Torah and had deliberately sought his own death in order that it might function as a salvific act on behalf of mankind, taking the place of adherence to the Torah as a means of salvation. The other was to derive this doctrine from the teaching of Jesus himself, and from his closest and earliest disciples, the leading figures of the Jerusalem Church. It was most important to disclaim any split (of any significance) between the Jerusalem Church and Paul, and to deny that their central doctrines came from Paul. It would have weakened the authority of the Pauline Church beyond repair to admit that its doctrines did not have the authority of the Jerusalem Church behind them. On the other hand, some explanation had to be offered for the patent fact that James, Peter and John, the leaders of the Jerusalem Church, had acted as if the Torah was still in force and had uncontrovertibly engaged in conflict with Paul from time to time. How deep was this conflict? What was it really about? These are questions that must be approached by using the totality of the evidence, and especially by noting the discrepancies between Paul's epistles and the accounts given in the Gospels and Acts. We shall note that our sources show a simultaneous desire to build up the authority of the apostles (so that Pauline Christianity can lay claim to this indispensable source) and to run them down (so that Pauline Christianity can claim to have the definitive version of Jesus' teaching as opposed to the teaching of anti-Pauline Jewish Christian teachers). So, in addition to denigration of the Twelve in the Gospels, we also, find in Acts particularly, a kind of downgrading of Paul from the status he gives himself in his epistles. The total result has to be a picture of Paul as one of the apostles, having equal, but not superior, status to them, yet leading them in a direction which they would not have taken without him, since their understanding of Jesus' purposes was, after all, inferior to his. Thus we end up with a picture of the twin apostles Peter and Paul, finally in total harmony, a picture that is, as we shall see, historically false.

The quarrel between Peter and Paul

In the book of Acts, no quarrel between Peter and Paul is recorded. But in the epistle to the Galatians, written by Paul himself, a serious quarrel is described. From this account, it appears that Peter visited Paul in Antioch, and at first adopted a friendly approach, sitting at table with Paul's followers and sharing a meal with them. However, at this point some emissaries from the Jerusalem Church arrived, and delivered some message, upon which, Peter, much to Paul's disgust, withdrew from the table. Here Paul narrates that he upbraided Peter for hypocrisy. This is certainly no trivial disagreement, yet not a word of it is allowed to enter the text of Acts, in which Peter and Paul are the best of friends throughout, with Paul taking the guiding role.

What was the cause of the quarrel between Paul and Peter in Antioch? Here most commentators take Paul's version entirely at face value, and interpret the matter as a hypocritical volte-face by Peter. Paul reports that 'when Cephas [Peter] came to Antioch, I opposed him to his face . . . I said to Cephas, before the whole congregation, "If you, a Jew born and bred, live like a Gentile, and not like a Jew, how can you insist that Gentiles must live like Jews?"'

(Gal. 2.11, 14, NEB). These are strong words, reflecting a conflict between Paul and Peter that has no echo in Acts.

One may ask what Peter was doing when he shared meals with the Gentile converts of Paul. Commentators have assumed that he was actually sharing forbidden foods, such as pig, having made a full transition from observance of the Torah. On this view, Peter, having made this radical transition from observant Pharisee to pork-eating Christian, suddenly had cold feet when emissaries from James arrived and pusillanimously removed himself from the table of the Gentile converts and started acting like an observant Jew again. Upon this Paul upbraided him, not for this vacillating behaviour, but for insisting that 'Gentiles must behave like Jews'. This is very puzzling, for Jewish law had never insisted that Gentiles must behave like Jews, and under the Gentile Covenant of the Seven Noahide Laws, it was clear that it was never any sin for a Gentile to eat pork or anything else, except 'a limb torn from a living animal'. At the Jerusalem Council, which took place some time before Peter's visit to Antioch, this position was confirmed by James: Gentile converts to the Jesus movement were to be allowed, but they must observe the Seven Laws, though James' version of these Seven Laws was slightly different from that of the Talmud, since he forbade Gentiles to eat 'meat of an animal that had been strangled' (that is, had not been drained of blood), an earlier interpretation of the Noahide Code deriving from Gen. 9.4 – this interpretation is found also in the book of Jubilees, but is contradicted in the rabbinic writings on the basis of Deut. 14.21.

So in what way was Peter contravening the Torah by eating at the same table as Gentiles, as long as they ate their food and he ate his? Clearly there must be some explanation of the rift between Peter and Paul, other than the confused explanation offered by Paul?

The explanation is probably that the emissaries from James had arrived not to announce that the decision of the Jerusalem Council had been reversed (the favourite explanation of commentators) but to inform Peter of information they had received that Paul had not been observing his side of the bargain struck at the Jerusalem Council: he had been declaring the Torah totally obsolete, and its provisions invalid for Jewish followers of Jesus as well as non-

Jewish adherents, or he had permitted Gentile followers to ignore even the few prohibitions laid upon them by James at the Council. At receiving this news, Peter withdrew from fellowship with Paul's branch of the Jesus movement. This was no weak vacillation but a decisive break between the Pauline movement and the Jerusalem community, of which Peter was one of the chief pillars. Peter is portrayed, however, by Paul in a contemptible light, and this became the strategy of the Pauline Church, as later evidenced by the Gospels.

In so far as Galatians reveals the occurrence of a serious quarrel between Paul and Peter, it is giving, however, a much more authentic account of events than Acts. On the other hand, in another respect, Acts is much more trustworthy than Paul in his epistles – in the accounts given of the Jerusalem Council. In Acts, it is clear that Paul plays a very subordinate role in this Council. He is summoned by the leader, James, and his chief officers, Peter and John, to answer charges and to make promises of his future behaviour; and he obeys this summons meekly. In Paul's own account of the matter (Gal. 2.6–10), however, things are very different. Paul attends the Conference as a full equal to James, Peter and John, and no final decision is delivered by James about the conditions under which Gentiles might be accepted into the Jesus movement. Instead, Paul is fully confirmed as 'Apostle to the Gentiles' and left to his own devices about how to go about this. Paul even refers to the Jerusalem leaders with hardly veiled contempt ('not that their importance matters to me', Gal. 2.6, NEB). Obviously, this was written when the split between Paul and the Jerusalem Church was nearing completion, though he still feels the need for their sanction for his own role.

The epistles of Paul and Gospels/Acts, taken together, form the main body of the Christian Scriptures, as they came into use in the Pauline Christian Church. Yet there are subtle differences to be observed between the approaches of the epistles, on the one hand, and Gospels/Acts on the other. Specifically, Gospels/Acts, wishing to preserve the link with the leaders of the Jerusalem Church, cannot quite take Paul at his own valuation as a kind of prophet, far outstripping in inspiration the apostle-companions of Jesus himself who formed the leadership of the Jerusalem Church. On the other hand, Gospels/Acts wishes to support Paul in denigrating these same leaders, to some extent, because they are aware that James, Peter and John stand for a kind of belief in Jesus which is very different from their own, being essentially in accordance with the Pharisaism to which Jesus himself belonged. These motivations lead to some interesting trends which require further analysis.

Lowering of status of Paul in Acts

Paul's account of his conversion to belief in Jesus gives him a much more grandiose role that that allotted to him in Acts. In Paul's account, after his vision of Jesus on the road to Damascus, he retires to the desert (like Moses or Elijah) to meditate for a period, and comes back with the conviction that he has been given a special mission to the Gentiles (like the prophet Jeremiah). Nothing is said about his resorting to Ananias in Damascus for instruction, or about his visiting Jerusalem to make the acquaintance of the leaders of the Jerusalem Church – these narrative elements are found only in Acts. Paul thus portrays himself as a prophet who has received a personal revelation, while in Acts, he is portrayed as a convert to an already existing revelation, and as a novice requiring instruction. We have already seen, too, that in his account of the Jerusalem Council, Paul gives himself a much more dignified role than that assigned to him in Acts. In his letters, Paul constantly refers to personal revelations which he received, subsequent to his original revelation on the road to Damascus. He bases his claim to apostleship, equal to that of the Jerusalem apostles, on these revelations, and even hints broadly that they make him superior to them. Indeed, if our evidence for the birth of Christianity were based only on Paul's epistles, we would not hesitate, on his own evidence, to characterize him as the founding prophet of Christianity, equivalent in status to Moses in Judaism. Even the central sacrament of Christianity, the Eucharist, on Paul's account (if the Greek is properly understood), was transmitted to him by the heavenly Jesus in a vision, not conveyed to him by the leaders of the Jerusalem Church.[1] In fact, Paul was the creator of the Eucharist, which was a rite not practised in the Jerusalem Church at all. The institution of the Eucharist comprised a new sacrament taking the place of the Jewish sacraments of the Temple and marking the advent of a new religion different from Judaism. The Jerusalem Church, however, remained loyal to the Jewish Temple, and regarded themselves not as a new religion but as a variety of Judaism.

Acts, however, has a very different picture to offer of Paul. Nothing is said about Paul's Moses-like sojourn in the desert. He is portrayed entirely as a convert to an existing religion and religious set-up, Christianity. Paul is the hero of the book of Acts, but only at the cost of a considerable reduction in stature. He is the indefatigable distributor of the Christian message, and he understands Jesus' purposes better than anyone else, but his links with the authority of the Jerusalem Church are carefully preserved.

Peter, on the contrary, is shown going through a process of education in which he gradually reaches the understanding of Jesus that Paul has from the first. Peter is horrified at first at the idea that the laws of Torah (on forbidden foods) are no longer in operation, and that Jesus' message is for all the nations, not just for the Jews. But he finally reaches this understanding. As representative of the Jerusalem Church, he has indispensable authority but limited understanding, which gradually improves. His slowness of apprehension continues a theme that is prominent in the Gospels themselves, which portray all the immediate disciples of Jesus as lacking the understanding which will eventually come to them through the educative influence of Paul. The limitations of understanding attributed to the Twelve in the Gospels are best understood as a polemic against the Jerusalem Church from a Pauline point of view – a polemic which must not be allowed to get out of hand, for otherwise the chain of authority which links the Pauline Church to the Jerusalem Church and thus to Jesus himself would be broken. Without the Jerusalem Church there would be an unbridgeable gap between the Pauline Church and Jesus, for it is never forgotten that Paul never knew Jesus in the flesh, and that the Twelve are the indispensable human link with Jesus. Moreover, the awesome authority of the Jerusalem Church cast a spell that lasted for several generations even after the Pauline Church split off from it.

The limitations of the Twelve in the Gospels

Again and again, the Gospels stress the lack of understanding on the part of the Twelve of Jesus' mission and intentions. One of the most striking of these passages concerns no other than Peter himself:

> From that time Jesus began to make it clear to his disciples that he had to go to Jerusalem, and there to suffer much from the elders, chief priests, and doctors of the law; to be put to death and to be raised again on the third day. At this Peter took him by the arm and began to rebuke him. 'Heaven forbid!' he said. 'No, Lord, this shall never happen to you.' Then Jesus turned and said to Peter, 'Away with you, Satan; you are a stumbling-block to me. You think as men think, not as God thinks.' (Matt. 16.21–3, NEB)

This startling indictment of Peter, whom Jesus has just appointed to be the Rock on which he will build his Church, is an indictment of the Twelve as a whole. They are revealed as totally lacking in understanding of Jesus' mission on earth. By calling Peter 'Satan', Jesus puts him in the same category as Judas Iscariot, into whom 'Satan entered', and who is only the most extreme example of apostolic hindrance of Jesus' purposes. But we must beware of accepting this repudiation of the Twelve by Jesus as historical fact. It is part of a propaganda campaign against the Jerusalem Church, in which Peter was a leading figure. It is an expression of the Pauline manifesto, which is, 'These great leaders of the Church, to whom you all look up, never really understood Jesus, until I, Paul, came along to tell them what Jesus intended.'

What then, according to the Gospels, was the actual expectation of Peter and the other disciples? What did they expect Jesus would accomplish? If we outline their expectations, we shall understand what motivated them to join Jesus' movement in the first place. We shall also gain some light on the hopes and beliefs of the Jerusalem Church which were so different from those of the Pauline Church that the Pauline Scriptures, the Gospels, are compelled to carry out a covert war against them in the guise of denigration of the Twelve.

The expectations of the Twelve may be gleaned from the following passages, which, however, convey a rather mixed message:

At this Peter said, 'We here have left everything to become your followers. What will there be for us?' Jesus replied, 'I tell you this: in the world that is to be, when the Son of Man is seated on his throne in heavenly splendour, you my followers will have thrones of your own, where you will be as judges of the twelve tribes of Israel.' (Matt. 19.27–8, NEB)

The mother of Zebedee's sons then came before him, with her sons. She bowed low and begged a favour. 'What is it you wish?' asked Jesus. 'I want you', she said, 'to give orders that in your kingdom my two sons here may sit next to you, one at your right, and the other at your left.' Jesus turned to the brothers and said, 'You do not understand what you are asking. Can you drink the cup that I am to drink?' 'We can,' they replied . . . When the other ten heard this, they were indignant with the two brothers. (Matt. 20.20–4, NEB)

Then a jealous dispute broke out: who among them should rank highest? But he said, 'In the world, kings lord it over their subjects . . . not so with you . . . You are the men who have stood firmly by me in my times of trial; and now I vest in you the kingship which my Father vested in me; you shall eat and drink at my table in my kingdom and sit on thrones as judges of the twelve tribes of Israel.' (Luke 22.24–30, NEB)

In the above passages, it appears that the Twelve have ambitions to have positions of worldly glory, sitting on thrones and judging the tribes of Israel. They have become reconciled, however, to the idea that before this can happen Jesus has to undergo death and they themselves may have to undergo the same fate. Yet their vision remains one of nationalism and glorious position in a royal court. The picture of rivalry and wrangling for position between members of the Twelve is hardly edifying. This is a transition passage, in which the Twelve are granted some understanding of Jesus' intentions, yet retain their primitive conceptions of the final result: ruling and judiciary power for themselves in a jealous hierarchy. The passage as a whole is hardly calculated to inculcate respect for the Twelve, and must be reckoned as part of the polemic against the Jerusalem Church.

The glimmering of understanding evinced here of Jesus' sacrificial role is, however, soon lost, it appears. We find that when Jesus finally suffers the death he has been foretelling, his disciples are totally puzzled:

> That same day two of them were on their way to a village called Emmaus, which lay about seven miles from Jerusalem, and they were talking together about all these happenings. As they talked and discussed it with one another, Jesus himself came up and walked along with them; but something kept them from seeing who it was. He asked them, 'What is it you are debating as you walk?' They halted, their faces full of gloom, and one, called Cleopas, answered: 'Are you the only person staying in Jerusalem not to know what has happened there in the last few days?' 'What do you mean?' he said. 'All this about Jesus of Nazareth,' they replied, 'a prophet powerful in speech and action before God and the whole people; how our chief priests and rulers handed him over to be sentenced to death, and crucified him. But we had been hoping that he was the man to liberate Israel . . . 'How dull you are!' he answered. 'How slow to believe all that the prophets said! Was the Messiah not bound to suffer thus before entering upon his glory?' Then he began with Moses and all the prophets, and explained to them the passages which referred to himself in every part of the scriptures. (Luke 24.13–27, NEB)

This is a very revealing passage. It shows that close disciples of Jesus (though apparently not members of the Twelve) were totally unaware of the mission of Jesus as understood later in the Pauline Church. They refer to Jesus as 'a prophet powerful in speech and action before God and the whole people', and their conception of his aims and their hope for him was that he would be 'the man to liberate Israel'. In other words, they thought of him as a Messiah-figure in the Jewish sense, someone who would restore to the Jewish people (Israel) its national independence, though no doubt they thought (in accordance with scriptural prophecies) that this 'liberation' would be the trigger for a world-wide movement of liberation from oppressive military regimes. Jesus' response to them is, 'How dull you are!', and this reproof is addressed not just to them but to the whole Jerusalem Church, which after Jesus' death continued to believe in him as a 'liberator'; one who had been killed by the Romans, but had nevertheless by a God-given miracle come to life again, and would come back shortly to continue his mission of liberation, and achieve his aim of restoring the independent Jewish state. To the Jerusalem Church, the resurrection of Jesus did not signify his deification. Such miracles of resurrection were attested by Scripture and never resulted in deification of the resurrected person (even Jesus was credited with such a miracle, but no one ever concluded that Lazarus was God).

Who are the two people who figure in this story, and who show such astounding ignorance of the allegedly often-repeated thinking of their leader? One of them is actually named – Cleopas – and this name is highly significant. After Jesus' death, his place as leader of the Jesus movement was taken by James, his brother. This was very natural if, as I argue, the Jesus movement was a monarchist movement in which Jesus was regarded as King of Israel. Even though James, Jesus' brother, had not been one of the Twelve and had played no prominent part in the movement during Jesus' lifetime, he was Jesus' nearest relative, and therefore, in a monarchical system, had to be appointed to be leader in his place, not as King indeed (since Jesus was believed to be still alive) but as Regent, occupying the throne until Jesus' return which was hourly expected. Peter, who had been appointed by Jesus as the 'Rock', continued to function as Grand Vizier or Prime Minister to the Throne. But on James's death in 62 CE, another close relative of Jesus was appointed to the office of Regent, at the head of the Jesus movement. His name? Simeon the son of Cleopas!

Simeon was Jesus' nephew, and Cleopas, his father, was Jesus' uncle. And the name of one of the two men with whom Jesus (miraculously unrecognized) conversed after his resurrection, and to whom he said, 'How dull you are!' was Cleopas. Clearly the choice of this name by the inventive narrator was no accident. He chose the name of the father of the current leader of the Jerusalem Church. The whole incident, therefore, is directed against the Jerusalem Church and its dullness in still thinking that Jesus came to 'liberate Israel'.

According to the book of Acts, Jesus' lengthy explanation to Cleopas and his unnamed companion had very little effect on the thinking of the Jerusalem Church, for right at the beginning of the book we find the following:

> He showed himself to these men after his death, and gave ample proof that he was alive: over a period of forty days he appeared to them and taught them about the kingdom of God . . . So, when they were all together, they asked him, 'Lord, is this the time when you are to establish once again the sovereignty of Israel?' (Acts 1.3–6, AV)

Again, the chief preoccupation of the apostles is a national one of liberation (though this liberation could have world-wide effects). The Pauline concepts of salvation brought about by the death of Jesus – rescue from damnation, immortality, access to heaven – seem to be not part of their thinking at all. Yet this passage can hardly be included in the roster of polemic against the Jerusalem Church, for Jesus does not reprove them nor does the author of Acts apparently regard them as being stupid. Indeed, the author of Acts testifies strongly that the apostles were faithful to the observance of the Torah, even though, according to Paul, the Torah was no longer valid.

The ambivalence of Acts on this point is a subject for discussion on its own, but it should be remarked that Acts does elsewhere testify to the abrogation of the Torah. This is particularly evident in the episode of Peter's dream, where Peter is represented as saying, 'I have never eaten anything profane or unclean' (Acts 10.14, NEB), in a context suggesting that this kind of behaviour is now outdated. But even this passage testifies that hitherto the abrogation of the Torah was unknown to Peter; he never heard anything of the sort from Jesus. On the whole, we may conclude that the book of Acts, unlike the Gospels, does not form part of the polemic against the Jerusalem Church, towards which it is remarkably sympathetic; but it does provide abundant evidence that the Jerusalem Church did indeed hold views that were very different from Pauline Christianity and that these views were derived from Jesus himself. Peter's testimony directly contradicts the popular modern theory of 're-Judaization'. Peter did not learn from Jesus to ignore the Torah, and then recoil from this anti-Torah teaching after Jesus' death; according to him the idea of the abrogation of the Torah was unknown to him during Jesus' lifetime and came to him only after Jesus' death. The leaders of the Jerusalem Church are portrayed in Acts as highly observant in the practice of the Torah; but they are not criticized as stupid for this, or as acting through misunderstanding the teaching of Jesus. The 'stupidity syndrome' of the Twelve is confined to the Gospels, where it is pervasive. The reason for this difference between Acts and the Gospels is that Acts is concerned to portray Paul as the teacher and educator of the Church not through acquaintance with the teachings of the earthly Jesus, but through communications from the heavenly Jesus. We may say that while the Gospels are concerned to denigrate the Jerusalem Church (in order to throw discredit on its teachings), the book of Acts is concerned to build up the Jerusalem Church again (in order to be able to claim its authority for the Pauline Church).

The Twelve as disloyal and cowardly

But the Gospel polemic against the Jerusalem Church is not confined to criticism of the Twelve as stupid in failing to understand Jesus' aims. There is also denigration of the Twelve as lacking in loyalty and courage, and since the Jerusalem Church was actually led by members of the Twelve, this is indeed a serious form of indictment.

First, there is the familiar episode of the treachery of Peter in denying his Master. Jesus is represented as foreseeing Peter's disloyalty, and also that of the other disciples:

After singing the Passover hymn, they went out to the Mount of Olives. Then Jesus said to them, 'Tonight you will all fall from your faith on my account; for it stands written, "I will strike the shepherd down and the sheep of his flock will be scattered." But after I am raised again, I will go before you into Galilee.' Peter replied, 'Everyone else may fall away on your account, but I never will.' Jesus said to him, 'I tell you, tonight before the cock crows you will disown me three times.' Peter said, 'Even if I must die with you, I will never disown you.' And all the disciples said the same. (Matt. 26.30–5, NEB).

In the event, when Jesus was arrested, 'Then the disciples all deserted him and ran away' (Matt. 26.56). As for Peter, his behaviour was even more disgraceful when Jesus was imprisoned:

Meanwhile Peter was sitting outside in the courtyard when a serving-maid accosted him and said, 'You were there too with Jesus the Galilean.' Peter denied it in face of them all. 'I do not know what you mean,' he said. He then went out to the gateway, where another girl, seeing him, said to the people there, 'This fellow was with Jesus of Nazareth.' Once again he denied it, saying with an oath, 'I do not know the man.' Shortly afterwards the bystanders came up and said to Peter, 'Surely you are another of them; your accent gives you away!' At this he broke into curses, and declared with an oath: 'I do not know the man.' At that moment a cock crew; and Peter remembered how Jesus had said, 'Before the cock crows you will disown me three times.' He went outside, and wept bitterly. (Matt. 26.69–75, NEB)

Peter and the other disciples are here depicted as acting basely beyond belief. Peter not only denies his Master, but does so twice 'with an oath'. An 'oath' does not mean a curse (though Peter employs curses too, which are mentioned separately) but a solemn declaration using the name of God. Peter was thus guilty not only of disloyalty but of perjury, by which he broke one of the Ten Commandments, which forbids taking the name of God in vain. He could hardly have acted more despicably. Some commentators take the line of defence that Peter and the other disciples were acting in accordance with the prophecy from Zechariah cited by Jesus, and therefore had no choice; their behaviour was fated and inevitable. This is a very feeble defence, especially as the prophecy concerned is very ambiguous and was obviously inserted into the narrative by the editor as a kind of ad hoc *pesher*. Judas Iscariot too is represented as acting in accordance with prophecy, and even on the instructions of Jesus; yet this does not reduce in the least the obloquy in which he is held. Disreputable actions are never regarded as excused by the fact that they are in accordance with prophecy.

But did the event of the disloyalty of the disciples ever happen? Far more likely is that the whole event is a slander concocted to lower the status of Peter and the other leaders of the Jerusalem Church. Peter's consummate courage is attested in the other events of his life; it is most improbable that he would have shown such pusillanimity at such a climactic moment. Some commentators take refuge in the thought that the narration shows the honesty of the Gospel narrative, which does not seek to hide the failings of its heroes, just as the Hebrew Bible does not hide the failings of heroes like Moses and David. But this narrative is in a different category. Moses shows a failing of impatience and anger; David succumbs to an overwhelming sexual temptation. This narrative, however, concerns mere contemptible weakness of character. Its outcome is clear: it lowers the status of the Twelve and constitutes an important ingredient in the polemic against the Jerusalem Church.

Yet the disloyalty of the key figure, Peter, is by no means the deepest form of betrayal depicted in the behaviour of the Twelve. One of the Twelve, after all, was Judas Iscariot, the archetypal traitor. One cannot say that the story of Judas's treachery contributed to the denigration of the Jerusalem Church in any direct way, since Judas Iscariot was ejected from the Twelve and his place was taken by another in the leadership of the Jerusalem Church. Yet the story of his betrayal does form a kind of apex of a trend of disloyalty discernible within the Twelve as a whole; so I think that it does make a kind of indirect contribution to the lowering of the status of the Twelve. I have shown elsewhere that the whole story of Judas's betrayal is mythical.[2] The story was unknown to Paul, who refers quite unselfconsciously to 'the Twelve' in relation to a period when Judas was supposed to have defected, and the number of the apostles was eleven (1 Cor. 15.5). The chief motivation of the myth of Judas Iscariot is not to denigrate the Jerusalem Church, but to denigrate the Jewish people, whose name Judas eponymously bears; he acts as a symbol for the alleged mass betrayal of Jesus by the Jewish people as a whole. But since the Jerusalem Church was in fact entirely composed of Jews, who remained loyal to the Jewish religion and did not worship the Jesus concocted by Paul out of his visions, some of the obloquy belonging to Judas Iscariot must have affected them too.

The leaders of the Jerusalem Church, James and his chief ministers Peter and John, were regarded with awe during their period of leadership, as several passages in Acts, and even certain passages in Paul's epistles, make plain. It was not an easy task to strip away the atmosphere of awe that surrounded them, and it was not in the interests of the Pauline Church to do so completely, since they relied so much on them for continuity with the Jewish past stretching back to Abraham which was one of their main selling-points. But some reduction had to be made in the status of these awesome figures, in order to make room for the new doctrines promulgated by Paul. The mechanisms for this reduction are found in the Gospels: the 'stupidity syndrome' of the apostles, by which they never grasped Jesus' self-sacrificial aims and his indifference to the cause of Jewish national liberation, and the serious defects of character which caused them to desert him at the climactic moment.

14

Jesus and Hillel

Hillel is the best-known of all the Pharisee leaders, and all that is known of him contradicts the hostile picture of the Pharisees that pervades the Gospels. It may be helpful, therefore, to give some account here of what is known about Hillel, since this may tend to make the central proposition of this book, that Jesus was a Pharisee, seem more acceptable to those who find it bizarre.

When Jesus sought to sum up the central message of the Hebrew Bible, he did so in the following words (Matt. 7.12, AV), 'Therefore all things whatsoever ye would that men should do to you, do ye even so to them: for this is the law and the prophets.' This is known as the Golden Rule, and Jesus presents it not as his own discovery, but as his distillation of the message of the Hebrew Bible. It is clear to all commentators that Jesus sees this formulation as related to a verse in the biblical book of Leviticus: 'Thou shalt love thy neighbour as thyself' (Lev. 19.18, AV) – a verse which, in another context, Jesus isolates (together with the commandment 'Thou shalt love the Lord thy God with all thy heart and with all thy soul and with all thy mind') as the Great Commandment, central to the whole content of the Hebrew Scriptures (Matt. 22.35–40, AV).

Of Hillel, it is said:

A Gentile once came to Shammai and said, 'Accept me as a proselyte on condition that you teach me the whole Torah while I stand on one foot.' Shammai drove him away with the carpenter's rule which he held in his hand. When he came to Hillel, however, he was accepted as a proselyte. Said Hillel, 'What is hateful to you, do not to your fellow; that is the whole Torah; all the rest is commentary; go and study!' (*b. Shabb.* 31a)

This is one of a number of stories in which Hillel is contrasted with his great contemporary Shammai, who did not have Hillel's patience with questioners, and who was less inclined than Hillel to adopt a lenient position in points of law. Hillel was the founder of a school of rabbinic thought known as the House of Hillel, while Shammai was the founder of a rival school, called the House of Shammai. The existence of these two schools has led to a theory (in my opinion entirely wrong, see below) that the Gospel vilification of the Pharisees can be explained as applying only to the Shammaiites, not to the Hillelites.

Shammai was an important leader among the Pharisees, second only to Hillel in his time, though subject to censure for his inclination not to suffer fools gladly. It should be noted, incidentally, that Shammai drove away the would-be proselyte 'with the carpenter's rule which he held in his hand'. The great scholar Shammai was a carpenter by profession, which gives him something in common with Jesus. The idea, commonly held, that Jesus' upbringing as a carpenter somehow disqualified him from entering the ranks of the Pharisees (regarded as rich aristocrats, or, more recently, as pen-wielding bureaucrats) is entirely wrong. Many of the most admired and respected Pharisees were working men who lived by the labour of their hands. Hillel, too, was a working man. He was a hewer of wood, not even skilled enough to be a carpenter.

It has been remarked that Hillel's version of the Golden Rule is couched in negative terms, while Jesus' version is positive in form: Hillel tells us not to do anything to another that would be unwelcome to oneself, while Jesus tells us to behave towards others as one would like others to behave to oneself. It has been argued that Jesus' formulation is superior, since it enjoins action, not merely refraining from action. On the other hand, some have found the negative formulation superior. Bernard Shaw, for example, criticized Jesus' formulation on the simple ground that your neighbour's tastes might be different from your own. If you love eating chocolates, you might (following Jesus' injunction) make a present of a box of chocolates to your neighbour, only to find that he hates chocolates. It is doubtful, however, whether either formulation is superior to the other; both express the same thought, care and love for the other. As it happens, some manuscripts of the New Testament express the principle in negative form.[1]

It has also been remarked that the Golden Rule is not exclusive to Jewish tradition, but is found expressed by not a few sages of other ancient religions (indeed it was not even new to Hillel in Jewish tradition, since a version of it appears in the book of Tobit, 4.15). It is after all not an esoteric idea, but one that occurs to every altruistic mind. This, however, is somewhat off the point. The nub of the matter is not the Golden Rule itself, but the fact that it is cited, by both Jesus and Hillel, as the central thought of the Hebrew Scriptures. As far as Jesus is concerned, this has been mistakenly understood to mean that he regarded the Golden Rule as the solitary kernel of value in a body of literature the rest of which was of little value (the Jesus Seminar, for example, cite 'the centrality of the love commandment in Jesus' teaching' in supposed refutation of the authenticity of his saying that the Law would never pass away). This is a misreading that was congenial to the Pauline Christian Church, which regarded the Jewish Scriptures as largely abrogated. But in context, it is very far from Jesus' meaning: the question he is addressing is, 'Of all the commandments found in the Hebrew Scriptures, which is the Great Commandment to which all the others are subordinate?' This by no means implies a repudiation of the minor commandments, but rather an explication of them.

As for Hillel, this was certainly his meaning, as he shows by his conclusion, 'The rest is commentary; go and study!' But what is worthy of remark, in view of the common view of the Pharisees as ingrained ritualists, is that Hillel, the supreme Pharisee, gives a summing-up of the Torah that omits all mention of ritual, and regards ritual as ultimately serving the needs of love of neighbour. It is remarkable too that Hillel, the Pharisee, puts love of neighbour even higher than Jesus, who subordinates it to love of God. Evidently, Hillel regards love of God as subordinate to love of neighbour; or perhaps like the hero of Leigh Hunt's poem, 'Abou ben Adhem' (and as given philosophical elaboration in modern times by Emmanuel Levinas) he regards love of God as finding its most fundamental expression in love of neighbour.

The idea that love of God and love of neighbour are the central ideas in the Hebrew Scriptures was by no means exclusive to Hillel and Jesus. This idea is pervasive in the whole Pharisee/rabbinic movement. Rabbi Akiva, the greatest of the second-century rabbis (with personal roots, however, in the first century) made the same judgement as Hillel. 'R. Akiva said, Thou shalt love thy neighbour as thyself – that is the greatest principle in the Law.' Akiva, unlike Jesus, does not call it the greatest 'Commandment' but the greatest 'principle' (*kelal*), a rather significant difference of vocabulary, since Akiva, unlike Jesus, did not see the matter in terms of commandments but of philosophical or moral axioms. After all, love is not something that can be commanded. Jesus is supposed to have lifted religious thinking out of the realm of heteronomy or obedience to command, yet here it is Akiva, not Jesus, who sees things in non-heteronomous terms. Even more interesting is that Akiva, like Hillel, but unlike Jesus, sees the basic principle of the Torah as love of neighbour, not as love of God. Not that love of God was in any way belittled in Pharisaic thought; for it was the Pharisees who elevated the injunction to love God (Deut. 6.5) to the central place in the Jewish liturgy. So when Jesus pointed to Deut. 6.5 as the Great Commandment, he was citing the accepted view of the Pharisee movement. Nowhere in his recorded sayings is Jesus more characteristically Pharisee than here.

It is in any case a great mistake to think, as many scholars do, that the Pharisees were not interested in searching for fundamental truths in the Torah, but instead regarded everything in it as equally significant. The Torah itself provides a list of fundamental moral truths in the Ten Commandments, which were regarded as the basic foundation of Judaism (and these Ten Commandments, it should be noted, do not contain any ritual laws, unless the observance of the Sabbath is regarded as such, a moot point in view of the desirability for rest-periods in any free, civilized community, together with the consideration that the Sabbath applied to animals as well as humans). But the Pharisees/rabbis considered that even the Ten Commandments were not sufficiently basic to act as a summary of essential moral truth; so they developed what they called the Seven Laws of the Children of Noah (Noahide Laws) as a code for all humanity, not just for Jews. Even these laws are eclipsed in brevity by the Three Laws of Martyrdom, that is, the three laws that must be observed at the cost of one's life (the laws against murder, incest and idolatry). So the question put to Jesus about priority among the commandments was one of the characteristic preoccupations of the Pharisees, who were by no means the commandment-obeying automatons portrayed in the caricatures so often offered, but were very concerned to know which laws were more important than others.

But how was it possible for both Hillel and Rabbi Akiva to state that all the laws of the Torah were grounded in love of neighbour? Many of the laws of the Torah, it may be said, are purely ritual (for example, the laws of purity, of forbidden foods, of the observance of festivals, and the sacrificial rites of the Temple). How can these laws be derived as 'commentary' from the command to love one's neighbour?

The answer lies in considering the purpose of the ritual laws. They may be said to have two purposes: (1) to bind together the Israelites as a functioning community; the patterning of time into a calendar of feasts and fasts is an important element here; (2) to reinforce the idea that the Israelites are a 'priest-nation', specially elected for the holy task of ministering as such to the whole world (the so-called 'holiness code', including laws of purity and restriction to certain foods, serves this purpose). In general, the ritual laws are essentially communal, rather than individual, laws; they are the means by which the Israelites feel bound to each other and have communal ties. Some modern thinkers have begun to realize the extent to which a sense of community contributes to the moral life; but even more influential than this is a sense of dedication, as belonging to a special community with a mission. Ritual does function in the interests of love of neighbour; not only in promoting love and bondedness of neighbours in one's own community, but by adding a note of noblesse oblige to one's behaviour to the whole of the rest of humanity. Judaism does not contribute to the view that 'every man is an island', nor does it regard humankind as a collection of Robinson Crusoes. At the same time, there is always the danger that what is essentially a means to an end may be mistaken for an end in itself. That is why the Hebrew prophets are constantly warning against the overestimation of ritual and its subordinacy to basic moral principles.

The rabbis, too, are always inculcating this lesson. Ritual is important, but must be kept in its place. No one is required to risk his life in order to observe a ritual law, for the preservation of life is a moral consideration far outweighing any ritual law. The paradigm case cited by the Talmud is that of David, who demanded of the High Priest that he should hand over the sacred loaves of the shew-bread to feed his starving men (1 Sam. 21). Nothing could be more sacred than the shewbread which lay in the innermost recesses of the shrine, but to save human life it could be eaten like any other bread. Jesus too made use of the same scriptural precedent when justifying, to some enquiring Pharisees, his permission to his starving disciples to pluck ears of corn on the Sabbath (though only one Gospel, Matthew, preserves the all-important detail that Jesus' men were indeed starving[2] at this time, the other Gospels being concerned only to portray Jesus as imperiously overruling the laws of the Sabbath, though he was in fact acting strictly in accordance with Pharisee thinking).

Some purists might object to the use of uniforms and badges of rank in an army, on the ground that this does not contribute to the purpose of an army, which is to fight against the enemy. But in fact it is not difficult to see that such ritual observances do contribute to the efficiency of an army as a fighting unit, turning it from a rabble into a disciplined body. The ascription of a role to ritual in the practical implementation of love of neighbour may follow a similar line of argument, and explain the centrality ascribed to love of neighbour by Jesus, Hillel and Akiva despite the multiplicity of ritual commandments in the Torah.

So far we have considered only one saying of Hillel, his famous enunciation of the Golden Rule. Almost as important, however, in setting the tone of the Pharisee movement, is his saying, 'Do not separate yourself from the community.' In this saying, Hillel rejects sectarianism, such as is found in other movements of the period, one of which was the Dead Sea Scrolls sect, about which we have a wealth of information. The essence of the sect was separation from the community, the majority of which was written off as irreclaimable.

In the great Day of the Lord which was approaching, only a remnant would be saved, those who adhered to the rules of the sect.
Even to enter the sect, a formal set of rules was laid down: an
apprenticeship had to be served, and expulsion was always a possibility. The watchword of the Pharisee movement, on the other
hand, was 'All Israel have a share in the World to Come' (*m. Sanh.*
10.1). The mission of the sages, who formed the core of the
Pharisees, was to the nation as a whole, whom they addressed in
popular meetings, using devices, such as parables, intended to
engage the interest of the ordinary people. This is the ideal
expressed by Jesus when he said that his mission was 'to the lost
sheep of the house of Israel'. Moreover, the Pharisees considered
that their mission was wider than this; that it extended beyond the
nation of Israel to the outside world. We have seen that the story of
Hillel about the Golden Rule shows him enunciating this not to a
Jew, but to a Gentile, who was showing some interest in joining the
Jewish religion, even though he made his approach on apparently
impossible terms, which, however, did not deter Hillel. The New
Testament itself testifies to this universalist approach of the
Pharisees, who, it says, would 'compass sea and land to make one
proselyte' (Matt. 23.15, AV) – though the Gospel-writer cannot
resist the impulse to qualify this apparent tribute to Pharisee uni-
versalism in a meanly ungenerous way by adding that they 'make
him twofold more the child of hell than yourselves'. Josephus too
testifies to the proselytizing activities of the Pharisees, and it was
shortly after the lifetime of Jesus that a whole nation, that of
Adiabene (the remnant of the once-great Assyrian Empire) became
converted to Pharisee Judaism.

It must be acknowledged, however, that among its varieties of
worship, Pharisaism contained certain sub-groups with some
sectarian-like characteristics, though in fact they did not comprise
sects. These consisted of a number of independent 'societies'
(*chavurot*) devoted to the practice of ritual purity beyond what was
legally required of non-priests. These societies, however, were
totally voluntary, and no one was regarded as sinful for not joining
one. These societies did, to some extent, cut themselves off from
ordinary Jews by having separate meals, in order to preserve their

condition of ritual purity. The purpose of these societies has been much discussed, but the most plausible explanation is that the members were performing a useful social service by being available to separate the priestly dues (*terumah*) from the crops at harvest time without causing them to incur ritual impurity which would prevent the priests from eating them.[3] Since most of the priests had no income other than these priestly dues, the *chaverim* were performing the service of making the lives of the priests viable. The purity societies, on the other hand, were balanced by other voluntary societies of an opposite but equally useful kind which cultivated *impurity* by devoting themselves to laying out the corpses of the dead for burial (this was never professionalized into a corps of undertakers). Even today (when ritual purity, in the absence of the Temple, is not an issue), this kind of society (known as *chevra kadisha*) is still in being among Jews. The existence of impurity societies in the same community as purity societies is very revealing. It shows that the cultivation of purity was never held up as a community ideal for all to follow. This point has been much misunderstood. Antisemitic scholars like Emil Schürer have seized on the purity societies to argue that they were characteristic of the whole Pharisee movement, which was nothing but a purity society itself, and was therefore a sect.

Unfortunately this same error has been perpetrated more recently by a Jewish scholar, Jacob Neusner, whose work was very influential at one time, but is now widely understood to be flawed. The purity societies never comprised more than a small minority of the Pharisee movement (though for a certain period after the Destruction of the Temple, and in memory of it, it became de rigueur, though never obligatory, for leading Pharisees/rabbis to belong to one or other of these societies).

As for Hillel, it is never stated anywhere that he belonged to a purity society. It is stated, however, that he attributed great importance to the duty of plain non-ritual cleanliness, since he regarded the human body with great reverence, stressing the biblical text that man was made in the image of God. A story illustrating this concern is the following:

When Hillel took leave of his students, he used to go off for a walk. His students asked him, 'Where are you walking to?' He answered, 'To perform a meritorious deed.' They said to him, 'And what is this deed?' And he said to them, 'To take a bath in the bathhouse.' They said to him, 'And is this a meritorious deed?' He answered, 'It is; if the statues erected to kings in the theatres and circuses are washed and scrubbed by those in charge of them . . . how much more should we, who have been created in His image and likeness, take care of our bodies, as it is written, "For in the image of God made he man [Gen. 9.6]"'. (*Lev. R.* 24.3)

Note that Hillel's concern had nothing to do with ritual purity, but only with dignity and cleanliness (ritual purity did not necessarily imply personal cleanliness, for it could be achieved by immersion in a muddy pool). This story reinforces the point made elsewhere in this book, that references to washing, whether of hands or cups, in the New Testament, should not be automatically and mechanically explained, as so often, as instances of ritual purity (see Appendix, pp. 196–205. There is no indication that Hillel was a member of a ritual purity society; such membership was not common among the Pharisee leadership in Second Temple times. With his maxim of 'Do not separate yourself from the community,' he would probably have been reluctant to undertake even this limited degree of separation.

Hillel was not in any way an unusual Pharisee, except in his possession of outstanding gifts and talent. He was a representative of the Pharisee norm. In this respect, he does indeed differ from Jesus, who, as explained earlier, was in some respects an unusual Pharisee. Hillel was not a charismatic. No stories are told about his performing miraculous cures or having powers of rain-making. He was not one of those charismatic Pharisees, such as Hanina ben Dosa, who were credited with such powers, but who, on the other hand, did not contribute to the theoretical development of rabbinic Judaism. Jesus was much more like Hanina ben Dosa than like Hillel in this respect. But the charismatic Pharisees such as Hanina ben Dosa (who were known as Chasidim, though they were far too individualistic to form a movement), formed a highly-respected ingredient in the Pharisee movement as a whole, which was by no means monolithic and contained many different religious types.

Hillel's concern for personal cleanliness as a religious duty contrasts to some extent with Jesus' unconcern with hygiene, typical of the Chasidim. In so far as careful washings were undertaken not just as a matter of dignity but as a precaution against possible dangers to health, the Chasidim were inclined to regard them as needless precautions showing lack of faith in the protection of God – as we saw in Chapter 3.

Jesus, no doubt, like other Jews, went regularly to the bathhouse, but he considered that the washing of hands before meals on health grounds was needless, just as his fellow-Chasidim objected to Pharisee regulations about throwing away liquids that had been left exposed. The mainstream Pharisees thought that such precautions were indeed unnecessary for people of such high spiritual stature as the Chasidim, who could count on special divine protection, but they themselves were legislating for ordinary people. Nevertheless, there was a certain tension between the normative Pharisees and the Chasidim on such points. Some scholars, for example, Geza Vermes, have seen in this tension an explanation of the conflict between Jesus and the Pharisees depicted in the Gospels. Jesus as a Chasid was at odds with the normative Pharisees. This explanation, however, is totally inadequate to explain the bitterness of the conflict as described in the Gospels, which includes even a strong desire on the part of the 'Pharisees' to bring about Jesus' death.

While the charismatics were not prophets, there was a thin line between their status and that of prophets such as Elijah, whose wonder-working activities were so similar to theirs. There were really two different kinds of prophets in the Hebrew Bible: the wonder-working peripatetic prophets such as Elijah and Elisha (who were very similar to the leading Chasidim), and the visionary, literary prophets such as Isaiah. Hillel himself, though not a wonder-worker, was regarded as 'worthy to receive the Holy Spirit', and this must mean that he was considered to have the kind of character that qualified him to be an Isaiah-type prophet.

Hanina ben Dosa specifically denied that he was a prophet, despite his Elijah-like activities. Jesus, however, when he first came on the scene prophesying the coming of the kingdom of God, was definitely claiming Elijah-like prophetic status. The real practical difference between him and Hanina was that Jesus, by claiming to be the precursor of the Messiah, the returned Elijah, was putting himself forward as a figure of strong political import, unlike Hanina, who avoided politics. Elijah, in popular messianic belief, was the precursor of the Messiah, who would 'liberate Israel' and break the Roman yoke. John the Baptist too put himself forward in an Elijah-role, and he paid the penalty for this political boldness by being executed by Herod Antipas (a pawn of the Romans), according to Josephus' account, which is much more credible than that of the Gospels. Later, the official Christian version was that John the Baptist saw himself as the Elijah-figure acting on behalf of Jesus, to whom he subordinated himself. But most of John the Baptist's followers did not see the matter in this way, and continued to regard John's movement as rivalling, not merely foreshadowing, Jesus' movement, even after John's death.[4]

Later in his career, Jesus moved from regarding himself as an Elijah-figure, precursor of the Messiah, and declared himself (prompted by Peter) to be the Messiah himself. He thus adopted an even more dangerous role that inevitably led to his death at the hands of the Romans, to whom he was handed over by the chief henchman and appointee of the Romans, the High Priest, much to the sorrow of the Pharisees, whose attitude is expressed in Acts by Gamaliel (the successor of Hillel).

Both Jesus and Hillel were Pharisees, but of very different kinds. Hillel never claimed to be a prophet or put himself forward as the Messiah; he had neither charismatic nor political features, whereas Jesus had both. But Jesus' daring claims were very much within the parameters of Pharisaism. Neither his claim to prophetic status nor his claim to the Messiahship would arouse the opposition of the Pharisees, who were constantly looking forward to the arrival of both Prophet and Messiah, and would expect them both to arise from within their own ranks. The average Pharisee concerned himself with studying the Written and Oral Torah, and by earnest study and practice of these, he hoped that God would have mercy and send the Deliverer. Hillel was the normative, mainstream Pharisee at his highest. His command of the Oral Torah in all its ramifications was legendary, and he also applied to it a rationalistic approach that enabled him to solve current problems for which there existed no traditional solution. He was in many ways an innovator, and this was not contrary to Pharisaic principles, which welcomed new approaches. Hillel is credited with the formulation of the Seven Hermeneutical Principles (*middot*) by which the Torah could be expounded in a logical way. As leader of the Pharisees, he is also credited with the introduction of new legal institutions (*taqanot*), by which abuses of the Law could be countered. The most celebrated of these was the *prosbul*, a legal instrument by which the Torah law demanding the remission of all debts in the Seventh Year could be circumvented except in the case of the truly destitute; thereby, he loosened credit and saved the economic life of the country, which required that loans should be available for economic enterprise. Hillel was a forward-looking leader, who regarded the Torah as a living instrument of change. He was just the opposite of the conventional picture of the Pharisees as rigid opponents of all change, applying an inflexible law. The picture given in the Gospels, of Jesus as opposing this alleged inflexibility and as being unique in proposing changes in the law, does not survive a study of the life-work of Hillel. This picture of Jesus is arrived at by ascribing to him reforms that the Pharisees had already made. The most prominent example of this is the account of Jesus' alleged reforming activity in healing the sick on the Sabbath: in fact, the Pharisees, long before the advent of Jesus, had permitted healing on the Sabbath. As mentioned above, some of the expressions attributed to Jesus, in his 'reforming' zeal, are actual Pharisee mottoes; for example, 'The Sabbath was made for man, not man for the Sabbath.'

A way that has been tried to explain the Gospel picture of Pharisaic hostility to Jesus is to turn to the figure of Shammai, Hillel's great contemporary and rival. In the years following Hillel's death in 10 CE, the Pharisees were divided into two parties, the House of Hillel and the House of Shammai, and Jesus must have been aware of the controversies in which these two parties were engaged. The records of the arguments between the House of Hillel and the House of Shammai are to be found in the rabbinic writings, and they show that, on the whole, the House of Hillel was more lenient in its decisions than the House of Shammai. The more severe temper of the House of Shammai no doubt stemmed from the character of its founder, Shammai himself, who, as shown above, was much less forbearing and sunny in nature than his great contemporary Hillel.

From these facts it was easy to construct a theory that the hostility against Jesus portrayed in the Gospels did actually exist, but it came from the Shammaiites, not from the Hillelites. In this way, it was possible to have the best of both worlds: the Pharisees as a whole could be defended from the Gospel charges (the Hillelites were much better than that), while the Gospels could be exonerated from the accusation of manufacturing misrepresentations of the Pharisees (these were correct, or at least, not too incorrect, representations of the Shammaiites).

The trouble with this theory is that it cannot be substantiated from the sources. There were differences between the House of Hillel and the House of Shammai, but they were all on such minor points that the vast gulf between them postulated for the purposes of this popular theory did not exist. As a matter of fact, if we look at the actual points of disagreement between the two Houses, we might easily come to the conclusion that Jesus was more in sympathy with the House of Shammai than with the House of Hillel.

For example, on the question of divorce, Jesus takes a very severe view. He forbade divorce altogether: 'What therefore God hath joined together, let not man put asunder' (Mark 10.9, AV). He said further, 'Whosoever shall put away his wife and marry another, committeth adultery against her. And if a woman shall put away her husband, and be married to another, she committeth adultery' (Mark 10.11–12, AV; see also Luke 16.18). Or at least this is the version of Jesus' view on divorce reported in the Gospels of Mark and Luke, a version that still holds the field in the Catholic Church. There is a rather more lenient version of Jesus' view of divorce in the Gospel of Matthew, 'But I say unto you, That whosoever shall put away his wife, saving for the cause of fornication, causeth her to commit adultery: and whosoever shall marry her that is divorced, committeth adultery' (Matt. 5.32, AV; see also 19.9). This latter version is more in keeping with the ruling of the Torah, which permits a husband to divorce his wife (Deut. 24.1, AV), but says as ground for divorce that the wife 'finds no favour in his eyes, because he hath found some uncleanness in her'. The Torah, on the other hand, does not appear to grant any power of divorce to the wife; so we may question why Mark considers the possibility 'if a woman shall put away her husband'.

We find that the House of Hillel and the House of Shammai have, as one of their disagreements, the question of divorce. On this matter, the House of Hillel is far more lenient than the House of Shammai, for it permits divorce on mere grounds of incompatibility, whereas the House of Shammai says that a husband may divorce his wife only if he finds that she has betrayed him sexually in some way (the disagreement obviously turns on the interpretation of the verse quoted above, Deut. 24.1, the House of Hillel putting the stress on the first clause 'finds no favour in his eyes', while the House of Shammai puts the stress on the second clause 'because he hath found some uncleanness in her'). But the point here is that both the Houses are more lenient than Jesus in the Mark version, while in the Matthew version, Jesus' view was exactly the same as that of the House of Shammai, but contrary to that of the House of Hillel. Thus if we take the question of divorce as a pointer to Jesus' general attitudes, we should have to say that Jesus' views were closer to those of the House of Shammai than to those of the House of Hillel – a conclusion that shatters the theory that Pharisee 'hostility' to Jesus can be explained as coming from the House of Shammai. We should have to entertain instead a possible hypothesis that not only was Jesus a Pharisee, but he belonged to the more severe wing of the Pharisee movement.

We may now take up the point raised above, 'Why does Mark refer to the case of a woman divorcing her husband, though the Torah does not seem to allow this as a possibility?' The explanation has been put forward that Mark, being a Roman, is here unconsciously slipping back into Roman law, which allowed wives to divorce husbands. But there is in fact no need to resort to such an explanation, for Jewish law, as administered by the Pharisees/ rabbis, did allow wives to divorce husbands, even though the Torah does not mention this as a possibility. This permission for a wife to divorce a husband was not a bone of contention between the House of Hillel and the House of Shammai; both Houses agreed with this reform, or, as they would have preferred to put it, interpretation of Torah law.

The interpretation ran as follows: when the Torah speaks of a husband divorcing or 'sending away' a wife, this refers only to the formal requirements of the divorce ceremony, which require the husband to hand over to the wife a divorce document, a formal requirement that must be complied with even in a case where it is the wife who is divorcing the husband. If a wife wants a divorce, she cannot simply 'send away' the husband, or give him a bill of divorcement, she must apply to the Court, who, if satisfied by her grounds of wanting a divorce, will then instruct the husband to carry out the formal requirements. The grounds allowed by Pharisaic/rabbinic law for a wife to divorce her husband are extraordinarily generous. Even if the husband wishes to go and live in a different town, contrary to the wishes of the wife, she is entitled to divorce him; or if he takes up some profession that makes him malodorous, tanning for example: there are many conditions of equal leniency.[5] So Mark was not wrong in assuming that Pharisaic law permits a wife to divorce a husband. Jesus, however, totally forbids it, which shows that he has failed in this instance to keep up with progressive trends in Pharisaism which were accepted even by the House of Shammai.

Jesus' ban on divorce has been the cause of much misery to unhappy couples through the ages, and one wonders whether he did actually forbid it so categorically, but merely expressed sorrow at the thought of it occurring – in concurrence with the rabbinic saying, 'He who divorces the wife of his youth causes the Temple altar to weep'; and of course the Pharisees endorsed the idealization of marriage found in the Torah itself (Gen. 2.24). The Pharisees/ rabbis did not like divorce, and would much prefer that it did not happen, but they felt that it was inhumane and contrary to natural law to force a couple whose marriage had broken down irretrievably to stay together, a view that the modern world, on the whole, endorses. Incidentally, Pharisaic law compelled a husband to pay a considerable sum as alimony to his divorced wife, and also to restore to her any money or property that she had brought into the marriage – a concept that did not enter Western Christian society until the nineteenth century. It should be added too that the leniency of rabbinic law in relation to divorce did not weaken the foundations of marriage. On the contrary, Jewish marriages have been remarkably stable.

Shammai himself, the founder of the House of Shammai, though he appears at times as a rather forbidding person in comparison with the genial Hillel, was by no means an ogre and cannot be held responsible for hateful characteristics such as the Gospels allege against the Pharisees. Some of Shammai's sayings are not at all inferior to the best sayings of Hillel. One of them was, 'Receive all men with a cheerful countenance.' This is hardly in accordance with some of the stories told about him, in which he shows an irascible temper. But it does show that he was aware of this defect in himself and desired to correct it.

The basic thought of Pharisaism is love of neighbour: but Pharisaism realized that society cannot be conducted on the basis of beautiful aphorisms. They have to be translated into practical terms, and this means considering thousands of detailed circumstances in which love of neighbour may be exercised. The consideration of these multifarious circumstances is called 'law'. Paul denigrated law, and thought that all one needed was love, and all the rest would automatically follow. Jesus on the other hand did not have this view. He subscribed to the view that one must pay attention to every jot and tittle of the Law, for this was the way to implement love of neighbour – yet like Hillel and other Pharisees, he did not think that the expression 'every jot and tittle' implied a static conception of the Law, but allowed room for reforms based on liberal and rational interpretation of its wording.

Appendix

The Washing of Cups

As explained in Chapter 3, there is a tendency among scholars to look for explanations of passages in the Gospels in terms of Jewish purity laws where such explanations are irrelevant. A prominent example of this kind of error, I believe, is J. Neusner's article that argues that Jesus' injunction to the Pharisees, 'First cleanse the inside of the cup . . .' (Matt.23.25–6) should be understood in the light of discussions in the Mishnah about the law of purity of utensils; and that further, the New Testament passage provides evidence of changes in that law between the composition of the Gospels and the redaction of the Mishnah.[1] Both these claims will be denied here. Instead, it will be argued that Jesus' injunction to 'cleanse the inside of the cup' has nothing to do with ritual purity, but is a matter of elementary, ordinary hygiene.

Neusner points out that there is a Mishnaic law which states that in certain circumstances a vessel can become unclean on the outside while remaining clean on the inside, while a vessel that is unclean on the inside is always unclean on the outside (*m. Kel.* 25.6). The inside therefore is determinative of cleanness for the Mishnah, or at least for the dominant authorities of the Mishnah, the House of Hillel. This law (Neusner argues) must therefore be later than the time of Jesus (or of the composition of the Gospels, if the saying is not authentically that of Jesus). For Jesus, taking his analogy from the law of purity of vessels, urges the Pharisees to regard the inside as determinative. But this (in the Mishnah) is what they already do. Therefore, the law of purity of vessels in pre-Mishnaic times must have been different; either the outside was determinative, or outside and inside were independent of each other. Otherwise, why should Jesus have urged the Pharisees, 'Clean the inside of the cup; then the outside will be clean too?' The New Testament passages thus throw light on the history of the law of purity: first the inside was not determinative, and later the law was changed and the inside became determinative. Neusner then embarks on complicated arguments to show that this conclusion can be reinforced by redaction criticism of the Mishnah itself, which, he alleges, shows traces of a previous law in terms of which the inside was not determinative.

Let us assume, for the moment, that ritual purity is relevant to the issue. Neusner reduces the saying of Jesus to the following: 'You cleanse the outside of the cup and plate but not the inside. Hypocrites: first cleanse the inside and then the outside will be clean.' Accepting for the moment this formulation of the saying, one notes that Neusner takes the first sentence to be a literal statement of Pharisee law and the second sentence to be a metaphorical application of the first, couched in the form of a recommendation to alter the existing purity law. But this is surely a most unnatural way to understand the two sentences. It seems much more likely (again assuming that there is a context of ritual purity), that Jesus is speaking metaphorically throughout. He is assuming that everybody knows that the inside of a cup is primary in matters of purity, and is using this knowledge to make an observation on hypocrisy. He is saying, 'You cleanse the outside of the cup in moral and spiritual matters, although *you* know very well that this is not the correct practice in matters of ritual purity.' Jesus is not recommending any change in the laws of ritual purity but using the existing laws to point a moral, just as he used the existing practice of whitewashing graves to point the same moral, without implying any criticism of that practice. Both in the statement, 'You cleanse the outside of the cup', and in the recommendation, 'First cleanse the inside', Jesus is speaking metaphorically of the state of the Pharisees' souls, though in using 'cup' and 'outside' and 'inside' he is taking metaphors (as we are now assuming) from the field of ritual purity. There is thus no evidence whatever in the saying that the law that Jesus is assuming is any different from the law found in the Mishnah.

Generations of Christian scholars, of course, have interpreted the saying very much as Neusner does.[2] It is understandable that Christian scholars, lacking knowledge of the Jewish sources or

inclined to regard the Pharisees as deficient in common sense as well
as other qualities, should have jumped to the conclusion that Jesus,
when he said, 'You cleanse the outside of the cup . . .', was referring
to some curious and illogical law by which the Pharisees washed
the outsides of cups and left the insides contaminated. Neusner's
problem is that he knows that the Jewish sources give evidence to
the contrary. Not doubting the prevailing literalist interpretation,
he looks for evidence in the Mishnah that there was once such an
odd custom among the Pharisees. Neusner's article at least serves to
show up the difficulties in the traditional Christian view of Jesus'
saying.

Strictly speaking, however, Neusner's enquiry is beside the
point. Jesus' saying is concerned with the *washing* of cups, not with
the extent to which they become unclean. It is unquestionable that
there was only one way of washing ritually-unclean vessels, whether
wholly or partly unclean: to immerse them totally in the water of the
Miqveh (ritual immersion pool).[3] Since there was no custom of
washing cups on the outside only, Jesus' saying, 'You cleanse the
outside of the cup . . .' must be taken metaphorically.

Instead of coming to this simple and obvious conclusion,
Neusner offers an interpretation in which Jesus is referring not to
purification methods but to areas of contamination, and is combin-
ing in his saying legal statement, legal injunction and metaphor. I
quote Neusner's own statement of his argument:

> Now when we are told, 'First cleanse the inside', what can be the
> state of the law? Granted, we have a moral teaching about the
> priority of the inner condition of a person. Yet for that teaching
> to be tied to a metaphor of the purity-rule about the distinction
> between the inside and the outside of a cup, the metaphor must
> be apt. If practice already is to regard the inside of the cup as
> determinative of the condition, as to purity, of the cup as a whole,
> what shall we make of the instruction first to clean the inside of
> the cup? We already do clean the inside of the cup first!

This is as if to say that if I tell someone, 'Put your house in order',
this metaphorical injunction will be inappropriate unless the person

addressed does not believe in keeping his *literal* house in order. On the contrary, it is just because the person addressed and the audience, if any, do believe that a literal house ought to be kept in order that my words have any meaning as applied to his spiritual or moral condition. Neusner's idea of how a metaphor becomes 'apt' is most strange. He thinks that any metaphorical injunction must carry with it literal implications; that when we tell someone to pull his socks up, this must mean that his literal socks are down – otherwise he could reply triumphantly, 'But my socks are already pulled up!', or, 'But I already believe in keeping my (literal) socks pulled up, so what are you telling me that is new?'

Let us now take a closer look at the texts to see whether, in fact, it is necessary to assume that they are concerned with ritual purity at all.

The two texts are as follows:

Alas for you, lawyers and Pharisees, hypocrites! You clean the outside of cup and dish, which you have filled inside by robbery and self-indulgence. Blind Pharisee! Clean the inside of the cup first; then the outside will be clean also. (Matt. 23.25–6, NEB)

When he had finished speaking, a Pharisee invited him to a meal. He came in and sat down. The Pharisee noticed with surprise that he had not begun by washing before the meal. But the Lord said to him, 'You Pharisees! You clean the outside of cup and plate; but inside you there is nothing but greed and wickedness. You fools! Did not he who made the outside make the inside too? But let what is in the cup be given in charity, and all is clean.' (Luke 11.37–41, NEB)

Neusner notes correctly that the way in which Luke connects the saying about the cleansing of cups with an incident involving the washing of hands is artificial. Also artificial is Luke's importing of the theme of charity. Matthew's version is more authentic, but Neusner proposes certain emendations in it. He wishes to excise the words 'which you have filled inside by robbery and extortion', arguing, 'the figurative "contents" of the cup or plates, "robbery and self-indulgence", do not fit the context of purity-questions nor the proposed remedy, "first clean the inside".'

This, however, is to beg the question. Only Neusner's unargued assumption that we are dealing not only with purity law but also with an unmetaphorical statement of that law makes him propose this excision. The words fit in excellently to a statement that is intended as metaphorical from the outset. As for Neusner's remark that the proposed remedy 'first clean the inside' is inappropriate to the context of purity questions, this seems to be a fleeting recognition that in fact there is no ritual purity law in the Mishnah or elsewhere that asserts that cleanness of the inside implies cleanness of the outside of a vessel. On the contrary, the law in *m. Kel.*, to which Neusner mainly refers, envisages precisely the opposite state of affairs in which a vessel is clean on the inside but unclean on the outside. Neusner juggles with the word 'determinative', saying that the Mishnah makes 'the inside of a cup . . . determinative of the condition, as to purity, of the cup as a whole'. He neglects to note explicitly, however, that the inside is 'determinative' only as regards uncleanness, not as regards cleanness. If the inside is unclean, the whole vessel is unclean; but if the inside is clean, the outside may be unclean. Thus when Neusner goes on to say that he regards 'First cleanse the inside, and then the outside will be clean' as 'the simplest and earliest version', he proceeds thereafter by ignoring the plain fact that there is no purity law analogy for this formulation. Yet the formulation is essential to Jesus' thought, which is that outward observance is useless without inner moral purity, but that when such purity exists, outward virtuous behaviour will follow inevitably. (Jesus is not saying that outward virtuous behaviour does not matter, any more than he is saying that tombs are just as well without whitewash).

Now if purity questions were the only possible context for Jesus' saying, we would perhaps have to struggle on and make some sense of that context. But as it happens, there is another context that makes much more sense of the whole matter and is entirely free of the confusions and illogicalities of Neusner's approach. This is the context of simple hygiene. It is far from being the case that the concepts of cleanliness and dirtiness were always associated in the rabbinic mind with matters of ritual purity. The category of personal cleanliness or hygiene was of great importance. Sometimes this category overlapped with the concept of ritual purity, but the two categories were nevertheless accurately distinguished.[4] Both categories had religious significance: ritual purity as a protection for holy foods and areas, hygienic cleanliness as part of the religious duty of preservation of human life and health, as well as the duty of respect for the human body as the creation and 'image' of God.[5]

There is thus no reason to bring in the concept of ritual purity in the exegesis of Jesus' remarks about the inside and the outside of a cup. All Jews were familiar with the difference between a clean and a dirty cup, and the image of a vessel that was clean on the outside but dirty on the inside as a metaphor of hypocrisy was perfectly intelligible to them, as was the similar figure of the whitewashed tomb which is 'full of dead men's bones and all kinds of filth'.[6]

Furthermore, the distinction between 'inside' and 'outside' was a familiar one, as evidenced by the Talmud, whenever it was desired to distinguish between sincerity and hypocrisy. A sincere person was called one whose 'inside was like his outside' (*tokho ke-varo*) (see p. 85), and there is nothing in this phrase that has reference to the topic of ritual purity.

Also very damaging to Neusner's thesis is the nature of the purity law which he is trying to make relevant to Jesus' saying. Firstly, the law is of a highly technical and limited character, without any of the charge of emotion or disgust attaching to impurities such as menstruation or gonorrhoea or a corpse. Being of such a technical nature, it is most unlikely that it would be used to symbolize moral corruption in popular homiletics, and it is certainly not so used in the Talmudic literature. Secondly, the distinction between the inside and the outside of a cup in purity law is certainly later than the time of Jesus.

The limited character of the law

The greatest defect of Neusner's analysis is that he fails to bring out or consider the limited character of the law. Why, on Neusner's analysis, do the inside and outside of a cup function separately only in the case of contamination by edible liquids? Why is it that a cup, if contacted, say, by a corpse, or a dead 'creeping thing', becomes entirely unclean even if touched only on the outside? No answer can be offered to this question from Neusner's standpoint because he thinks that the distinction between inside and outside was primary. The view of the Talmud and of traditional Jewish exegesis (which Neusner rejects) is that the distinction between the inside and out-side of a vessel was secondary, and was linked to the Rabbinical decree that unclean edible liquids were to become capable of transmitting uncleanness to vessels.[7] *This* view makes sense of the limited character of the law: it is limited because it is intended to have the function of alleviating the effects of the decree about liquids.[8] Consequently, the distinction between inside and outside of vessels does not operate except in relation to the decree about liquids.[9] This explains fully why 'biblical' sources of impurity, such as corpses or dead 'creeping things' are not affected by the distinc-tion between inside and outside when coming into contact with vessels (other than earthenware vessels, see note 9).

Furthermore, the Talmudic and traditional view (again rejected by Neusner) is that there is *no dispute* between the House of Shammai and the House of Hillel on the relation between outside and inside: both hold that a cup contaminated by liquids becomes fully unclean only if touched on the inside; if touched on the outside, the inside remains clean; and that this is a concession and alleviation in recognition of the unbiblical, rabbinical origin of the decree about liquids. The Talmudic view thus makes sense of the topic as a whole, while Neusner's view is unintelligible unless certain aspects are viewed in isolation.

There is thus no reason to suppose that there was ever a time when outside and inside were distinguished by both Houses but disputed as to primacy. The only dispute recorded between the Houses in the matter was *whether the decree about liquids should be enacted*: the Shammaiites were in favour, the Hillelites against. Once the decree was enacted by majority vote, both Houses agreed that its operation should be limited by making a distinction between inside and outside, so that external contact with liquids would have only superficial consequences on vessels.

The date of the law

If the distinction between inside and outside of vessels is logically dependent on the decree about liquids, the date of the distinction must be contemporary with or subsequent to the date of the decree. According to the Talmud (*b. Shabb.* 13b and 14b) the decree that unclean liquids should become capable of contaminating vessels was one of the Eighteen Decrees enacted during the war against Rome (66–70 CE). The list given of the Eighteen Decrees in this passage, however, is subject to doubt.[10] Even if we suppose that the decree was enacted at some earlier period of the activity of the Houses, that still makes it later than the time of Jesus, though earlier than the composition of the Gospels.

We have to choose, therefore, between two hypotheses: that the authors of the Gospels invented a saying of Jesus based on a highly technical and limited purity law; or that Jesus was actually the originator of the saying, but was not referring to purity questions but simply to common parlance, which knew then, as now, that there is a difference between a physically clean cup and a dirty one, and knew too that a cup with a dirty inside is worse than a cup with a dirty outside, and that a perfunctory wiping of the outside of a cup may leave the inside dirty, while a thorough cleansing of the inside will inevitably entail the cleansing of the outside too.

The above considerations make it unnecessary to undertake a full discussion of Neusner's complicated argument from redaction criticism of the Mishnah. In any case, a full critique of Neusner's argument would have to take into account his methodology as displayed in his *History of the Mishnaic Law of Purities*, and would take us far beyond the range of the present discussion. A few remarks, however, may serve to show the subjective and debatable character of this type of argument.

Examining *m. Kel.* 25.1, Neusner points out that this passage merely enquires into the definition of 'inside' and 'outside', and does not state any primacy of one over the other. He therefore concludes that this passage was written at a time when no such primacy existed. One would like to know how better a discussion of a topic involving the inside and outside of a vessel could be introduced than by making a careful definition of 'inside' and 'outside'. There seems to be perfectly logical justification for postponing discussion of primacy at this point for a few sentences, and therefore no conclusion can be reached from the passage's silence on the subject of primacy. One might as well argue that Caesar's sentence, 'Gaul is divided into three parts,' was written at a time when he did not know the names of the tribes inhabiting those parts.

On the other hand, Neusner shows the opposite fault of over-credulousness in relation to *m. Ber.* 8.2. All that this Mishnah says is, 'The House of Shammai says, They wash the hands and afterwards mix the cup. And the House of Hillel says, They mix the cup first and afterwards wash the hands.' It is the Tosefta and the Talmudim that give an elaborate and implausible interpretation of this dispute in terms of liquid-impurity and the distinction between inside and outside of a cup. The Mishnah itself is utterly silent about liquid-impurity, inside and outside. Yet here Neusner draws no deductions from the Mishnah's silence, but swallows the Talmudic interpretation whole.[11]

Neusner's attempt to reconstruct the history of the purity law of the inside and outside of a cup, by redaction criticism of Mishnaic passages, should thus be regarded with caution. His overall interpretation of the Gospel passage has certainly not been (appreciably) strengthened by it.

As a summing-up, we may take another look at Neusner's thesis as a whole and see if it makes sense. He is saying that Jesus did an odd and puzzling thing: he sought to inculcate a moral lesson by proposing a change in the law of purity of vessels. This is rather as if someone were to try to teach a moral lesson by proposing a change in the law of parking cars: 'You teach that cars should be parked at the side of the road, but I propose that they should be parked in the middle of the road, in order to symbolize the virtue of avoiding extremes.' Surely there are much better ways of teaching a moral lesson than to legislate symbolic bye-laws. On the other hand, it is perfectly understandable that a preacher may take a metaphor from some aspect of life, which he uses as an illustration without seeking to change it into something else. Jesus, like the rabbis of the

Midrash, was a preacher who took his metaphors from plain, ordinary life, and was much more likely to use the image of everyday washing-up of cups as experienced by every household than to use an illustration from an esoteric and technical department of the law, especially as that department did not exist at the time.

Indeed laws are so many-sided and symbolisms so pliable that no worthwhile argument can be based on the suitability of some symbolism for derivation from some law. Neusner's argument is thus hopelessly imprecise, and can yield nothing of value for the history of rabbinic law. The best explanation is the simplest: that Jesus was talking about clean and dirty cups as a straightforward metaphor for clean and dirty personalities, both cups and personalities having an outer and an inner aspect; and the relevance of Jesus' saying to the history of ritual purity is nil.

Notes

Chapter 1

1. Neusner (1971).
2. Saldarini (1989).
3. See Reif (1993).
4. Sanders (J. T.) (1987).
5. There are, however, other aspects of Acts which do confirm Saldarini's postulation of a desire to assert continuity between the Gentile Christian Church and the Jerusalem Church (see pp. 165–6). This desire is particularly evident in the treatment of Peter as increasingly turning away from adherence to the Torah, and also in the scaling-down of Paul's very high self-assessment as expressed in his epistles: both tendencies work towards a narrowing of the gap between the Gentile Christian Church and the Jerusalem Church.
6. Sanders (E. P.) (1985), p. 250.
7. Kümmel (1975).
8. Kümmel (1973).
9. Coggins and Houlden (1990).
10. Sanders (J. T.) (1987).

Chapter 2

1. See Maccoby (1991a), ch. 4; (1991b).
2. This similarity was noted by C. G. Montefiore in his Commentary on Matthew (Montefiore, 1927, vol. II, p. 235), but he did not understand the full implications.

Chapter 3

1. See Maccoby (1999), p. 59.
2. For a more complex instance of the importation of ritual purity considerations into a matter of simple hygiene, see the Appendix, where Jesus' remarks about the 'inside and the outside of a cup' are examined.
3. Vermes (1973).
4. Crossan (1992).

Chapter 4

1. Crossan (1992), pp. 322–3.

2. Crossan, in accordance with his criteria of attestation (impressively worked out in his *The Historical Jesus* (1992), pp. xxxi–xxxiv), would argue that an episode that appears in all three Synoptic Gospels has only one attestation, since these Gospels are so dependent on each other (Matthew and Luke are frequently simply reproducing material taken from Mark). I suggest, however, that this is an over-simplification. Matthew and Luke frequently modify material taken from Mark in the interests of their own standpoints. If, however, Matthew and Luke fail to alter material taken from Mark which militates against their customary standpoints, this becomes a case for reflection. How could Matthew and Luke retain Jesus' injunction to the leper despite its inconsistency with their repeated portrayal of Jesus as repudiating the Law? The answer can only be that the tradition was too strong to be repudiated. Here the principles of *tendenz* theory (see Chapter 12, p. 157, for fuller explanation of this term) come into play. A saying that contradicts the *tendenz* is particularly authentic. Unfortunately, *tendenz* theory is often neglected by modern scholars, and it plays no part in Crossan's theory of attestation.

3. Douglas (1993–4), pp. 109–30.

4. Borg (1998), p. 98; see also Jeremias (1969), pp. 310–12.

5. Borg (1998), p. 99, n. 42.

6. See *b. Kidd.* 82a; *m. Kidd.* 4.14 (cf. *y. Kidd.* 4.11.66b; and Jeremias, 1969, pp. 303–9).

7. The Talmud contains two types of material, halakhah and aggadah. Halakhah is legal material, embodying binding decisions reached by a rabbinic majority. Aggadah consists of stories, parables and aphorisms of individual rabbis. These are not regarded as having legally binding force. See Maccoby (1988), pp. 17–22.

8. For full discussion, see Maccoby (1999), pp. 3–12.

9. For more extended discussion, see Maccoby (1988), pp. 142–4.

Chapter 5

1. In this story, one rabbi, Eliezer, called on support for his opinion, expressed in debate, from a voice from Heaven (BAT QOL) which duly came, but was overruled. This does mean in a sense that God himself was overruled, but certain distinctions need to be made. Rabbi Eliezer was not claiming to be a prophet. Nor does the story mean that during the prophetic age, a prophet, such as Isaiah, would have had to submit to the majority decision of a rabbinical council. On the contrary, the rabbinic age, by definition, was that age in which the guidance of prophecy was lacking and majority vote of rabbis had to be substituted for it. The Talmudic story actually uses the term BAT QOL in order to make plain that prophetic inspiration played no part, since it was a dictum that 'When prophecy ceased, its place was taken by the BAT QOL.' Thus the occurrence of a BAT QOL (literally 'a stray

voice') could be taken as a confirmation of an opinion arrived at by constitutional means, but could not supersede it. The probable meaning of a BAT QOL is 'the voice of someone speaking outside' (perhaps the voice of a child) that says something so opportune that it was taken as having an element of supernatural coincidence. If Rabbi Eliezer had been confirmed as a prophet (and therefore as the inaugurating figure of a new prophetic age) his authority would have been greater than that of any rabbinic council. But he did not make this claim, but simply sought miraculous confirmation of his opinion in order to secure the vote of his colleagues, as he did with the previous miracles he had employed, and which had been similarly overruled. Thus when God is represented as accepting the decision against the BAT QOL as a defeat for himself, he is not meant to be saying, 'I abandon the institution of prophecy for ever,' but only 'I accept the present non-prophetic state of affairs as valid even in the face of semi-incursions of the Divine which still occur in these non-prophetic days.'

2. This story, as well as the story of Rabbi Nathan, seems to suggest that even in a prophetic age, not all decisions would be made by the prophet. Certain areas of decision (particularly administrative or calendrical decisions) would still be left to the Council, and God himself, in those areas, would accept the Council's decision. It would be a mistake to divide the prophetic age from the rabbinic age (in rabbinic theory) by too hard-and-fast a line. After all, even Moses was unable to manage without a Council. It has been fashionable in recent years to speak of the Talmudic 'rabbinization' of biblical figures – the most prominent example being Moses himself, who is designated 'Moshe Rabenu,' or 'Moses our Rabbi'. There is no doubt that a process of 'rabbinization' did take place in rabbinic thinking about the scriptural age and this at times had anachronistic results; but the idea that the rabbinic age had qualities that had existed and had been necessary and desirable even in the prophetic age, and that the transition from one age to the other, while highly perceptible, was not entirely abrupt is one which deserves respect. Thus it is well within rabbinic thinking that Jesus, even though he has just claimed both prophetic and messianic status, could hand over certain powers of religious decision to Peter, and declare that such decisions would be recognized 'in heaven'.

3. This verse is actually missing in many good texts of Matthew. It is found invariably, however, in texts of Mark 12.40, which is probably the origin of the charge from which it was interpolated at some point into Matthew and later into Luke 20.47. There is thus great doubt about the provenance of the charge which is actually untypical of the charges made against the Pharisees even by their worst enemies.

Chapter 6

1. See Cohen (1990).
2. Deines (2001), p. 501.

Chapter 7

1. Rivkin (1978).

Chapter 8

1. There is also a more sophisticated approach to the matter which claims to be 'scientific', basing itself on the principle of Occam's razor. If a saying is found in a second-century text, on this principle, it can never be reliably dated to any period before the text in which it appears, even if the text itself attributes it to an earlier period. This is a principle much employed by Jacob Neusner and his disciples. It often leads to a confusion of thought: the notion that a saying cannot be dated *with the utmost certainty* before a particular time easily slides into the dogma that it never existed before this time. If this principle were consistently applied, we should have to give up most of what passes for history. If we accept, however, that probability, rather than certainty, is the guide to the study of history, we face a more complex situation. We have to accept the possibility that an attribution to someone preceding the authorship of the text may be correct, and many factors come into the assessment of whether it is correct or not. Neusner himself accepts that some attributions are correct, and he worked out a system for assessing this, but his sieve is far too fine, and condemns many very probable attributions to undeserved rejection. Moreover, we have to consider the probability that some sayings are actually *older* than the person to whom they are attributed (for an example of this see p. 93). The minimalist approach of the Neusner school leaves voids in the narrative which are sometimes filled up (especially by Neusner himself) with wild conjectures very much at variance with the alleged scientific standpoint (see Maccoby, 1984). A more recent school of scholars has taken a more commonsense, probabilistic approach, and has concluded that Pharisaism and rabbinism are continuous. Philip S. Alexander, for example, writes, 'the traditional view that there was a close link between the post-70 rabbis and the pre-70 Pharisees is probably correct' (Alexander, 2001, p. 263).

2. Jeremias (1972), p. 12.

3. For a more expanded version of this aspect see the version of the parable in Luke 14.16–24; and for an even plainer allegory, which does not involve a king but a householder and a vineyard, in which not only the householders' servants but finally his son, an obvious allegory of Jesus, is killed by his tenants, see Matt. 23.33–41.

Chapter 9

1. Graves and Podro (1953).
2. See Petuchowski and Brocke (1978).
3. Sanders (E. P.) (1977).

Chapter 10

1. *b. Shabb.* 31a, where the principle of love of neighbour is expressed in the form of the Golden Rule: 'What is hateful to you, do not to your fellow-creature.'

2. *Sifra* 89b; *Gen. Rab.* 24.7: Rabbi Akiva said, '"Thou shalt love thy neighbour as thyself" is the greatest principle in the Law.'

3. See Casey (1991).

4. See Acts 5.36, and Josephus, *Antiquities* 20.97, for Theudas. See Acts 21.38, and Josephus, *Antiquities* 20.167, for 'the Egyptian'.

5. See Maccoby (1980), pp. 139–49.

Chapter 11

1. MMT (*miqtsat ma'asei ha-Torah*), is also known as the Halakhic Letter or by its fuller abbreviation 4QMMT. The title may be translated as 'Some Precepts of the Torah'. The document purports to be a letter sent by the leaders of the Qumran sect to the priestly leaders in Jerusalem, reproving them for adopting certain practices which are otherwise known only from second-century rabbinic documents. Most scholars take the view that this document is reproving the Jerusalem priests for compromising too much with the Pharisees; it shows that there is continuity between the religious practices of the Pharisees and those of the rabbis.

2. Rengstorf (1960).

3. Davies (1965).

4. There is one source (*b. Sanh.* 107b) which portrays Jesus as having been a disciple of a famous rabbi, Rabbi Joshua ben Perachia, and this story does at least put Jesus into a rabbinic milieu, even though the story itself is clearly unhistorical, since it places Jesus in an era over a hundred years too early.

Chapter 12

1. Funk *et al.* (1993), pp. 140–1.

Chapter 13

1. See Maccoby (1991a), ch. 4; see also Maccoby (1991b).

2. See Maccoby (1992).

Chapter 14

1. Several manuscripts (D and some others) include the Golden Rule in its negative form among the basic principles to be observed by Gentile converts set out by James in Acts 15.20. The negative form of the rule is found also in Irenaeus.

2. See Matt. 12.1. The Greek word *epeinasan* is translated by NEB, in mild

fashion, as '(were) feeling hungry', but a more correct translation is 'were famished' or 'were starving'. In any case, it seems reasonable to suppose that people reduced to eating raw ears of corn must be very hungry indeed. Some extreme exponents of the 're-Judaization' theory have explained Matthew's introduction of this word as a deliberate attempt to bring Jesus' conduct in line with Jewish law (since the Gospel of Matthew, on this theory, was written for a Judaizing community). According to this theory, the earlier reading is that of the other Gospels, who omit the word *epeinasan*. This theory acknowledges, at least, the crucial importance of the word in any adequate exegesis of the episode, something that others have denied or glossed over by employing a misleading translation.

3. See Spiro (1980).

4. See Acts 18.25, which describes Apollos as a follower of John the Baptist, unaware of the teaching of Jesus, even after Jesus' death. Apollos is reportedly brought into line, but the passage provides evidence that John the Baptist did not impart to his followers a notion of subordination to Jesus. The Mandaean movement claimed John, not Jesus, as their founder, but scholars disagree about the historical authenticity of this claim.

5. The formal requirement for divorce that the husband must hand the bill of divorcement to the wife (and not vice versa) has, however, led to trouble, when an obstinate husband refuses to obey the instruction of the court. The difficulty is all the greater in that the law requires that this should be done willingly by the husband. Nevertheless, at the time when rabbinical courts had penal powers, it was the regular practice in such cases for the husband to be flogged until he agreed to perform the ceremony. As for the requirement of willingness, this was circumvented by the concept that every Jewish man, in his heart, wants to obey a Jewish court, and the flogging is merely helping him to overcome the temptations besetting him. When Jewish courts ceased to have penal powers, however, the problem deepened, and there arose the misfortune for some women of being a 'chained wife' (*'agunah*), who could not obtain a divorce and could therefore not marry again. In modern Israel, where courts have penal powers again, a recalcitrant husband is put in prison until he obeys the court's decision. Outside Israel, the problem of the *'agunah* has become a scandal. Various legal solutions have been offered; notably the exercise of the power of a Jewish court, attested in the Talmud, to annul a marriage; but current legal authorities are too timid to exercise this bold option. In Jesus' day, the leading Pharisee authority, Gamaliel, was famous for his courage in using rabbinic powers to counter social abuses, even if this meant temporary abrogation of a Torah law (see Palestinian Talmud commenting on *m. Git.* 4.2).

Appendix

1. Neusner (1976).

2. See, for example, Strack-Billerbeck, *Kammentar zum Neuen Testament*, ad loc. Some commentators, however, regard the cleansing of cups to be, in general,

an 'outward' observance and do not distinguish in their exegesis between the exterior and the interior of the cup. The 'inside' of the cup becomes unclean because it contains stolen goods (Loisy), not because it is levitically unclean; or the 'inside' refers only to people, not to vessels (Wellhausen).

3. See Maimonides, *Mishneh Torah*, *Miqv.* 1.1. 'All unclean things, whether people or vessels, whether Biblically or Rabbinically unclean, have only one remedy: immersion in the ritual pool.' See *m. Miqv.* 5.6, 6.2, etc.

4. E.g. *b. Hul.* 105 a–b: the 'last washing' at a meal is distinguished from the 'first washing' as being hygienic rather than ritual, and for that reason more important. See also *m. Tem.* 8.4: liquid left uncovered at night is forbidden for hygienic reasons (a snake may have drunk from it and left venom). This is misunderstood as a ritual law by Vermes (1973), p. 81. Dr Stefan Reif has pointed out to me that there is evidence that a hygienic washing was distinguished from a ritual washing by a difference in the blessing pronounced. See Abrahams (1899), p. 42, with references.

5. See, for example, *Lev. Rab.* 34.3; *b. Shabb.* 50b. For hygiene with particular reference to cups, see Maimonides, *Mishneh Torah*, *Ma'akhalot 'Asurot*, 17.29: 'The Sages have forbidden . . . eating and drinking out of filthy utensils which offend against one's natural fastidiousness'. The Talmudic source is *b. Mak.* 16b, a saying of R. Bibi bar Abaye, quoting as biblical authority Lev. 20.25, a verse frequently cited by the rabbis when combating unhygienic or unaesthetic practices. I owe this reference to Dr Louis Jacobs.

6. The verb *katharizo* used in both Matt. and Luke can be used of literal, spiritual or ritual cleansing. For the literal use, see, for example, Septuagint Prov. 25.4, *katharisthetai* referring to the purification of silver from dross.

7. See *m. Parah* 8.5–7. It was deemed to be biblical law that edible liquids, like other foodstuffs, were incapable of transmitting uncleanness to vessels but only to other foodstuffs. The reason for the rabbinical decree was that certain little-regarded liquids (for example, the spittle of a person with a 'running issue') were so capable (see Lev. 15.8), and since there was danger that the effect of these liquids would be ignored (see *b. Nid.*7b), it was thought best to extend the rule to all liquids. The various types of ritual uncleanness (in descending order of gravity) were largely notional. It is important to grasp that there was no sinfulness, and, in most cases, no stigma, for a person who was not a priest, in being ritually unclean. Indeed, it was frequently a meritorious act to become unclean, for example, when burying the dead. Sinfulness only entered the picture when a person, being unclean, entered holy places, or caused holy food to become unclean by allowing it to come into contact with unclean substances or persons. If a person voluntarily undertook to 'eat ordinary food in cleanness' that is, to avoid imparting uncleanness even to ordinary food, then by failing in this undertaking he incurred the same blame as anyone who failed to keep a vow; but no sacrilege was involved. To eat ordinary food 'in cleanness' did not mean to remain in a state of cleanness perpetually (this was neither possible nor desirable), but to perform certain ablutions

before eating; and it did not require the same degree of cleanness as was required of a priest eating holy food. The emphasis always was not on personal ritual cleanness, but on the protection of food or areas from uncleanness. Neusner's central axiom that the ideal of the Pharisees was 'that the ordinary folk should behave as if they were priests' has led him to give a distorted version of the above facts in his various writings.

8. See *b. Bek.* 38a.

9. The exception to this rule is the case of earthenware vessels, which can be rendered unclean only from the inside (see *m. Hul.* 1.6; *t. Hul.* 24b–25a, expounding Lev. 11.33). The outside of an earthenware vessel cannot be made unclean by direct contact, even by a corpse. It was in connection with this law that the distinction between the inside and the outside of a vessel was first made. The question may be asked, 'May it not have been to this biblical law that Jesus was referring when he spoke of the inside and outside of a vessel?' (Neusner does not consider this possibility). The answer is that this cannot be the case. As far as biblical law is concerned, an earthenware vessel cannot become unclean on the outside only. If contaminated on the inside, it becomes wholly unclean, but the remedy is not washing but breaking the vessel (Lev. 11.33). (There is a disagreement among medieval Jewish authorities about whether the rabbinical decree that liquids could contaminate the outside of vessels included earthenware vessels. The best opinion seems to be that it did not: see Rabad on Maimonides, *Mishneh Torah, She'ar 'Avot ha-Tume'ot* 7.3. If, however, it did, this merely puts earthenware vessels in the same category as other vessels in this one respect, so Jesus cannot be referring to them specially.) Rabbinical law of the inside and outside of vessels in relation to liquids was based to some extent on definitions of inside and outside previously developed in expounding the biblical law of earthenware vessels. It is not impossible to imagine a homily based on this biblical law, but Jesus, speaking in terms of washing, cannot have had it in mind.

10. See Weiss (1924), I, p.186; also Zeitlin (1915), pp. 22–36.

11. It is interesting that Maimonides *(Mishneh Torah, She'ar 'Avot ha-Tume'ot* 7.2 and Introduction to *Toharot* in his Commentary on the Mishnah) makes a halakhic decision (that liquids made unclean by hands cannot contaminate vessels) contradictory to this Talmudic passage. Maimonides' decision has been much discussed, but it is evident that he regarded the Talmudic commentary on *m. Ber.* 8.2 as unauthoritative, especially in the light of *b. Shabb.* 14b and *y. Hag.* 3.1. Maimonides here (unlike Neusner) shows a lively and sceptical critical sense, regarding the Talmudic discussion on *m. Ber.* 8.2 as an academic exercise, not as a correct explanation of the Mishnah. He overrules also the argument of the Tosefta, cited in the Babylonian Talmudic discussion, which also gives a ritual purity exegesis of the matter (*t. Ber.* 5.26). It should be noted, however, that the Tosefta (slightly later than the Mishnah and considerably earlier than the Talmud) contains strong traces of a previous exegesis that was not in terms of ritual purity. For example, the 'alternative explanation' (*davar 'aher*) that the House of Hillel

believed that 'the washing of hands should come immediately before the meal' is evidently a remnant of an explanation in terms of simple, natural priority (similar to the explanation given concerning the priority of the blessings). Even this remark of the Tosefta, however (which appears also in the very brief discussion in the Palestinian Talmud of the passage in *m. Ber.* 8.2), is explained in terms of ritual purity in the Babylonian Talmud.

References

Abrahams, Israel, 'Some Fragments of the Passover Hagada', *Jewish Quarterly Review* 10 (1899).

Abraham, Israel, *Studies in Pharisaism and the Gospels*, 2 vols., Cambridge: Cambridge University Press, 1924.

Alexander, Philip S., 'Torah and Salvation in Tannaitic Literature', in D. A. Carson, Peter T. O'Brien and Mark A. Seifrid, (eds.), *Justification and Variegated Nomism: Volume 1: The Complexities of Second Temple Judaism*, Tübingen: Mohr Siebeck/Grand Rapids: Baker Academic, 2001, pp. 261–301.

Beare, Francis Wright, *The Gospel according to Matthew*, San Francisco: Harper & Row, 1981.

Borg, Marcus J., *Conflict, Holiness and Politics in the Teaching of Jesus*, Harrisburg, PA: Trinity Press International, 1998.

Brandon, S. G. F., *The Fall of Jerusalem and the Christian Church*, London: SPCK, 1951.

Bultmann, Rudolf, *History of the Synoptic Tradition*, ET of *Geschichte der Synoptischer Tradition*, Göttingen, 1921, Oxford: Oxford University Press, 1958.

Casey, Maurice, *From Jewish Prophet to Gentile God*, Cambridge: James Clarke, 1991.

Charles, R. H., (ed.), *The Apocrypha and Pseudepigrapha of the Old Testament*, 2 vols., Oxford: Oxford University Press, 1913 (repr. 1963).

Charlesworth, James H., (ed.), *The Old Testament Pseudepigrapha*, 2 vols., New York: Doubleday, 1983.

Coggins, R. J. and Houlden, J. L., (eds.), *A Dictionary of Biblical Interpretation*, London: SCM Press/Philadelphia: Trinity Press International, 1990.

Cohen, Stuart, *The Three Crowns*, Cambridge: Cambridge University Press, 1990.

Crossan, John Dominic, *The Historical Jesus*, New York: HarperSanFrancisco, 1992.

Davies, W. D., *Paul and Rabbinic Judaism*, London: SPCK, 1965.

Deines, Roland, *Die Pharisäer*, Tübingen: Mohr Siebeck, 1997.

Deines, Roland, 'The Pharisees Between "Judaisms" and Common Judaism', in D. A. Carson, Peter T. O' Brien and Mark A. Seifrid, (eds.), *Justification and*

Variegated Nomism: Vol. 1: The Complexities of Second Temple Judaism, Tübingen: Mohr Siebeck/Grand Rapids: Baker Academic, 2001, pp. 443–504.

Douglas, Mary, 'Atonement in Leviticus', *Jewish Studies Quarterly* 1/2 (1993–4), pp. 109–30.

Eusebius, *Ecclesiastical History*, trans. K. Lake (Loeb Classical Library), London: Heinemann/Cambridge, MA: Harvard University Press, 1926.

Fisch, Menachem, *Rational Rabbis*, Indiana University Press, 1997.

Funk, Robert W., Hoover, Roy W., and the Jesus Seminar, (eds.), *The Five Gospels: the Search for the Authentic Words of Jesus*, New York: Polebridge Press, 1993.

Golb, Norman, *Who Wrote the Dead Sea Scrolls?*, London: Michael O'Mara Books, 1995.

Graves, Robert and Podro, Joshua, *The Nazarene Gospel Restored*, London: Collins, 1953.

Herford, R. Travers, *The Pharisees*, Boston: Beacon Press, 1962.

Horsley, Richard, *Jesus and the Spiral of Violence*, San Francisco: Harper & Row, 1987.

Jacobs, Louis, *Studies in Talmudic Logic and Methodology*, London: Vallentine Mitchell, 1961.

Jeremias, Joachim, *Jerusalem at the Time of Jesus*, Philadelphia: Fortress Press, 1969.

Jeremias, Joachim, *The Parables of Jesus*, London: SCM Press, 1972.

Kümmel, W. G., *The New Testament: The History of the Investigation of Its Problems*, London: SCM Press, 1973.

Kümmel, W. G., *Introduction to the New Testament: Revised Edition*, London: SCM Press, 1975.

Levinas, Emmanuel, *Difficult Freedom: Essays on Judaism*, trans. Seán Hand, London: Athlone Press, 1976.

Loisy, A, *Les Évangiles Synoptiques*, Paris: Emil Nouri, 1908.

Maccoby, Hyam, *Revolution in Judaea*, 2nd edn, New York: Taplinger, 1980.

Maccoby, Hyam, 'The Washing of Cups', *Journal for the Study of the New Testament* 14.3 (1982), pp. 3–15.

Maccoby, Hyam, 'Jacob Neusner's Mishnah', *Midstream* 30.5 (May 1984), pp. 24–32.

Maccoby, Hyam, *Early Rabbinic Writings*, Cambridge: Cambridge University Press, 1988.

Maccoby, Hyam, *Paul and Hellenism*, London: SCM Press/Philadelphia: Trinity Press International, 1991.

Maccoby, Hyam, 'Paul and the Eucharist', *New Testament Studies* 37 (1991), pp. 247–67.

Maccoby, Hyam, *Judas Iscariot and the Myth of Jewish Evil*, London/New York: Peter Halban, 1992.

Maccoby, Hyam, *Ritual and Morality: The Ritual Purity System and Its Place in Judaism*, Cambridge: Cambridge University Press, 1999.

Montefiore, C. G., *The Synoptic Gospels,* 2 vols., London: Macmillan, 1927.

Moore, George Foot, *Judaism in the First Centuries of the Christian Era*, Cambridge, MA: Harvard University Press, 1927.

Neusner, Jacob, *The Rabbinic Traditions about the Pharisees before 70*, Leiden: Brill, 1971.

Neusner, Jacob, 'First Cleanse the Inside', *New Testament Studies* 22 (1976), pp. 486–95.

Parkes, James, *The Foundations of Judaism and Christianity*, London: Vallentine Mitchell 1960.

Petuchowski, Jakob J. and Brocke, Michael, (eds.), *The Lord's Prayer and Jewish Liturgy*, London: Burns & Oates, 1978.

Reif, Stefan C., *Judaism and Hebrew Prayer*, Cambridge: Cambridge University Press, 1993.

Reitzenstein, R., *Die Hellenistische Mysterienreligionen*, 3rd edn, Leipzig/Berlin: B. G. Teubner, 1927.

Rengstorf, Karl-Heinrich, *Hirbet Qumran und die Bibliothek vom Toten Meer*, Studia Delitzschiana 5, Stuttgart: W. Kolhammer, 1960.

Rivkin, Ellis, 'Defining the Pharisees: the Tannaitic Sources', *Hebrew Union College Annual* 40 (1969–70), pp. 234–8.

Rivkin, Ellis, *A Hidden Revolution*, Nashville: Abingdon, 1978.

Saldarini, Anthony J., *Pharisees, Scribes and Sadducees in Palestinian Society*, Edinburgh: T&T Clark, 1989.

Sanders, E. P., *Paul and Palestinian Judaism*, London: SCM Press, 1977.

Sanders, E. P., *Jesus and Judaism*, London: SCM Press, 1985.

Sanders, E. P., *Judaism: Practice and Belief 63 BCE – 66CE*, London: SCM Press, 1992.

Sanders, Jack T., *The Jews in Luke-Acts*, London: SCM Press, 1987.

Spiro, Solomon J., 'Who Was the Haber? A New Approach to an Ancient Institution', *Journal for the Study of Judaism* 11 (1980), pp. 186–216.

Strack, Hermann L., and Billerbeck, Paul, *Kommentar zum Neuen Testament aus Talmud und Midrasch*, 4 vols., München: Beck, 1922.

Vermes, Geza, *Jesus the Jew*, London: Collins, 1973.

Weiss, I. H., *Dor Dor ve-Doreshav*, New York/Berlin: Plat & Minkus, 1924.

Winter, Paul, *On the Trial of Jesus,* Berlin: Walter de Gruyter, 1961.

Zeitlin, S., 'Les Dix-huit Mesures', *Revue des Études Juives* 68 (1915), pp. 22–36.

Index of Scriptural References

HEBREW BIBLE

APOCRYPHA

NEW TESTAMENT

MISHNAH

OTHER TANNAITIC SOURCES

BABYLONIAN TALMUD

PALESTINIAN TALMUD

MIDRASH

POST-RABBINIC SOURCES

GREEK SOURCES

Index of Names and Subjects